India - China Relations

Issues and Challenges

India - China Relations

Issues and Challenges

Dr. Sanjay Kumar

Associate Professor

Department of Defence Studies

Meerut College, Meerut (UP)

Dr. Bina Rai

Associate Professor

Department of Political Science

R.G.P.G. College, Meerut (UP)

Dr. Neelam Kumari

Associate Professor

Department of Chemistry

Meerut College, Meerut (UP)

Goel Publications

New Delhi - 110002

India- China Relations: Issues and Challenges

First Published in 2021

₹ 995

ISBN 978-81-953481-0-7

Published by : **Goel Publications**
G Floor, 4855/24, Ansari Road,
Daryaganj, New Delhi-110002
Tel. : 09999819813
E-Mail: goelpublications@gmail.com

Laser Typesetting : Aarati Computers, Delhi-110 009

Printed at : Balaji Offset, Delhi

Printed in India

Contents

Preface

As key emerging powers in the international system, India and especially China have received much attention in recent times. The likely emergence of China and India as new major global players – similar to the rise of Germany in the 19th century and the United States in the early 20th century – will transform the geopolitical landscape, with impacts potentially as dramatic as those of the previous two centuries. In the same way that commentators refer to the 1900s as the "American Century," the early 21st century may be seen as the time when some in the developing world, led by China and India, come into their own. A combination of sustained high economic growth, expanding military capabilities, active promotion of high technologies and large populations will be at the root of the expected rapid rise in economic and political power for both countries.

Relations between the two Asian giant, India and China have experienced profound upheaval over the past five decades, ranging from benign warmth in the 1950s and hyper-tension in the 1960s and 1970s, to rapprochement in the 1980s and readjustment in the 1990s. A close examination of Chinese and Indian perspectives on the fundamentals of the emerging international order reveals that Sino-Indian differences on many issues of both bilateral and global significance are stark. The major problems in India-China relations are the unresolved border issue that is getting more complicated with increasing Chinese military capability in Pakistan occupied Kashmir (POK); Sino-Pak military nuclear and missile collaboration; and China's String of Pearls strategy to encircle India.

Nevertheless, from the Indian and Chinese point of view, the relationship between them has a global significance. The real significance of India-China relations lies in the significant role that both countries can play in the twenty-first century. However, the global significance of this bilateral relation has been overshadowed by the prolonged issue of border dispute. The border issue is at the core of India's mistrust of China and the uncertainty about its future intentions. Both sides after several rounds of bilateral dialogue have an unsettled 3000 kilometers plus long border. This is creating a recipe for instability, tensions and even conflict. India has charged China for deliberately keeping the border issue unresolved so that it can continue to serve as a pressure point on India. Both sides after discussion have reached an understanding to exchange maps of their respective perceptions of the Line of Actual Control (LAC) in order to identify the physical extent of the disputed areas was suddenly terminated by the Chinese side without explanation. During Prime Minister Vajpayee's visit to China in 2003, India proposed a 'political solution' to the issue, to which end Special Representatives (SRs) of the two countries were nominated and given a mandate to establish a set of guidelines (which they have done) for proceeding towards resolution. The SRs have met more than dozen times without any real breakthrough.

In order that the ongoing border dispute does not hamper the relations from prospering, both sides have agreed to a hot line and a new mechanism at the Foreign Office level to contain any escalation of incidents at the border. The settlement of the border issue would open up avenues for board cooperation between the two countries.

At the political level of cooperation, India and China have set up a multi-channel and multi-level political dialogue platform, with frequent bilateral visits for in-depth discussions to resolve difficult issues and problems. On 26 September 2011, the first Sino-Indian Strategic and Economic Dialogue was launched, in which Chinese and Indian economic and foreign affairs policymakers began frank and direct discussions. Besides, leaders from both countries have frequent meetings in bilateral, regional and global forums.

On the defence and security front, both sides have developed an understanding on the need to fighting the menace of terrorism which poses a serious threat to global peace and security. Based on this, military ties between the Indian and Chinese armed forces have been building since December 2007, when India and China: Constrained Cooperation 329 the first joint counter terrorisms exercise Hand-in-Hand was held at Kunming. After the terror attack in Mumbai in November 2008, a joint military combat exercise was conducted from 6 to 14 December 2008 in Belgaum, Karnataka, which featured joint tactical man oeuvres and drills, with a 137-strong Army contingent from the 1st Company of the Infantry Battalion of the Chengdu Military Area Command and troops from the 8 Maratha Light Infantry Battalion of the Indian Army.

On the economic front, India-China trade relations have improved significantly in recent years that China has become India's largest trading partner in goods. The bilateral trade has reached over US$ 70 billion in 2011 and is expected to reach US$ 100 billion by 2015. The economic dimension of the relationship has acquired a new dynamic with the institutionalizing of a Strategic Economic Dialogue between the two countries. Besides, the two-way investment links between the two countries are also increasing. Overall, India's strategic thinkers should carefully analyse China's moves which have the potential to adversely affect India's interests and take effective steps to safeguard these interests. On the other hand, it would be in India's interest to pursue areas of mutually beneficial engagement, both in a bilateral and in a multilateral framework.

We would be failing in our duty if we do not acknowledge several other Personalities, Mentors and colleagues who contributed in their respective capacities to the success of this volume. We would like to thanks Lt Gen Dr. R.N. Singh, Lt.Gen Dr. Nitin Kohli, Lt. Gen Dr. J.S. Negi, Prof. Gopalji Malviya, Prof. Rajendra Prasad, Prof. Gautam Sen, Prof. Prashant Agarwal, Prof. Vijay Khare, Dr. Dhirendra Dwivedi for their cooperation for this book.

We must be thankful to Raj Publications, for bringing out this book timely and in proper manner. Finally, we sincerely hope that this book will generate considerable debate among scholars, academicians, experts and policy makers of both countries and open up new vistas for dialogue on the future of India-China Relations.

Dr. Sanjay Kumar
Dr. Bina Rai
Dr. Neelam Kumari

List of Abbreviations

LAC	—	Line of Actual Control.
PoK	—	Pakistan Occupied Kashmir
PLA	—	People's Liberation Army
NCP	—	National Comprehensive Power
US	—	United States
NATO	—	North Atlantic Treaty Organisation
ASEAN	—	Association of Southeast Asian Nations
NEFA	—	North Eastern Frontier Agency
PoW	—	Prisoners of War
CCP	—	Chinese Communist Party
NPT	—	Non Proliferation Treaty
NAI	—	National Archive of India
USI	—	United Service Institute of India
B.C.	—	Before Christ
A.D.	—	Anno Domoni
C.E.	—	Common Era
GDP	—	Gross Domestic Product
B.C.E.	—	Before Common Era

CIE	—	Companion of the Order of the Empire of India
JHSS	—	Journal of Humanities and Social Sciences
IOSR	—	International Organisation of Scientific Research
LAC	—	Line of Actual Control
SASAC	—	State-owned Assets Supervision and Administration Commission
KKH	—	KaraKoram Highway
LOC	—	Line of Control
JWG	—	Joint Working Group
PRC	—	Peoples Republic of China
CBMs	—	Confidence Building Measures
CICIR	—	China Institute of Contemporary International Relations
BDCA	—	Border Defense Cooperation Agreement
GOC	—	General Officer Commanding
PM	—	Prime Minister
CPC	—	Communist Party of China
CPAFFC	—	Chinese Peoples Association for Friendship with Foreign Countries
CEO	—	Company Executive Officer
FDI	—	Foreign Direct Investment
HDI	—	Human Development Index
UNDP	—	United Nations Development Programme
JSG	—	Joint Study Group
WTO	—	World Trade Organisation
MoU	—	Memorandum of Understanding
MNC	—	Multi National Companies.

JTF	—	Joint Task Force
RTA	—	Regional Trade Agreement
JEG	—	Joint Economic Group
SED	—	Strategic and Economic Dialouge
NDRC	—	Nation Development and Reform Commission
CCP	—	China's Communist Party
COAS	—	Chief of the Army Staff
MAC	—	Military Area Command
PLAAF	—	Peoples Liberation Army Air Force
PLAN	—	People's Liberation Army Navy
A2/AD	—	Area assess and Area Denial
CNS	—	Chief of Naval Staff
IAF	—	Indian Air Force
CAS	—	Chief of Air Staff
COSC	—	Chiefs of Staff Committee
SKAT	—	Suryakiran Aerobatic Team
USSR	—	Union of Soviet Socialist Republic
CTBT	—	Comprehensive Test Ban Treaty
CWC	—	Chemical Weapons Convention
BWC	—	Biological and toxin Weapons Convention
NSG	—	Nuclear Suppliers Group
PNE	—	Peaceful Nuclear Explosion
UN	—	United Nations.
CMF	—	Combined Maritime Force.
SHADE	—	Shared Awarness and De- confliction
EEZ	—	Exclusive Economic Zone
EU	—	European Union

EAC	—	East Asian Committee
ARF	—	Association of Regional Forum
APT	—	Asia-Pacific Telecommunity
APEC	—	Asia-Pacific Economic Cooperation
EAS	—	East Asia Summit
TRA	—	Taiwan Relations Act
SCS	—	South China Sea
UNCLCS	—	United Nations Commission on Limits of Continental Shelf
UNCLOS	—	United Nations Convention on the Law of the Sea
ONGC	—	Oil and Natural Gas Commission
IOR	—	Indion Ocean Region
COPH	—	Chinese Overseas Port Holding Company
SPDF	—	Sychelles Peoples Defense Force
SCO	—	Shanghai Cooperation Organisation
MGC	—	Mekong Fanga Cooperation
BIMSTEC	—	Bay of Bengal Initiative for Multi-Sectoral Technical and Ecological cooperation
SAARC	—	South Asian Association on Regional Cooperation
FTA	—	Free Trade Area
CAFTA	—	China ASEAN Free Trade Agreement
BRIC	—	Brazil-Russia-India-China
BCIM	—	Bangladesh-China-India-Mayanmar.
ARC	—	Asia Relations Conference
SEATO	—	South East Asia Treaty Organisation
BFTA	—	BIMSTEC Free Trade Area

SAFTA	—	South Asian Free Trade Area
CAR	—	Central Asian Region
ESCAP	—	Economic and Social Commission for Asia and the Pacific
ECAFE	—	Economic Commission for Asia and Far East
TAR	—	Tibet Autonomous Region
CIA	—	Central Investigation Agency
PRC	—	Peoples Republic of China
EPG	—	Euro Patho Genomics
IJC	—	International Court of Justice
UNSC	—	United Nations Security Council
UNGA	—	United Nations General Assembly
RIC	—	Russia- India –China
DPRK	—	Democratic Peoples Republic of Korea
CENTO	—	Central Treaty Organisation
NCNA	—	New China News Agency
CFR	—	Council on Foreign Relations
CMC	—	Central Military Commission
CGS	—	Chief of General Staff
CCPC	—	Chinese Communist Party Congress

1

Historical Background

Natural environment forms the background of all human existence. Human culture originated in a place where population grouped in a considerable number and maintained permanent relations. An area irrigated by rivers and protected by natural barriers was required by primitive men to support a large population. Looking at the world map it is evident that it is no coincidence that all early known civilizations developed along the Nile Valley in Egypt, the Tigris-Euphrates valley in Babylonia and the Ganges in India. There is a traditional belief that Chinese civilization originated in the Hwang Ho (Yellow River) valley or its tributaries.[1]

According to anthropologists, the Peking man, who lived in North China about 500,000 years ago, already possessed certain characteristics peculiar to Chinese race. The Upper Cave Man, who lived about 50,000 years ago, also in North China, was a modern Chinese in appearance and more advanced in culture than his ancestors of 450,000 years earlier and both were ancestors of the Neolithic men in North China i.e. they belonged to Paleolithic age.[2] Though the civilization of China is wholly Mongolian, it does not prove that the northern roots are the only ones from which it grew. If it grew first in the Tarim valley, then unlike all other civilizations (including the Mexican and Peruvian) it did not grow out of the heliolithic culture. The Chinese mingle with such kindred peoples as the Siamese and Burmese, and seem to bridge over towards the darker Dravidian peoples and towards the Malays.

It is quite clear from the Chinese records that there were southern as well as northern beginnings of a civilization, and thatthe Chinese civilization that comes into history 2,000 years B.C. is the result of a long process of conflicts, mingling and interchanges between a southern and a northern culture of which the southern may have been the earlier and more highly developed. By 100 B.C. the Chinese had heard of India, who's power had spread across Tibet and into Western Turkestan, and they were trading by camel caravans with Persia and the western world.

The Chinese belief of this universe is centered on Pangu, who emerged from a cosmic egg tocreate the universe. His head became the mountains, his flesh fields, and his bones, rocks. His hair became trees and vegetation, and his breath, winds and clouds. His sweat was rain, and the insects, which finally found themselves on his body, were the people.

Of the five legendary rulers, the first, Fuxi and Nuwa (a brother-sister pair) domesticated animals, built farmhouses, taught people to fish with nets, introduced fire, channeled rivers, created writing, and focused their mythical energies on the Yellow River. The second, ShenNong, introduced agricultural techniques and medicine through herbs and other means. The third Huangdi, the Yellow Emperor, quelled barbarian's tribes, established a calendar, and created an infrastructure for plow carts and other vehicles, besides developing agriculture practices that is followed into the twentieth century. His wife, the first empress, practiced silk cultivation. In these first three mythical reigns, the idea of a Chinese state was created. It is the last two rulers, Yao and Shun, who exemplify the core ruling myths of Chinese civilization and have appeared prominently in the rhetoric of Chinese politics for more than three millennia.[3]

The account of early cultural heroes is interesting because they reveal what many Chinese historically have thought were most important about their past, these cultural heroes presented developments that enabled people to live differently from beasts. Cang Jie invented Chinese characters, or written Chinese language. Shen Nong invented agriculture. Sui Ren discovered the use of flint to produce and use fire. The Yellow Emperor (Huangdi) invented boats and the bow and arrow. His wife discovered the secret of making of silk.

Yao Chao shi invented houses and shelters. Yao perfected a calendar and the means of tracking the movements of planets and stars. He eventually chose a proficient government minister named Shun, ratherthan his own son, as his successor. Shun, as a King, perfected the government bureaucracy and spelled out the four classic punishments for criminals (fines, beatings, banishment and death). Yu, also known as Yu 'the great' efficaciously channeled the flood waters through a network of ditches and canals and latter rose to be the founder of the Xia dynasty, also known to be the first recorded dynasty of China.[4]

The Middle Kingdom

While the people of other nations have until recently thought of China as a remote nation, the Chinese have long regarded their country as the center of the civilized world. Since before the birth of Christ, the Chinese have called their land Zhongguo—"Middle Kingdom"—as if to say that other cultures was satellites of theirs. China's comparative quarantine from the nations of Europe led to the development of a distinctive civilization, encouraging the Chinese to think of themselves as culturally superior. With one exception, the frontiers of China have long been secure. To the west lay Tibet and Central Asia, Mongolia to the north, Manchuria to the northeast, and to the east and south, the Pacific and

Southeast Asia. The weakest of China's borders was on the northwest. There, the wild Central Asian nomads often invaded the frontier. The Gobi Desert was a main invasion route into North China. It was blocked, however, by a great Chinese emperor, Qin Shihuangdi who during his reign (221-210B.C.) extended the Great Wall from the Pacific in a western direction, which was an effective barrier against the nomads, he fought on horseback with bows and arrows and had no artillery or siege weapons.[5]

Peking man was an advanced hominid whose limbs and trunk were of averageextents. In 1959 the cave at Zhoukuodian was reopened and newly excavated materials shed light on a band of hunters and food gatherers which thrived there some 500,000 years ago. As a tool-maker with the knowledge of fire, Peking man had a varied diet of edible leaves, nuts, roots and meat from animals. The most primitive hominid so far discovered, is Yuanmou Man who existed in Yunnan province over 1.7 million years ago. Possible use of fire is suggested by the presence of ashes and charred bones near the place where the fossil teeth of Yuanmou Man were unearth.

It was within the last 10,000 years that the ancestors of the Chinese people were ready for a settled way of life, based on agriculture.[6] Chinese society has progressed through five major stages - Primitive Society, Slave Society, Feudal and Semi-feudal Society, Semi-colonial Society, and Socialist Society. The rise and fall of the great dynasties forms a thread that runs through Chinese history, almost from the beginning.

The Early Chinese Dynasties

Xia dynasty was the first ever recorded dynasty of China. The establishment of the Xia Dynasty (21st - 17th century BC) is an important milestone in the history of Chinese civilization and marks the end of the Primitive Society and the beginning of the Class Society. It is the first dynasty in Chinese history, which lasted nearly 500 years including the reigns of 17 emperors. It is thought that most of the Xia people were probably inhabited in the western area of Henan Province and southern Shanxi Province. Yuthe Great was the first one to set up the dynasty under the Abdication System (choosing the leader according to their ability). After he died, his son Qi broke up this system and made himself the Xia emperor. From that time onwards, the 'Abdication System' gave way to the 'Hereditary System'. Following the system of hereditary, 15 offspring's of Qi succeeded him after his death. Among them, emperors like Shaokang, and Huai made great contributions to the development of Chinese society. However, there were also many totalitarian emperors during this period such as Taikang, Kongjia, and Jie.Xia dynasty achieved many firsts; for the first time, people had started living mainly through agriculture, using tools made of stone or bone. The jade ware at that time was quite delicate and bronze vessels were well smelted. Craftwork made of bronze embedded with jade had also appeared. Commodity exchanges were developed. A calendar system of both lunar and solar movements was used.

Shang dynasty was the outcome of the fall of Xia dynasty. (c. 1600-1028 BC). The Shang civilization was beyond doubt a high civilization. It lay in north-western Honan, alongside the Shansi Mountains. It was a peasant civilization with towns. They built rectangular houses in a style still found in Chinese houses. The Shangs buried their Kings along with their belongings. They hadsculptures in stone, an art which disappeared and came back post-Christian times under the influence of Indian Buddhism. The ancient Chinese were also mathematically sophisticated. They used the decimal system as early as fourteenth century B.C., during the Shang dynasty. They also made use of zero by leaving a blank space. Chinese were the first ones to make use of compass. Bronze implements and vessels were used. The earthenware vessels were very akin to porcelain. Silk was already in use. The people of Shang dynasty were agriculturists; however their implements were still primitive. Capitals of the dynasty were changed many times. Population of Shangs would be between 4-5 million at that time. The Shang people had attained very high material and intellectual level. They followed a religion with many nature deities, especially of fertility.[7] Warfare during the Shang period, both offensive and defensive, was apparently frequent. To collect tribute and supply the court with all its needs and luxuries must have necessitated a great deal of "power politics" and scavenging in regions far away from the capital. The presence of various musical instruments, such as triangular stones, bells, and ocarinas; the dagger axes indicated a high degree of material culture.[8] With the burning of the Shang King all by himself, the Shang dynasty ended.[9] Zhou dynasty lasted from ca. 1122-221B.C. This was the first dynasty to unite most of China under a single government. The capital was moved eastwards to Luoyang in the present day Henan Province. Due to this shift the historians divided Zhou period into Western (1027-771B.C.) and Eastern Zhou (770-221 B.C.).With the royal line broken, the power of the Zhou court diminished; the disintegration of the kingdom hastened. The eastern Zhou period is divided into two sub-periods. The first from 770-476 B.C., is called the spring and autumn period, after a famous historical cronical of the time; the second is known as the Warring States period (475-221 B.C.). Eastern period is known to be the shaping period of Chinese culture. The Zhou clan which was a semi-nomadic in nature was from the North-western fringe of the Chinese world. Feudal monarchy existed as the form of the government. The rulers were the nobles with family names and they practicedancestral worship. Divination marked very important decisions or events. Peasants during this period were physically separated from other classes but were a key element. The philosophers of this period proclaimed the doctrine of the "mandate of heaven", the notion that the ruler (son of heaven) governed by divine right, but his dethronement would prove, he had lost the mandate. It was the Zhou dynasty which invented the famous chopstiks.

Although it is not certaint as to when metallurgy began in China, there is reason to believe that bronze wasapparently developed autonomously. The era of the Shang and the Zhou dynasties is generally known as the Bronze Age of China, because bronze, an alloy of copper and tin, used to develop weapons, parts of chariots, and ritual vessels, played an important role in the material culture of the time. Iron appeared in China towards the end of the Eastern Zhou dynasty. This dynasty also saw the written script evolve into its modern form.

Importance of Zhou period will always be best known for the rise and fall of its feudal political structure and its cultural and intellectual efflorescence. There were, however, several amazing technological and scientific innovations during this period. The trace harness was invented in fourth century B.C., agricultural revolution. By sixth century B.C., the Chinese were using iron plows which were very scientifically designed and came into use in Europe only during seventeenth century.Different kinds of coins and knifes were reinvented and used extensively.

During this period straight-line cropping was already practiced in China but the same came to Europe only in eighteen century A.D. In second century B.C., Chinese medical practitioners had discovered that blood circulates throughout the body and understood fully that the heart pumped the blood. Elaborate pumps and circulatory networks were used for teaching the students. The Chinese had discovered natural gas and used it as a heating source approximately preceding western natural gas drilling by 2300 years. A Moist book dating to fourth or third century B.C. states, "The cessation of motion is due to the opposing force... if there is no opposing force... the motion will never stop.[10]

Warring States period saw the Chinese invent and use crossbow on the battlefield. They were also the first in the world to use chemical and especially poison gas weapons on the battlefield.[11] In divinations and religious practices, human sacrifice in burials and rites were substantially lessened as new ways of worship were indoctrinated in the people. Zhou dynasty was also known as the iron dynasty. The technology pertaining to iron in this era had preceded that of European regions. Iron was extensively used for the protective gear of the army. Also recording and documentation became more pronounced.

Confucius, a philosopher was born in 551 B.C. during this periodConfuciuswas the greatest philosopher-teacher of the Zhou period and other times of China. Connected to his birth, the Eastern Zhou has the uniqueness of China's recorded history, since people of this dynasty facilitated collection and compilation of varied types of records and documents. During this period, the ancient form of religion declined and transformation into the Confucianism and Daoism took place.

It is also during this time that military thoughts and technical advancement opened doors.Confucius represented the emerging class of administrators and advisors, who were needed to aid the rulers, deal with the ever-present need of diplomacy with other states and internal administration. He took to the task of creating a class, based on virtue, which would take over the high position of the government and lead the people by their example. On the other hand Taoism philosophy was based on simplicity. They believed that Legalism should be followed in totality andthat every aspect of life should be ruled by a set of strict and impersonal laws.The philosopher Lao Tsu founded the religion and taught of a naturalistic "path to life." The religion was centered on the three jewels of the Taoist faith: compassion, moderation and humility. They believed that wealth and military strength gave the ruler actual power. The doctrine of Confucius was "to be true to the principles of our nature and to exercise them benevolently towards others. He opened a school for the sons of nobles at a great personal sacrifice. He was a descendent of a Shang King and a minister of justice. In his opinion, a stronger civilization could be developed if individual could be taught to accept the idea of ren or humanitarianism. He had compiled the wisdom of Shang and Zhou dynasties in five classics. Yiging, i.e. Book of changes; contained the thinking of prehistoric oracles. Shujing was the book of history; included the statements of rulers and ministers. Shijing was the book of Odes; anthology containing 305 poems, folk songs and ceremonial lyrics, ritual group of texts and Qunqiu; springs and autumn annals, was a brief cronical of events in the state of China. The essence of Confucianism, as it developed, was allegiance to human values rather than any religious rites. It was more a system of ethics than a religious movement. It offered a way to world peace through the extension of family love, through which development of the masses rather than the enrichment of a few rulers could be achieved. He made education almost holy to Chinese. In his wisdom, those born with possession of knowledge were the highest class, those who learn and get possession are next and those who are dull and stupid and yet do not learn are lowest. The world was peaceful for those who knew their place and respect the authority of superiors. People had five basic relationships to the world i.e. to parents, brother, mates, friends and the government. Although the emperor is the ultimate authority but people can disobey him if he becomes tyrannical or breaks the ancient law. Confucianism believed that authority is based on ideals and behavior rather than physical power. His two followers who spread Confucius after his death were Mencius also called as Chinese Saint Paul or second sage and Xunzi.[12]

Daoism was another philosophy during Zhou period, preached by Laozi (Lao-tze). His teachings were widely accepted among intellectuals. His book Daodejing, meaning, classic of the way and values. He preached people to renounce their brutal ambitions, aggressive designs and desires, and to strive to regain the inner balance, congruence, and wise apathy which exist in nature. He attempted to achieve inner peace in the midst of the savage conflicts of his times. To reassert the importance of personal values, pleasures and happiness; in contrast to the emptiness, the pitiful transistorizes of worldly achievements. His philosophy viewed the world as made up of two balancing forces. Yin; meaning female and passive elements in the nature symbolised by the earth, darkness, even numbers, or a broken line and Yang; which embodied the male and active element, symbolized by heaven, light, cold, odd numbers, or an unbroken line.[13] This religion had its drawbacks. For example, Lao Zi promoted the idea of a return to a small state with a small population; people did not socialize though they lived so near, ultimately preventing social development.

Chinese intellectuals resorted to a hermitic way of life whenever they met setbacks and when they were successful, they would say "the less hermitry was to live in the remote areas while the great hermitry was to live in the court". The inner worldly and outer worldly attitudes made the Chinese intellects hover between the active Confucianism and the passive Taoism.Taoism was suppressed by the Qing rulers as well as by the foreign invaders consequent upon the Opium War. It has been faced with a huge impact from foreign culture but it remains an influential system of thought among the Chinese people. Qin (pronounced "cheen") prevailed militarily over all other states and unified China under its rule in 221 B.C. The Qin then imposed its name on rest of China, and it is from "Qin" that name China evolved. Qin was relatively anquarantined, rugged, semi frontier region located in the very fertile valley of Wei River, a tributary of the Yellow river. Its natural geography made it easy to defend but very difficult to capture, apparently managed to keep its economy and polity relatively unscathed. The Qin government was also anviolent recruiter of administrative and military talent. Qin transformed itself from a feudal government ta a highly centralized, unitary state.[14] Qin was a legalist who believed that people were bad and therefore necessarily had to be controlled and regulated to inculcate discipline. He developed a system of bureaucracy. The empire was divided into 36 provinces and further districts two government officials were put in charge of each district. The workers of that time were well trained and paid in a systematic manner. A network was setup to enable the emperor to know the pulse of every person. Land reforms were instituted by virtue of which land was taken away from nobles and given to peasants to work with specific tasking; this barred the nobles to rise against the emperor. Law implementation group was made to ensure law code was followed by all. He also attempted to combine the Great Wall into one continuous wall as a safety measure against the intruders from northwestern border. Anyone who would violate law code was sent to construct the wall and it was considered a punishment. Many people perished during this construction. However it was an advantage during war and a majorobstacle from the raiders from North western borders.

He practiced total censorship. 400 scholars who refused to turn in books were burnt or killed. He burnt all the books of Confucius.The Qin army was highly disciplined. Every soldier of Qin was a match for many opponents. Sima Qian, a great Chinese historian had said that the country of Qin was a state whose position alone predestined its victory. Qin was known as the "wildest beast" of China.[15]

Han consisted of two dynasties: the Western Han (206 BC - 24 AD) and the Eastern Han (25 - 220). During this period, 24 emperors ruled the dynasty. Many excellent Emperors like Gaozu, Wen, Jing and Wu contributed towards good governance and new inventions. These wise Emperors took effective measures during their reign, making the Han Dynasty a period of peace and prosperity. During this dynasty, China was considered a world power of that time flourishing in unparalleled successes in literature, arts, culture and technology. The achievements of that time still influence the lives of the Chinese people today.

Han dynasty was created by its leader Liu Bang an uneducated peasant. He had been a bandit and soon became an ally of his state's ruler, who needed his help to quell the rising violence. He defeated his only rival, Xiongnu, who was a Hun. When Liu Bang died following his refusal for medical treatment, his widow thereafter ruled for eight years.

Reign of Han Wudi again saw breaking down of feudal barons. Wudi was a dedicated Confusionist. He strengthened the civil service system by basing appointments on written examinations which tested knowledge of Confucianism. Wudi expanded towards south and added "Annam" (in Vietnam), five states in Southern China, Xinjiang and Korea to the Chinese territories.[16] The writing brush and ink was introduced and it came into wide use. Many classics were edited and the first dictionary was compiled. Coming of Buddhism increased cultural ties with India and parts of Middle East.

During this period Chinese harnessed the power of rushing water in streams and rivers. They invented waterwheel that transmitted power from a running stream to the large bellows of an iron casting operation. The Chinese also built the first ever suspension bridge in the world, 1800 years before such bridges were known in the West. They were the first ones to invent paper. The Chinese during this period also invented hang gliding and parachuting.[17] Han strove to create a strong central government. They restored the classical literature of China, established the first public school system and invented paper, porcelain, wheel barrow, compass and a primitive seismograph. They chose to rule by merit. Han period was marked by military expansion, even up to Europe. The Taoist secret service also known as Yellow turbans ended the Han rule. Sima Qian, China's greatest historian produced his great work "Shiji" (Records of the Grand Historian) during Wudi's reign. Sima Qian was castrated by Wudi for publicly coming to a captured general's moral defense thereby being deprived of the opportunity to produce male offspring to carry on his name. However he channeled his paternal instincts into historical writing. A popular historical novel about this period, called the Romance of the Three Kingdoms, is one of the China's all-time favorite literary works.[18]

Buddhism was first brought to China from India by missionaries and traders along silk route that connected China with Europe in late Han period (202B.C.-220A.D). Indian Buddhism was by then already 500 years old but had not flourished in China because of Confucian beliefs. There were two main divisions in Buddhism. Firstly, Theravada, which involves strict meditation and a close reading of the original teaching of Buddha. This is prominent in Sri Lanka and South East Asia. Secondly, Mahayana, which included various forms such as Zen, Pure Land and Tibetan Buddhism also known as Lamaism. Mahayana Buddhism also accepted contemporary Buddha's like Amitabha. During the Three Kingdom period, Buddhism was studied as an independent subject. Luoyang in North China became a major study center where there was focus on translation of scriptures. In 401 A.D. Kumarajina, a scholar was invited to Chanjang together with 3000 other scholars who translated 74 sutras. The royal families in China were passionate towards this religion and granted monks and nuns considerable privileges. Numbers of temples and monks mushroomed during this period. Bodhidharma came to China during this period. He visited Guangzhou and became the first patriarch of Zen Buddhism, the formation of which marked the independent development of the faith in China. Entry of Buddhism in China was at a time when Confucianism and Taoism were the prominent religions in China and rivaled India in historical antiquity and cultural pluralism. Due to similarities with Taoism, it gained a foothold in China. Shih-Kao, a patrician monk and Lokakshema, a Kushna monk from Indian subcontinent and Central Asia gave impetus to the new religion including translation of many Buddhist texts from Pali and Sanskrit to Chinese. Buddhism reached its glorious heights between 6th and 10thcentury A.D. during Sui and Tang dynasties.

Confucianism which had gone into hibernation due to coming of Buddhism again revived in 11 century due to non-religious activities of Buddhist monks and monasteries. Buddhism had also started facing challenges from the increasing popularity of Brahmanism and aggressive policies of Islamic rulers of the Indian sub-continent. Buddhism lost its dynamism when communist government of China succeeded in officially putting an end to the practice of religion by abolishing all forms of public worship and closing down all the monasteries.

Most of the Buddhist textbooks were the translation of Buddhist texts from India. Concepts such as monasticism and separation of the individual from the society were against the communitarian nature of the Chinese society.

Advocating abandonment of ties to family was also hard for ancestor worshipping Chinese to accept. Shaving of heads was strongly against Chinese traditions. The individual attainment of nirvana would be beneficial to the empire was not clear to the Chinese. To thrive in China, Buddhism had to transform itself into a system that could exist within the Chinese way of life. The obscure Indian sutras were made compatible with ancestor worship and participation in Chinese hierarchical system. Today the most popular form of Buddhism in mainland China and Taiwan is Pure Land School.

After the Han period, China suffered social disorder from A.D 222-581. It entered another quasi-feudalistic period. It tended to be an armed camp. The power was held by landed gentry, who commanded private armies. For three hundred years China lay wide open to invasions by tribes from Mongolia, Central Asia and Tibet. However some scholarly Taoists of that period discovered medicinal herbs, the magnetic compass, and the invention of gunpowder. At the end of Six Dynasties Period, general named Yang Jiang won Nanjing and ended a long period of chaos and formed Sui Dynasty.

Sui dynasty saw the reign of Yangdi who was the most talked about .He contributed a lot to public works projects. He forced a million laborers to dig a canal from his palace in Luoyang to the Yangzi River and perhaps an equal numbers to repair the Great Wall.[19] During this period, industry made new advances and shipbuilding technology reached a new high level. Steps to improve national economy like equal divisions of fields and tax moderation system were carried out. A grand canal of more than 2.5 miles long, between north and south China enhanced national water transportation. He carried out a change in the Political system wherein the examination system became more profound. Wae with Gaoli (Korea) became one of the major causes of the downfall of this dynasty. Tang Dynasty was founded by one of the last emperors of Sui dynasty. (A.D 581-618), spanned over three centuries of Chinese history. It is regarded as one of the most glorious periods in a unified empire. It was an era of cultural brilliance, territorial expansion and great economic prosperity. During this period China was the richest and most powerful political unit in the world. Trade flourished over silk route, overland and by sea. Large numbers of foreigners visited China for trade especially in Changan, present day Xi'an, which had also become one of the most cosmopolitan cities in the world, only after Baghdad. This was during Xuanzong's rule. During Tang rule China was the most powerful and prosperous countries in the world, particularly in economy, culture and military strength, which reached its unparalleled advanced level.

Bridge building techniques, music, and visual art penetrated into China in the Tang period. With both China and India being the oldest civilizations and neighbors' would have certainly exchanged many more inventions.[20]

The famous astronomer, Monk Yixing, was the first

to successfully measure the length of the meridian line. The well-known King of medicine, Sun Simiao, wrote medical book Qianjin Fan (Thousand Golden Prescriptions). Novel writing also became more prominent. The earliest engraved printing in the world was printed in the form of translation of Diamond Sutra.

The study of medicine was the highest contribution of Tang Dynasty, as it is practiced worldwide even today. The illustration of using herbs or organic materials was developed and spread during this period. A study on diabetes was conducted successfully. Study of complex chemicals to create gunpowder was also one of the contributions of this period. Gas cylinders and air conditioning was also invented during this rule. Study of law and mathematics had become very prominent.

Tang Dynasty had a very strong military based on Fubing system, a local military system that could be mobilised quickly in times of war. It involved militiamen between ages of 21-60 who were allocated area of land for their livelihood. Officers were given extended commission. Regular soldiers reported for duty in the provincial capital depending on the distance of their residence. Army was under the Army ministry, which had 634 units called Zhechougfu, each consisting of 800 to 1200 men. This system was abandoned in favor of full time regular Army in the 8th century.

Song dynasty lasted 300 years i.e., (960-1279) and the founder was Zhao Kuangying also known as "Grand Progenitor of the Song". He was famous for the "exchange of military authority for a cup of wine". Song became a weak dynasty militarily. Hebelieved in merit, than aristocracy. He eliminated any possibility of military and social challenges to his position by centralizing all authority. This period also saw rice cultivation reach its heights in quantity and various varieties.

During this period the Chinese exchanged goods such

as Indian and Persian cotton cloth, precious gems, incense and perfumes. Chinese ships were seen all through the Indian Ocean and began to displace Indian and Arab merchants in the South Sea. Chinese ships were larger than the Indian ships and technologically more advanced. However Indian ships frequented the city of Zayton, now Guangzhou for sale of their products.

People of Song dynasty had risen to world leaders in ship building, water tight bulk heads, improved buoyancy and protected cargo. They improved the steering system and introduced oars and sails in the ships which could hold several hundred men. Compass was further refined and made to be used for maritime navigation.

Military engineers during this time found gunpowder to be helpful in siege warfare, leading to the development of many types of rockets, cannons, bombs and mines. The "Wujing Zongyao" a military manual written in 1044 C.E. records the first true gunpowder formula and its production in bulk quantity. The mannual has four parts, including institutions, frontier defense, campaign anecdotes, and divination. The book can be seen as an encyclopaedia of Chinese military arts till the Song time. Its topics range from military strategy and organization, to infantry and cavalry training, the production and employment of weapons, and famous campaigns of earlier periods. Large number of illustrations in the book makes it a valuable of the military technology of the time. Su Song was famous for having designed and constructed mechanical clock tower which showed time, day, phase of the moon and position of certain stars and planets in the sky.

Economic reforms movement brought about government granaries for storage of grain, which was used as price control mechanism. Song also brought about "public services act". To improve both the budget and the army, the emperor reduced the number of troops and replaced a large numbers of standing army with militia of loyal farmers. There was commercial expansion; some Islamic forces in the west of China opened a new trade. New prosperous cities were found which could accommodate ships from India. Printing was given a new shape with a kind of ink made from lampblack, the so called Indian ink.[21]

China during this long period again saw ups and downs like in other dynasties, however with a changed outlook. Due to the persistent military threat from the West and North, the Song Dynasty reached a new height of Confucian civilization. Merchant wealth and ownership of vast land were not important for gaining political power as against educational qualifications.[22]

The Mongols

Mongols came to China as a result of the in-house fight. The Mongol Empire was one of the largest land empires in the history. The Mongols were par excellence people from the steppes who believed in freer life of animal husbandry and hardened battles over very rough and tough terrain. They believed in creating a great steppe empire by extending their rule as far stretched as possible. A small tribal chieftain called Temuchin who fought for his survival when challenged to maintain his position became more and more popular with each victory due to his skills in tribal warfare. His success story got the entire steppe under one rule and they came to be known as Mongols. He gained the name of Genghis Khan. Meaning, all encompassing chief.

The capital of Mongol empire was shifted twice, at Karakoram and later at Peking. The Mongols while in China exploited and enjoyed the products of the conquered Chinese and the other foreign people. With the predominance of the Mongols, Chinese were again left out of the main stream and alienated in their own land by the ruling Mongols. Although the Mongols were good in warfare on the horseback, for siege and capture tactics of walled cities, they had to learn the use of large catapults and explosive missiles from the Chinese.

The Mongol conquest of China shattered the Chinese economy, thousands of Chinese were butchered and plenty of collateral damaged suffered. The Mongols had divided the population into four ethnic groups, basically to malign the Chinese in their own land. The well- known traveler Marco Polo, who came to Kublai Khan's court also, talks about Mongols disregard for the Chinese.[23]

Hans were discriminated socially and politically, all important posts were a monopoly of the Mongols. However in Yuan dynasty established by Kublai Khan, development of novel and written vernacular along with musical instrument of western culture became very popular. Many people converted to Islam in Northwest and Southwest of China. Christianity and Lamaism also flourished.

Mongols had traditionally supported variety of faiths, due to which the Confusionist influence declined at the royal court. Public projects like communication system including the extension of Grand Canal, shipping of surplus grains from south to less fertile land in the north and construction of roads continued. However the campaign against Japan and other Southeast Asian Countries, faulty taxation, lavish expenditure, tarnishing traditional Chinese superiority by discrimination, in-house fights amongst the Mongols and the plague that killed many people ultimately weakened the vast Mongol empire which now showed signs of a break. Mongols failed to administer thisugly situation which led to a strong rebellion in 1352 starting from Guangzhou, and spreading throughout China, finally leading to founding of a new dynasty in 1387 called Ming under Zhu anzhang.

The Later Chinese Dynasties and Period Upto 1962

Ming Dynasty (1368-1644 A.D) was the last Dynasty in China ruled by ethnic Hans. It was another peak dynasty in Chinese history like the Han Dynasty. This was a period of transformation in traditional Chinese society. The culture and traditions that were broken by the Mongol rule were again restored and expanded. Painting was given impetus especially in expressive calligraphic style. Pro agricultural policies and reforms were introduced along with newer and improved innovations such as water-powered plows and crop rotations were implemented. Regional crops were grown along with 'National Market' system to enable export. This period started showing signs of decline of feudal society and origin of capitalism. Sea trade was at its height and extensive trade was taking place with Southeast Asia and Japan.

This Dynasty had started giving importance to Foreign Relations. Exchange of goods developed the economy and their goods were in demand in Europe and Western countries. The most talked about voyage was undertaken by Zheng He, probably the largest in the maritime history of the world in 1405. The fleet reached America 70 years before Columbus and circumvented the globe and almost a century before Magellan.

One of the areas explored was Taiwan, leading to an exodus of Chinese immigrants to this island. Han Chinese in Taiwan had assisted in a rebellion in the mainland to overthrow the rulers of the Qing dynasty. This has become a part of Chinese history and one of its excuses to base its claim on Taiwan. During Ming Dynasty, China had 31% of worlds GDP says Joseph Needham, sinologist. The burden on peasants was reduced considerably and emphasis was laid on removing corruption and rewarding exemplary punishments.

The world's largest encyclopedia called "Yongle Chengzu" was written during this time. Silver and fire arms were important items which were traded during this time. The improvement in medical practice and innovations was at its peak. "Bencao Gangmu" i.e, compendium of material medicine was published during this period by Li Shizhen who was one of the greatest medical practitioners of his time and was the first one to identify gallstone, used ice to treat fever and developed unique technique of disinfection. Prevention of small pox was discussed and practiced 200 years before Edward Jenner introduced inoculation in England.[24]

Every dynasty that ruled China developed some or the other area. In the Ming period, besides other spheres, the military was given a further boost. Gunners were introduced in infantry along with full-fledged gun powder based military technology. The system of use of chariot in land warfare was re-introduced, this time by innovating fitting of guns on them. It would be prudent to note that in 14thcentury; only 10% of Ming infantry were gunners. However in 16th century almost entire infantry was converted into modern gunners. The employment of firearm along with chariots became a main-stream strategy of Ming era, which means that strategists during that period actually added further teeth to the infantry by giving it mobility and lethal firepower, and converting the chariot into a defensive shield against bows and arrows. Catapults of very effective technology was developed which could throw explosives for destruction of walls and used in seize operations.

The capability of Chinese navy was also made more modern and lethal in middle of 16th century wherein 70% of all warships was based on firearms. Proper use of firearms, cannons, rocket launchers and other weapons was advocated keeping in mind the distance at which they would be effective. This tactics was successfully used against the Japanese pirate ships. This firearm tactics of the Chinese during that time was more superior to that of the west. There was a consolidation of the army which by now had a standing army of one million. However since the Chinese did not have any military opponent then, and due to the inward looking policy of the Chinese, there was no pressure to further enhance or improve the technology. Comparatively the westerners who were at war with each other and competing for new technological discoveries were resolute in making more sophisticated weapons.

Ming dynasty was also responsible to create the greatest of the governmental and social stability in human history. The lost agriculture base was rebuilt and 16th century economy was stimulated by more easy and faster maritime trade.

Some of the outsiders felt that Tibet was never part of China and talked of it being independent of China during the Ming Dynasty. However the Chinese historians take an opposing view of it. Chinese mention that Ming had established itinerant commenderies, overseeing Tibet administration.

The overall theme of the military history of the early Ming was the decline in the importance of offensive warfare. It became important for the emperor to keep the Mongols at bay in order to claim the mandate of heaven, however, any further territorial conquest was debatable, and was also generally opposed by the civil officials.[25] In the period between ca. 755-960 the Confucian opinion was permanently suspicious and disdainful of the military, and in the ensuing Song dynasty this opinion had been inculcated in the Chinese society as a whole. There was a general agreement in Emperors and the civil officials that the military be confined to an instrumental role, and should be accustomed to obeying orders and this was seen as more important than a victory. However early Ming contradicted this and made military more powerful than the civilian officials and also paid them more.

With the change in time, by 1435, the civil services elite finally won out completely over the military. This situation arose due to the fact that more and more capture of extended land required military to be predominant. In the later years it was necessary to have more contacts with foreign world for which Confusionist thought was mandatory i.e., to have elite people from the civil service examination.[26] It is evident from history that the early Ming policies had a long lasting effect and are followed till date. Important areas such as warfare, geographical basis of power, military institutions, foreign affairs, the civil service and governmental administration could be distinguished analytically but in practice, decisions affecting a particular area was taken by different rulers or set of people.

Response to a contemporary situation in one area could call for a decision in another. Therefore wars were undertaken in order to defend or extend the land frontier, the civil service was established to provide logistics for the army, and foreign relations were centrally controlled to prevent any future war. The civil service was consistently able to veto policy changes, whether they came from the grand secretaries or the eunuch dictators. As an example, shifting the capital away from the dangerously exposed site of Peking should have been a priority after 1612, but though it was proposed, it was not done. Political and military unity co-existed was a fact for a long time in imperial China.The Ming Dynasty was one of the most important periods of the emergence of the Chinese character which can be seen even today, it impacted the Manchu or the Ching dynasty which was the last dynasty of China.

Ching Dynasty was founded by Tungus people, the descendants of the Jurchen who had ruled North China earlier under the name of Chin. The Chin founder had named his people as Manchu's, who became the people of Manchuria. Manchu's were Mongols horsemen turned merchants and were a mixed of Mongolian, Korean, Chinese and Jurchan. Taking advantage of the chaos in China's Ming Dynasty in 1644, the Manchu's moved further to south. They had formed an alliance with a Ming loyalist general who had sought for help.

The Manchu's were very wise. They led the military campaigns with diplomatic expertise, taking the Chinese Hans alongside and therefore managed to extend their rule right up to Pamir Mountains and establish protectorate on what China today calls as Xizang and better known as Tibet. Manchu's had expanded China to twice its size and also doubled its population from 200 million to 395 million by granting trade concessions to Islamic rulers in central Asia and monarchs in Southeast Asia. To guarantee their power the Manchu's, now the Ch'ing Dynasty maintained their own military identity by bringing their banner forces into China, placing them in garrisons around the capital Peking and in strategic locations around the country. (They had divided themselves into 8 banner men, banner man being a social/military organization transcending the old tribal groupings.) There numbers being small, they had to rely on regular Chinese armies for an affective and numerically superior military power. Although the Chinese Hans were more sophisticated and learned, Manchu's prevailed over them and with every Han there was a Manchu placed in the government and other department. They had managed to keep their identity separate from the Chinese Hans.

Kangxi dictionary was a massive effort on part of the Manchu's to help them conquer China both spiritually and militarily because they knew that they have to go the Chinese way when in China and therefore assimilated a great deal of Chinese culture. They continued the Confucian court practices and temple rituals. This period again saw discrimination with Han Chinese. The major threat to China was always from the West or the North. However since the people who threatened were already ruling in China, the threat was now perceived from the sea from Southern coastal area from where Western traders had started flocking.

From the outset, the Manchu's traditionally followed Confucian cultures than any previous alien dynasty. This helped them gain Chinese sympathies. They ensured their affective command and control which prevented any Han official from establishing a local power base. In the period between 1736 and1796, the Chinese territory under the

Manchu Dynasty reached greatest glory in terms of territorial expansion and domestic prosperity. The Westerners and the Europeans both regarded China as the greatest Eastern culture to imitate.

Increase in population, declining crop production, massed corruption and in-house fight had started failing Manchu's, whose power began to be interfered by westerners and the Europeans apparently by land and sea. This situation was never anticipated by the Chinese who felt secure from just the Great Wall and the vassal states created around them thinking this to be a good enough buffer. Having known about the massive trade facilities in China, these countries started making a bee-line here in quest of good trade. The Chinese felt that they were self-sufficient and foreign goods were of no use to them. Moreover the trading would involve payback in silver, which the Chinese did not like. The British then paid this from Indian kitty while the Americans from Central America.

The forced trade by West introduced Opium brought from India in plenty, which the Chinese had later banned, causing two wars and ultimate subjugation of Chinese in giving trading rights and latter loosing some of its territory to the foreigners. This was indeed a very humiliating chapter in the history of modern China. An era of revolts and rebellions, administrative failure of governance, bankruptcy, floods and drought, corruption, and humiliating defeat by west, all put together shattered an ordinary Chinese who was made an extra terrestrial in his own country. Millions of people were killed due to plague and hunger.

The Treaty of Nanking established formal equality between the rulers of China and Great Britain. This ended the Chinese perception of 'Mandate of Heaven'. This also undermined the ideological sense of dynastic rule, a first step in the destruction of the imperial order. Perhaps opium played an important role in the transformation of imperial virgin China into a modern strong China by arousing

Chinese nationalist feeling. All the coastal and inland cities which were flocked by western people by force and against the wishes of the Chinese are today the modern centers of their economy.

Confucianism again stepped in as a defender of the Chinese social fabric embedded in its tradition very strongly, but not for long. It was becoming clear that imperialism was coming to an end and there was a probability of a breakup of dynastic rule and advent of a nation-state theory. Sun Yat-sen of peasant origin near Canton having seen the sufferings of the Chinese started an uprising on October 10, 1911, that led to collapse of the Manchu government and takeover of power by the regional military forces in which Sun was elected the first President of Republic of China. This period of transition as well as military and political chaos was also a period of intellectual ferment. Acceptance of Western form of social life and equality of sovereign states overthrew the basic concepts of the Chinese polity; the Mandate of Heaven and the principles of Confucian political order.

It is difficult to say whether it was Westernization or Modernization that killed the spirit of traditional literary language of the past and its replacement by a new written language amongst the students of that time as also their being impressed by pragmatism and materialism. The Republic of China in its inception was politically unstable due to nonavalaibility of a clear minded direction. Two schools of thought emerged in the fight to freedom. The rivalry between the communists and the nationalist saw an ideological difference, slowly building up towards a civil war, this time amongst the inhabitants of China itself, and not from a raider from outside.[27]

The Chinese future was now hanging between communists, under Mao Tse-tungand Nationalists, under Sun Tat-sen on one side and the Common enemy Japan on the other. Although the aim of both was freedom of imperial China, but the manner in which they wanted to obtain this was different. From 1928 to 1949, China's history was characterized by three major wars. Prolonged fight coupled with the unpopularity of the Nationalist government and its lack of willpower to fight the communist, resulted in its defeat. On the First of October 1949 China was declared as the People's Republic of China by the communists. Drastic reforms in almost all the sectors were taken to strengthen the shattered economy and the badly humiliated image of one of the oldest civilization in the world.

In order to stabilize the country economically and culturally two political decisions were taken, The Great Leap Forward of 1958 and the start of Cultural Revolution in 1966.[28] During 1960, one of the worst famines occurred, which along with the previous two failures caused more than 20 million lives in a matter of four years. During this period Mao Tse-tung had become very unpopular and had to resign. It was during this period that the Chinese waged an unexpected war against India in 1962.

The Early Indian History

India is probably the earliest seeds of human habitation and the oldest inhabited region on the planet. It is supposed that human samplings lived in parts of India even in the second ice age because their remains have been traced in parts of Punjab and of South India as early as between 400,000 and 200,000 B.C. However the earliest known man in India belonged to what is known as the Paleolithic or Old Stone Age, when men earned his living by gathering food and by fishing and hunting. The community was small and nomadic in habits. Rough type of quartzite chipped rock was used for hunting. The human beings belonged to the Negrito branch of the Negro race that are known to have lived along the maritime coast from Arabia to China and their descendants may be found in Andaman Island.The relics of Old Stone Age have been discovered in several parts of India, particularly eastern coast of India.

Neolithic age was the outcome of the Proto-Australoids whose arrival in India is supposed to have marked the advent of the Neolithic or the New Stone Age, relics of which have been discovered in many parts of India. Human beings living in this age were acquainted with the use of improved weapons and methods of agriculture. They lived in huts made of mud and bricks and knew the technique of painted pottery. They tamed animals like ox and goat. The walls of their houses were decorated with colored paintings. Spinning and weaving cloths was practiced and going out into the sea on homemade boats was a common practice. The dead were buried in the tombs. The earliest remains of the New Stone Age dating back to the fourth millennium B.C. have been found in Baluchistan and lower Indus Valley.

Metal age transition is not marked but it is believed that metals in the form of copper was being used and a matured civilization already existed in large areas watered by Indus at least 3000 years before the birth of Christ. On the basis of evidence recorded in the Atharvaveda it appears that iron was already in use in Northern India in 1000 B.C.

Dravidians followed the metal age that were seen as evidence of racial elements. The Dravidians were experts in use of metals, pottery with polychrome decorations. They lived a settled life and practiced cultivation of land. By now people were aware of the defensive system that was necessary around their domestic area, and had constructed forts around their villages. Use of bows and arrows, spears and swords were common in their armory. The Dravidians were organized in small states for ease of administration and were ruled by the King. They worshipped Mother-Goddess and totem-symbols. Theypracticed burying of the dead and adopted cremation as a disposal method. There were also traces of the Dravidians having established trade centers along the Southern coast-line, Ceylon and the Indian Archipelago. Most of the Dravidians had settled in southern part of India.

Indus Valley Civilization, like all other civilizations in

the prehistoric times also evolved near a water source; China near Yellow River, Egypt near Nile, Mesopotamia near Tigris-Euphrates and India near Indus. The most prominent example of the Indus Valley Civilization are the ancient sites of Mohenjo-Daro in Larkana district of Sind and the other at Harappa in Montgomery district, now both in Pakistan. The Indus Valley Civilization developed in around 3d millennium B.C., more than 1000 years earlier than it did in China. The system of living was very matured and advanced. People practiced agriculture and grew wheat, rye, cotton and rice amongst other cereals. They had good irrigation system including control of water from rivers and rain water. Fish was also eaten besides other non-vegetarianfood. Disciplined community living with proper two, three rooms along with drainage, sewage system and soak-pits with mortar and burnt bricks were constructed with elaborate system of ventilation.Citadels with high walls were constructed evenfor more priestly people who were dominant in running the administration of the community. The most important finding was the construction of the Great Bath which was meant to take community bath, was more related to religious requirement rather than hygiene. This may have been connected to the Maha Kumbh mela held in India every 144 years. Trading and commercial facilities existed with Mesopotamia, China, Burma, Persia and Egypt,and the quality of products was superior to the products from other places. Cotton was extensively used as textile, which the western world saw only after 2000 to 3000 years later.

Meditation, yoga, Goddesses worship and art were prevalent during this time. Metals like gold, silver, copper and bronze were used to make utensils, ornaments and other items of weaponry, however use of iron was not traced. People believed in peaceful, well ordered and disciplined life and probably because there was no invader for almost a thousand years, there was no requirement felt for more active military organization or sophisticated armaments. The relics of the streets, houses, public assemblies, citadel and state granaries are suggestive of an advanced technique of city planning and organization. Measurement system in terms of Weights and distance of different variety were in use. The civilization crumbled between 1500 and 1000 B.C. The reasons could be invasion of the Aryans, natural calamity, and change of climate or natural catastrophe.

Earliest Literature and the Epics of the Indo-Aryans are known collectively as Veda, which means 'knowledge'. The Vedas i.e. religious texts and historical information (Rik, Sama, Yayurand Artharva-together with the Samhitas, Brahmans, Aranyakas, Upanishads and Vedangas) constitute a huge mass of literature, composed over a long time and mark the transition from prehistoric to historicera which Kautilya also mentions in his description of Arthashastra. The contents of the Vedas are collection of metrical hymns, prayers, spells, or charms, mixed in some cases with prose passages. Most of the hymns are invocations addressed to the gods and have a religious bent of mind. Passing from the Vedic lyrics to the Sanskrit epics, an extreme transformation in grammar, vocabulary, style, social conditions and religion is experienced. Two voluminous poems in the form of epics described as Ramayana and Mahabharata believed to be contemporary were composed by Valmiki and Vyasa respectively.[29]

The Aryans invaded the Indian subcontinent somewhere in 1500, and came to dominate most of the original Dravidian people. The Aryans spoke a language related to the western European languages, and came from the Russian steppes. They produced the Vedas, which subsequently gave India its Vedic religion. The Aryans also developed the caste system called as Kshatryas and the Brahmins under whom various regional groups like vaishas, who were peasants and Shudras who the Dravidians were included. The hierarchical society lasted officially until the British rule, and continues informally even today with all casts intact. Around 500 B.C., Siddhartha Gautama, better known as the Buddha preached a stoic life style involving moral living and meditation that developed into the rich philosophy of Buddhism. Another philosopher, Vardhamana, called Mahavira, and his follower Jina, who believed that suffering, was due to the mixing of spirit with base matter, which must be separated from each other by means of fasting, asceticism, and chastity translated into a religion called Jainism. Monarchy was the prevalent form of government, although the concept of republics was not wholly unknown. The institution of monarchy probably owed its origin to military necessity and was sought to be justified on grounds of divine sanction. Kingship was hereditary with exceptions. The society was patriarchal and father was the head of the family. Musical instruments like flute, lute, harp and drums were used for singing and dancing. Intermarriage and eating together was quite popular. The status of women was higher than it was to be in later centuries. Girls were allowed to move around freely and take part in social functions. Horse sacrifice was a popular religious ceremony observed by the royal families. The economic life of Aryans unlike that of Indus Valley people was distinctly rural. Agriculture was the main occupation and value of commodities or land was determined in terms of cattle. Religion was basically the continuation of primitive faiths i.e., terrestrial, celestial and atmospheric. The great epic Mahabharata as per the historians is probably not older than fourth century B.C. and not later than fourth century A.D. Similarly Ramayana assumed its present form over a long period intervening between the third century B.C. and the second century A.D. Deconstruction of the two epics reveals that the two epics complement each other. They are part of a grand 'Vedic' continuum.

Buddhism, founded in 5th or 6th century B.C.E. is a world religion which spread in and around the ancient kingdom of Magadha, in Bihar and is based on the teachings of Siddhartha Gautama Buddha. It is the spiritual solution of the awakened one, Buddha, is regarded as one of the three most widespread major world religions. Prince

Siddhartha, who became Shakyamuni Buddha, lived in central north India from 566 to 486 B.C.E. After attaining enlightenment at the age of thirty-five he started preaching. In the first phase the historic Buddha expounded the teaching and his disciples preserved it. In the second phase were the interpretations of the teaching, from 4th century to the first century. The third phase was the rise of Mahayana Buddhism which occurred approximately from 1st to the 7th century C.E. The last and the fourth phase were of Buddhist Tantra which took place after 7th century which migrated to Tibet. Buddhism spread to various parts of Asia from 250 B.C.E. to 7th century C.E. The five principles of moral code of refrain from killing, stealing, adultery, indulging in falsehood and drunkenness along with six fundamental virtues of charity, purity, patience, courage, contemplation and knowledge did bring about a change in the thinking and made an everlasting impact on the minds of the people, which exist in the human character of the Indians till date. Buddhism spread to China, Tibet and other west Asian countries through the Silk Route in 1st century B.C. Buddhism declined in India due to the withdrawal of royal patronage. The Muslim rulers and the Huns also contributed to its decline. The famous Chinese travelers Fa- Hien and Hiuen-Tsang observed that the faith had lost its pristine purity. There was inefficiency of the church organization and non-availability of a Supreme Head to control and take the belief forward.[30]

Foreign invaders and prevalence of Buddhism in lands beyond India invariably brought into it, the impact of foreign nations, beliefs and cults and molded it to suit its own society resulting in losing the credibility of it being purely of Indian origin. The assimilative character of Hinduism transformed the old ideas into a new mould. Buddhism and the contemporary Jainism shared much with the cotemporary Brahmanical sacrificial religion, since all sprang from mystical and philosophical notions explored in the Upanishads, which were still in composition at around 500 B.C.E. Differences nevertheless remained between Brahmanicalsects and their competitors; one example of which pertains to the concept of Karma.[31] Buddhist condemned the Brahmanical sacrifices because they involved the slaughter of animals.

Jainism came into existence when later Vedic civilization between 1000B.C -600B.C. had come to an end and there was a rise of empires and small kingdoms. They were basically farmers and valued bulls and cows. Jainism evolved from the word Jin referring to one who has vanquished his passion or conquest of own self in bondage. It is a religious faith of Thirthankaras who were the 24 gurus of Jainism, and had shaped the foundation of the Jain thought, the last two being Parsvanath and Lord Mahavira. Jainism believed in ahimsa, i.e., non-violence. Mahavira had no faith in God but believed in the existence of a omnipotent power in all the souls. The history of these two is recorded by Bhadrabahu, 150 years after Nirvana of Mahavira in a text called Kalpasutra. It had an exceptional prosperous period of domination of various religions. Mahavira is also known to be a contemporary of Buddha. Jainism was even more essentially moralistic in its outlook than Buddhism, with an even greater emphasis on austerity and mendicant monasticism as the sole route to salvation. Their teachings found an audience similar to that of Buddhism in the complex villages and towns. There seem to be much similarity in both the teachings. Greeks happen to be the first Europeans who came in contact with the Jains. They considered that religion is eternal and imperishable; it is without any beginning and will never cease to exist. It is that Indian religion of peace, whose doctrine proclaims that every being has a soul with potential divine properties; its goal is self- control. Jains do not believe in creationism, they believe that,nature follows its own law. Jainism does not believe in God as a creator, survivor, and destroyer of the universe, but as a perfect being. It was dissipated with the rise of Hinduism and more importantly Islamic barbarians who plundered and destroyed most of the Jain culture. Unlike Buddhism, Mahavira's sect did not spread beyond India, but it remains a living tradition there.

Hinduism is one of the oldest religions in the world. Unlike China, where the emergence of the Confucian socio-political order was well documented, and once established, the system showed remarkable historical continuity. The evolution of the Hindu socio-religious system was not only undocumented but it continued to add new schools of philosophy, cults and rituals throughout its evolution and captivated many religions and allowed them to flourish side by side. Origins of the religion are traced to the Indus Valley Civilization. Its development was influenced by many invasions over thousands of years, the major one being Aryans who brought Vedism. It has grown to be the 3rd largest religion after Christianity and Islam. It is 13% of the world's population and remains arguably the most tolerant of polytheistic religions. Hinduism revolves around Brahmanism. Meditation is practiced, with Yoga being the most common. It has the deserved reputation of being highly tolerable of other religions. The most important of all Hindu text is the Bhagwat Gita, part of the epics of Mahabharata and the second one being Ramayana. The Vedic hymns evolved Brahmins, Kshatriyas, Vaishas and Shudras. Two further developments also contributed to the evolution of Hinduism; firstly, the creation of new sacred ideas that were preserved in a variety of textual traditions and secondly the founding of institutions, especially that of the temples, by which Hinduism was to be maintained as the central, evolving religion of the majority of people of the subcontinent. The dominance of the Brahmins manifested in a uniquely Indian-religious-social system known as caste. One of the positive attributes of the caste system was that it allowed for the coexistence of people with many levels of culture within the country, and also for the peaceful absorption of many racial groups that entered India prior to the coming of Muslims. The alternative would have been, as history has shown in other parts of the world, mutual extermination or enslavement. The rise in popularity of local deities and personal gods led to iconolatry and the building of temples, which became a well-established part of

Hindu religion by the Gupta period (320-480C.E.). What makes Hinduism the most tolerant of religions is its syncretism nature and its acceptance of the fact that there are many paths that lead to God, and that God accept all of them. Karma and sansarawere the concepts of Buddhism, Jainism and Hinduism as well.

Mauryan Empire rose when fascinated by the conquests and glory of Alexander the great, Chandragupta had met him at Taxila and desired to emulate him. Soon after the death of Alexander at Babylon in 323 B.C., Chandragupta along with his friend, minister and counselor, Chanakya who was exiled from powerful Nanda kingdom of Magadha, raised the old cry of nationalism and arouse the people against the foreign invaders. Chandragupta demonstrated extreme acumen under the guidance of Chanakya (a Brahmin teacher at Tkshashila) and within a span of two years annexed Pataliputra and established the Maurya Empire, in the year 322 B.C.E. Other great Greek invaders like Seleucus, Eudemus and Peithon were also defeated and the largest ever empire in its time was created. A small portion of the Indian subcontinent named Kalinga was later captured by his grandson Ashoka bringing the entire India and some of its neighbors under the Maurya Empire. Megasthenes, the ambassador of Seleucus, had left a record of the entire episode.

Successive rulers like Bindusara, hissonand Ashoka the grandson of Chandragupta, both followed their predecessors' in a kingly way, further building on the culture and ethics left by their fathers. During their rule the discipline of the entire empire was at its peak. There was a proper organizational control and the administrative units of the kingdom were further divided for better command and control. There was a proper system of tax collection. Agriculture was regulated in many ways, so were rates of interest. Periodical inspection of food, markets, manufacturers, and slaughter house was carried out. Weights and measurements were standardized. Punishments were rigorously given to people who would disobey rules and regulations. Trade had flourished not only within the empire but also outside.

Silk called Chinapatta was also made in India, and often compared with the Chinese silk. The import of Chinese silk indicates existence of trade contact with China as early as 4thcentury. The economy of the empire was outstanding because of its systematic and well organized administration and diplomatic relations. Although the ultimate authority was vested in the King, the smaller zones enjoyed great deal of autonomy and decentralisation. One fourth of income was spent on public works and army was maintained adequately. Iron was used widely. Major turning points in the Indian economy were improvement in communication and transportation, increasing use of coins and metals like iron, improvement in trade and commerce, and infrastructure. Many urban centers grew during this period. The Indian economy was an agrarian economy by this time.

There was an irrigation department which looked after the canals and a navigation department for harbors', ferries, bridges and boats and ships. It had a strong navy alongside of the army. Naval capability had developed in India since Rig Vedic times. History is more often than not, the creation of its geographical environments, and geography of India facilitated this, being surrounded by sea from three sides. Hiuen Tsiang, a Chinese traveler to India also speaks about presence of strong navy during King Harshas rule. Ashoka maintained diplomatic relation with Cyclone and Hellenistic monarchies of Syria, Egypt, Cyrene, Mesopotamia and Epirus. The kingdom of Kamarupa played an important role in the naval history of ancient India. The naval battle between the Jats and Sultan Mahmud in 1025 A.D. is also a reminder of various other examples of the naval history of ancient India.[32]April 05 1964 is celebrated as the National Maritime Day of India. On this day in 1919 naval history of India was created when S. S. Loyalty the first ship of Scindia Steam Navigation Co Ltd journeyed to UK.

Ashoka (272- 231 B.C.) The grandson of Chandragupta Maurya was one of the most distinguished emperors of Maurya dynasty and remembered as one of the greatest emperor of India. He was popular for not only providing outstanding administration to his people but also for spread of Buddhism especially after the Kalinga war. He furthered his father's and grandfather's kingdom in every respect, and embraced and preached Buddhism not only in India but also in other Countries including China and Tibet. His creation of Ashoka Pillar became the official emblem of the Government of India.

He was a great warrior of his times and had fought many wars with victory. The Kalinga war transformed him completely. The sufferings of the people muted from the Kalinga war made Ashoka denounced violence and adopt peaceful life. While the war changed his attitude towards humanity, peaceful life which he wanted to persue after the war was misunderstood as his weakness which brought about a collapse of the empire. Shunga dynasty was formed for a short period followed by another major dynasty known as Gupta Dynasty in 320 A.D.

Kautilya was also popularly known as Chanakya. He was a Brahmin by caste and was a professor of economics and political science in the ancient Tkshashila University. He was the brain behind the rise of Maurya Empire. He had served both Chandragupta and his son Bindusara as their chief advisor and was famous for his diplomatic and martial foresight and vision. He wrote Arthashastra, an ancient treatise which highlights the monetary and fiscal policies, welfare, international relations and war strategies in detail. His writings of governing a state made him popular not only in India but also outside. According to him, the ruler should use any means to attain his goal and his actions require no moral sanctions. He has also often been linked to Machiavelli.

Due to a misunderstanding, he was driven out of the Nanda Empire, which he took to heart and pledged to destroy the dynasty. Later his acumen in warfare strategy became the cause of fall of Nanda Dynasty. He was loyal to his king and therefore hardly refrained from doing anything in pursuit of achieving his aim; he was unscrupulous enough; yet he was also wise enough to know that this very purpose might be defeated by means unsuited to the end. Long before Clausewitz, he is reported to have said that war is only a continuance of state policy by other means, but at the same times adds that the objective must always be the betterment of the state as a result of war, not the mere defeat and destruction of the enemy.[33]

Alexander's invasion affected the North Western parts of India to a great extent, and was an important landmark in the history of India. At that time Greeks knew about the Indian richness through the Persian rulers, who gained revenue from India in the form of Gold. Herodotus a Greek historian also knew about this. Alexander entered India after conquering Persia. He crossed Indus and faced King Ambi in Taxila who was ready to accept Alexander's supremacy. However another King, Porus gave him a tough fight but ultimately lost to Alexander's supremacy with dignity; impressed with his determination, Alexander let Porus rule his kingdom and made him an ally. Further movement to cross river Ganges was made difficult by his own army who were now tired of a long campaign and did not want to challenge the militarily strong kingdom of Nanda's.

The strenuous campaigns of Alexander restored the fabric of imperialism and laid the foundation of closer contact between India and the Hellenic world. The Macedonians had welded the political atoms into one unit and thus paved the way for the permanent union under the Maurya. Peshawar and the old university of Taxila became the meeting place of men from many nations. There the Indians met the Scythians, the YuehChih, the Iranians, the Bactrian Greeks, the Turks, and the Chinese. This meeting was the one which was historical and perhaps the one to start the relations between China and India resulting in establishing the first Chinese embassy to India in 64A.C.[34]

Gupta Dynasty (320-550 C.E.)followed after the fall of the Kushan Empire around fourth century A.D. due to its political and military collapse, there was again disintegration of the Indian Subcontinent into smaller regions and kingdoms, all taking their own way. Being weak, it was invaded by various foreigners and barbarians or Mlechchhas from the north western frontier region and central Asia. However, one great ruler Chandragupta-I successfully thwarted any design and threw out the foreigners, laying the foundation of Gupta Empire which was to reign for the next 300 years. The reign of Gupta Empire was called as the Golden Age of the Indian history.

This period produced many prominent personalities like Kalidasa and Aryabatta, who brought the greatest of literary work and developed the concept of Zero and decimal system based on number 10. Panchatantra and Kamasutra were written during this period. There was a renewed enthusiasm in religions. Vishnu and Shiva came to be prayed. Due to extensive trade, and interaction of the Indians with others, the culture of India became the dominant culture around the Bay of Bengal, profoundly and deeply influencing the culture of Burma, Cambodia and Sri Lanka. The Gupta Empire established a strong central government which also allowed a degree of decentralization. Physicians developed herbal remedies to treat various illnesses and developed plastic surgery and vaccination against smallpox, which had been used in China and Europe much later. There was peace, progress and prosperity. Fa-Hien, the Chinese pilgrim, who visited India during the rule of Chandragupta-II, speaks highly of the efficiency in administration during this period.[35]

Agriculture was the main profession; however a significant progress was made in trade and industry. Guild system came to be practiced. Improvement in relations with outside world was made through trade and commerce by land and sea route. Military was strengthened and better organized. Great importance was given to education by means of establishing Nalanda University with an amazing 1:9 teacher student ratio.

Gupta Empire had amassed plenty of wealth due to flourishing trade with other countries. It had the distinction of becoming the wealthiest Empires, and therefore also most peaceful as compared to its contemporary dynasties elsewhere in the world. Many reforms were carried out in the administration and financial matters. The empire declined and ultimately disintegrated due to very heavy expenditure carried out to stop invasion of Hephthalites. Moreover expecting financial bankruptcy the smaller kingdoms started declaring their own freedom. The barbarian invasions of the 5th and 6th century A.D. marked a turning point in the history of India. Politically, the Hun inroads hastened the decline of the Guptas. All this chaos led to the intermingling of the foreigners with the Indians on the social level, paving the way for social predisposition and the admittance of Indianised foreigners into the fold of Indian history. However the Huns failed to build a lasting hegemony in India in contrast to their victories in the west.

Chola Empire (753- 1190C.E.) had ruled the southern part of the Indian sub-continent until 13th century. The main source of origin was river Kaveri. The Empire extended upto Sri-Lanka and Maldives. They had centralized form of government. They left behind a legacy of Tamil literature and the famous and artistic temples of the south. They were the center of economic activity in the south, both via land and sea. Hinduism was followed extensively; mainly people worshipped Vishnu and Shiva, although other religions existed side by side. Trade and commerce flourished and people lived peacefully. The army was divided into three groups; archers, forest soldiers, cavalry and elephants. They possessed around 60,000 elephants and the total strength of army was 150,000. Maritime history of Cholas was very rich and innovative. Different kinds of ships and boats were available and land fights fought on deck boards. The Cholas's redefined the trade culture from pre-emporia to emporia, China under the Sung dynasty, contemporarily also witnessed this in eleventh century A.D.

The Muslim and Mughal Empire

The main aim of all Muslim rulers behind invading India was the immense wealthof India. The conversion of the Arabs to Islam gave an impetus to various activities including commercial trade during the earlier contact with India. There is evidence of a naval expedition led by the Arabs against the western coast in about 637 A.D. However, a well-planned and more ambitious territorial expansion was the next Muslim contact with India in terms of the Arab invasion of Sindh in 715 A.D. by Mohammad Bin Qasim. Many people were massacred and lower Indus valley came under Muslim occupation.

After many others, Mahmud Ghazni invaded India several times, howeverhis sixteenth expedition specifically targeted the Somnath Temple in 1025 A.D. to acquire the wealth that he could take away to maintain his huge army. India was known to have been the richest country in the world, even richer than China because of its climatic conditions and agriculture and other precious jewellery and stones. His seventeenth and last attackin India was against the Jats in 1026 who had tried to stop him when he was going back with the booty. Anandapala and Chalukya Bhimadeva-I of Gujarat offered great resistance to Mahmud Ghazni for a long time but failed to stop him. (Goel Sita Ram & Shouri Arun, Heroic Hindu Resistance to Muslim Invaders; 636-1206 A.D.).

Thereafter Muhammad Ghori invaded India and established a Turkish empire. He was a strategic warrior and a lover of arts and culture. To maintain his huge army and continue to expand his empire outside the Indian sub-continent he required wealth for which he turned towards India, which was still the wealthiest country in the world. Inspite of a very brave resistance by Prithviraj Chauhan and other allied Hindus he managed to plunder the Indian wealth, after being defeated by Prithviraj Chauhan in the first battle of Tarain in 1191 A.D.[36]

The other successors like Khilji, Tuglaq, Sayyid and the Lodi established short-lived dynasties of Turkic and Pashtun origin in and around Delhi which was also known as Delhi Sultanate. They were all disliked for their anti-Hindu stance like banning chewing of beetle, financial reforms which were against Hindus. In the end one of their own courtier invited Babur to invade India in 1526 A.D which ended their rule and came the Mongols. The impact of his invasion was immense, as it proved for the first time, the weakness of the Hindu rulers in securing their territories from foreign invasion; secondly it paved the way for new dynasty called as the Slave dynasty and lastly, it carried the germs of communalism and anti-religious feelings towards the non-Islamic religion. The only solace it gave was a temporary insulation from the Mongol invasion till Timur invaded India in 1398. In spite of all this chaos, various necessities forced the Hindus and the Muslims to meet each other resulting in evolution of a common language; a convenient compromise between the two languages resulted in the formation of Urdu.[37]

Vasco da Gama a great Portuguese explorer, landed in Calicut on 20 May 1498. His first trip to India is considered as a pinnacle of world history as it marked the beginning of the first wave of the global multiculturism. The rivalry in the naval hegemony between Portugal and Spain made both countries to look for a sea route to India having known of its vast resources in spices and other valuables. The visits to India by the Portuguese there after became a routine under other voyagers to trade and station their commercial and later administrative heads to control the spice trade via sea route. At this point of time Portuguese were the only naval power who controlled the sea, before Japan and USA came into the sea. He had led a politico- diplomatic expedition. However circumstances thereafter graduated towards developing a Portuguese empire in India and therefore holding Goa by Alfonso de Albuquerque, a great strategist. Later as a spring action Diu, Bassein and later Daman were conquered from 1535 to 1559 A.D. This opened the gates for Dutch, Danish, French and British. The Portuguese power started to decline before they could expand to the whole of India; their system of mixed marriages produced a degenerated race that did not possess the military qualities; their administrative system was also ineffective with rampant corruption; the religious intolerance persuaded destruction of Hindu temples; with the decline of Vijayanagar; Goa lost its importance as a trade Centre, leading to more and more claimants arriving into India to loot the vast wealth.

Mughal Empire in India was started by Timur, the grandfather of Babur. However it was Zahirudin Muhammad Babur also popularly known as 'Babur 'was the founder of the Mughal Empire in India, which lasted for more than 330 years. Babur was a descended of Timur on his father's side and Chengez Khan on his mother's side. In his quest to rule a larger territory than Farghana, he wanted to invade India, whose wealth he had heard about from his grandfather. His task was made easy, when on the invitation of Dalut Khan Lodi and Alam Khan of Delhi Sultan, he invaded India. In his fifth and the last invasion he defeated Ibrahim Lodi in the first battle of Panipat in April 1526.

His literary work Tuzki-i-Baburi, also known as Babur Namah is a well-known and a popular work in India. The impact of Babur's invasion was once again the depletion of Indian wealth and its religious and cultural sentiments besides the forced conversions of Hindus to Muslims. It cracked the socio-religious-politico fabric of India but could not break it because of various strong Hindu rulers who often gave a tough resistance. Humayun, Babur's son was simultaneously plundering the other part of India amongst resistance from Afghan rulers. Before he could consolidate, he was defeated by Sher Shah and later died by falling from a library stairs.

Akbar, son of Humayun was the next to accede to the throne, as declared by Humayun on the day of his victory over Sirhind on June 22, 1555. Bairam Khan was the friend, philosopher, and guide of Akbar. Akbar's first major achievement was the defeat of Himu at the second battle of Panipat in 1556. This was against a very strong opponent with a great deal of military might. However Akbar with his presence of mind and better tactical skills carried out a flanking attack, thereby creating confusion in the large force. Slowly he captured major portion of India and side by side inviting other European visitors for business. He instituted a highly efficient bureaucratic system of mansabars (military governors), who were directly responsible to him. Great agricultural, revenue and judicial reforms along with compatible religious environment made him popular as a great ruler. He followed the policy of absorbing Hindu chieftains into Mughal nobility, and giving them their due, which paid handsome dividends resulting in the old Indian ideal of a united India again taking shape by rejuvenating a political unification with cultural fusion[38]. He sowed the seeds of making Hindustan a financial capital of the world which was later seen during the reign of Emperor Shahjahan. Akbar's revenue in 1605 was stated from official accounts to be about 17,500,000 shillings[39]. He died in 1605 after three weeks of illness.

Nur-ud-din Mohammad Jahangir, in short also known as Jahangir or Salim, the eldest son of Akbar succeeded his father, in 1605, after he had revolted against his father for the throne. He followed his father in all aspects of administration, education and religion. He was a lover of poetry, art and architecture. He named his wife as Nur Jahan and gave her the authority of ruling the Empire. He was fond of liquor and women. Although he did not have an expansionist tendency, his empire expanded because of his subordinates and his fathers' everlasting name and strengths that came as inheritance. He was popular for giving justice for which he enacted Twelve Decrees, which are a remarkable thoughts facilitating liberalism and foresight.He maintained his foreign relations and developed alliance between Ottomans, Mughal and Uzbeks against Safavids. He crushed revolt of Khusrau, won over Mewar, subjugated Afghans and Bengal and Annexed Kangra. He was deadly against 5th Sikh Guru Arjan Dev and killed him for having helped his revolting son against him, despite of having amply proved that the help was inadvertent and on humanitarian grounds. He also threw away the Portuguese for having misbehaved, looted and killed Muslims who were proceeding for Haj.

He lost Qandahar to Shah Abbas, in 1622 due to his son's failure to fight against the enemy. His son was more interested in snatching the throne rather than focusing on the fight with the enemy. He felt insecure about the throne which reminded him of the same situation that he had created for his father, Akbar. He died due to prolonged illness in November 1627. It is evident that his empire was becoming weaker in military power. Selfish luxury drained the resources of the country. He was the first one to officially open relations with the East India Company of Britain against the Portuguese.[40]

Shahjahan also called as Ala Azad Abdul Muzzafar Shahabuddin Mohammed Khurram was the next descendent of the Mughal throne amongst dispute between two brothers. He ruled from 1628 to 1658 and was the 5th Mughal Emperor. His reign was called as the Golden Age of Mughal architecture and was the most prosperous in the dynasty. While he had inherited a good governance set up and plenty of wealth from his predecessors, his love for lavish spending and art and architecture resulted in construction of world famous structures like Taj Mahal, the seventh wonder of the world, Red Fort, Moti Masjid, Jama Masjid, Peacock Throne; the most precious throne in the world, establishing of imperial capital (also called Old Delhi), and commissioning of 777 gardens including Shalimar Bag.

His rule was not very peaceful due to regional rifts. He was a good military commander but had to face the brave Rajputs of Mewar and Lodi in Deccan. He executed Guru Gobind Singh in Punjab, drove out the Portuguese from Hooghly, and recaptured Kandahar in 1638 from Safavids. In spite of all this, trade was at its best and India saw one of the most prosperous times and it is said that during his time India had the highest GDP in the world.[41]

Aurangzeb, the third son of Shahjahan, declared himself the successor after killing his brothers, and keeping his father under house arrest for eight years till he died. As a ruler, he exhibited qualities of a brave, cunning, strong and an efficient administrator and a military man. He ruled for 48 years and perhaps lived the longest amongst the Mughal Emperors. He had abandoned the religious tolerance of his predecessors and adopted anti Hindu, Sikh and Christian stance. He destroyed many temples and churches and instead build Mosques on them. He had expansionist intensions and expanded his empire because finances required for enlargement were not a problem due to the flourishing trade.

He made his military, an epitome of strength. Production of cannons had reached the highest during his time. However the Sikhs and the ever dominant Marathas and Raj put's constantly kept harassing him with their attacks and draining his resources. As a result of continuous battles his resources started depleting and he had to resort to imposition of heavy taxes from the people; anti people policies further reduced his popularity with the regional kingdoms. TheRajput's were so far loyal to him because they had no other choice, but having got the first opportunity they openly revolted against his son to settle scores.

Pashtun rebellion (1672-1674) closed the Attack- Kabul road and later the Grand Trunk road, which effected overland trade and inherent security which was available by friendly Pashtu's from the northwest. He broke up with the Portuguese and made an alliance with the British to continue trade. Expensive gifts were sent outside India during Haj. He executed Guru Teg Bahadur in 1670 for increasing popularity and his rejection to forced religious conversion. Shivaji's guerrilla tactics over two decades had drenched him of his resources including one fifth of his manpower. Highpoint of imperial centralization under Aurangzeb coincided with the start of imperial downfall. He soon lost his hold on the great Empire which started breaking into small kingdoms like Hyderabad, Oudh, and Bengal etc. Bahadur Shah-I, his son lacked both the will and the strength to administer such a vast Empire which started breaking and gave way to the British East India Company to strengthened its roots in India for the next more than stwo centuries. It may be noted that, perhaps it was only during the reign of Akbar that an attempt was made to reconcile to the Hindus of India. He sought to be the ruler of all Indians and thereby strengthen the base of his empire. His liberal and conciliatory policies were aimed at winning over not only the Hindu ruling classes but also the Hindu masses. It would be pertinent to understand that number of invaders were always numerically less than the Hindu population and therefore only a few conversions were forced under fear, most of the Hindus who converted was because of the mystical teaching of the Sufis converged with indigenous devotional forms of worship, making this form of Islam well adapted to the Indian condition;[42] In the beginning it was observed that both religions could co-exist in a less bitter environment like Buddhism and Jainism. However after Akbar, all other rulers did not allow Indians any freedom of expression and a free hand to do their own business. It was made a rule rather than an exception to make them live in a state of poverty; so that no surpluses were left with the Hindus to organize themselves in any kind of a force which could challenge the invaders. Islam also had indirect social impact. The Brahmanical institutions which were under the royal protection had seized to exist. The status of women declined. Moreover, the invaders maintained a form of military feudalism in their administrative structure, whereby they recruited mostly Muslims and only handpicked Hindu loyalists in their army.

Looting was the only aim, of all these invaders, however when there was no or less resistance offered; cruelness, butchery and destruction became a habit and routine of the invaders to suppress and threaten the poor and defenseless people. Hindu dominated India had always experienced tolerance of other religions, but from Mahmud of Ghazni till Aurangzeb the sub-continent saw religious animosity, antagonism and mutual suspicion between Hindus and Muslims. Feeling of alienation within owns land crept in due to the second class treatment mooted to the local Hindu population of India.

The invaders who were Muslims from outside India, living on Indian soil, making a fortune out of Indian wealth, did not identify themselves as Indians; maintaining their original identity, did manifest into differences on basis of religion which was later further exploited by the British. They cleverly exploited the Hindu-Muslim divide of the ethos and ideology of masterly attitude of Muslims towards the Indians.

Inception of East India Company and British Rule

Trade with India had been carried out for a long time, however, with the Chinese it started during the spread of Buddhism and later it started with other countries. It started withspices, because these fetched more value than gold. However Vasco da Gama's discovery of India in 1498 was the begening of an organized trade. Soon other players broke the monopoly of the Portuguese, when Dutch and British slowly entered this trade. In 1600, the British East India Company was chartered by Queen Elizabeth-I, to obtain spices cargoes; simultaneously therearouse a need to meet the growing demand of raw material due to industrialization and the wars. After the Battle of Plassey, in 1757, the Dutch power declined and the British gained the upper hand.

It has been said that the British Empire was picked up in a "fit of absence of mind." Nowhere was this truer than in the case of India which gradually came under British rule, not by the efforts of Britain's government, but by those of the British East India Company, founded in 1599 by a group of merchants in search of nothing more than "quiet trade." However, circumstances would prevent these peaceful intentions, and over the next 250 years the British would find themselves more and more in the role of conquerors and governors than traders.

Not only would the British have a profound effect on India's history, but the "crown jewel of the British Empire" would also affect Western Civilization. This is reflected in such English words as bungalow, verandah, punch, dungarees, and pajamas, bonda, rasam, samadhi and customs as smoking cigars, playing polo, and taking showers, as well as more profound influences in the realms of religion and philosophy.

The Mughal rule was fast declining due to faulty policies of Aurangzeb, famine ensued enlarge in many parts of India, the Portuguese were heading towards declining and self-destructive role due to annoying the locals, different stakeholders were fast emerging like honey bees on to the wealth that India still possessed. The French started providing military training to the locals to gain sympathy and acquire land for their trade, but failed. British seeing the light of the day under Robert Clive and thereby gaining trade hegemony and subsequent monopoly made their base stronger. The 3rd battle of Plassey in 1757 between Britain and Siraj-ud-daulah, the battle of Panipat between Ahmed Shah and the Marathas in 1759, battle of Buxar between Britain and Mir Kasim after which Lord Clive became one of the richest Briton,At the time of his death, his wealth stood at over £500,000. The war of Mysore with Tipu Sultan, Anglo-Sikh and Anglo-Gurkha war and later the war of independence with Laxmibai, Subhas Chandra Bose, Mahatma Gandhi and Pandit Jawaharlal Nehru amongst so many others are some of the prominent ones. Almost all these battles ended up in payment of extraordinarily huge sum of compensation to the British. There are ample examples of Indian money being used in England. The plunder by the British in Bengal and the compensation paid by India was used to finance the industrial revolution in England.[43]

This British dominance impacted India in many ways. They started influencing the Indian administration by installing their own candidate on the Mughal throne and subsequently claiming the wealthy province of Bengal. The control of the affairs in India rested with England which was 7000 miles away or nine months of travel at that time. The absence or the delay of decision on company matters, left India wide open to exploitation by the company and its employees. Soon the company started getting bankrupt while individually, people were making fortunes from Indian wealth. Moreover the growing number of Christian missionaries coming to India to preach Christianity clashed with the more flexible beliefs of the Hindu majority and the strong beliefs of Indian Muslims. Next, the British were bringing in modern technology (especially railroads) and new business methods, which disrupted the traditional, slower paced culture and economy of India.

Robert Clive laid the foundations of the British Empire in India after he arrived in 1743 as a civil servant. He had managed to win the battle of Plassey with Nawab Siraj-uddullah of Bengal by bribing and instilling the fear of gun into the ranks and file of Nawab's army. Jawaharlal Nehru in his book, Discovery of India writes that Clive promoted treason and forgery to win, and thus sowed the seeds of unsavory beginning. Dual system of government established by him proved a failure. Lord Cornwallis was the first Governor General under the new act and held office between 1786-1793. He defeated the mighty Tipu Sultan of Mysore in the 3rd Anglo-Mysore war. He brought about administrative and financial reforms in the company's rules to stop further irregularities and simultaneously settled the revenue and land system of Bengal. He brought some positive changes in the criminal administration which was more humane and softer on the Hindus. He brought about police reforms and civil services system into the administrative sphere.

Lord Minto was both the Viceroy and the Governor General of India. He had to repair the ill feelings that Lord Curzon sowed due to the partition of Bengal. He was targeted by the great Indian revolutionaries for his faulty policies when he passed the Indian Press Act which was non-democratic. He passed the Morley- Minto reforms to give some power to the inclusion of an Indian in the legislative assembly but was rightly understood as foundation of Hindu-Muslim differences.

Warren Hasting was the first Governor General of Bengal from 1772-1785. He fought the first Anglo-Maratha war and the second Anglo- Mysore war. He was inclined towards the socio- economic-political satire of India and carried out extensive interaction with the locals. He founded the Asiatic Society of Bengal, and also wrote the introduction to the first translation of "The Bhagwat Gita" to English. Famous for his boldness and foreign policy, he had to face impeachment on his return to England for crimes and delinquencies.

Lord William Henry Cavendish- Bentinck the first Governor General of British India, wanted to improve the financial position, and therefore took some extreme anti people steps like cutting the wages of the military men and encouraging education of English language for future use of Indians in the bureaucratic services. He even wanted to demolish the Taj Mahal and sell of its marble and the Agra cannon of Akbar (an artifact piece) to collect money. He abolished sati and discouraged female infanticide. Some of his totalitarian policies sowed the seeds of mutiny in the minds of the people. He could visualize the threat from the Russians to the northern and northwestern borders of British India and therefore made a soft approach with Maharaja Ranjit Singh of Punjab and signed many treaties with him to his advantage.

Lord Dalhousie was in India from 1848 to 1856. He was a visionary and in spite of having a small tenure he contributed a lot to the British India's development for English cause. He introduced the Doctrine of Lapse, which was quite unpopular with the Hindu concept of rule of a kingdom. He was the first to lay the rail track from Bombay to Thane, first to lay telegraph lines from Calcutta to Agra and encouraged private enterprise to develop other rail network. He encouraged recruitment of Gurkha in the British-Indian Army and started the Engineering collage at Roorkee. He passed the widow remarriage Act.

He consolidated the entire communication system including the Ganges Canal. He carried out reforms in civil service, land and revenue, social policies, Foreign policy and military upliftment. Europeanization and consolidation were the keynotes of his policy. He enlarged the legislative council. He moved the Army Head Quarters from Calcutta to Shimla, moved Bengal Artillery from Calcutta to Meerut.

Lord Canning was the last Governor General and the first Viceroy from 1856 to 1858. The 1857 mutiny took place during his time and thereafter the rule was passed on to the Crown. He withdrew the Doctrine of Lapse to be able to ease down the problems with the Indians. He passed the

Council Act 1861. He got the universities established in Calcutta, Bombay and Madras. He reorganized the British Indian Army and restored the financial stability.

Lord Rippon handled the Indian problems by putting himself in their shoes. He was largely hailed by the Indians for pro-Indian policies. When he failed to satisfy the British on the Ilbert Bill which was democratic and pleased the Indians, he resigned. He introduced the First Factory Act in 1881 thereby making the working conditions better for the Indians and also relaxed child labor.

Lord Curzon was in India from 1899 to 1905. He had two successive terms. He was very susceptible to the Russian danger in the north western borders of the British India. He had sent Colonel F.E. Younghusband, C.I.E. on a mission to northwest for recce and created North West Frontier Agency. He was serious about the office functioning and ensured its meticulous and efficient working. He expanded and developed the existing infrastructure in railways, and established the Railway board. He showed interest in better education system, agriculture and different means of communication. During the period of Lord Hardinge, construction of Delhi started from 1912 onwards, and finished in 1929. After the visit of King George-V and Queen Mary, the capital was shifted from Calcutta to New Delhi. Defense of India Act was passed in 1915. Start of world war involved Indian Troops being sent to far of countries under the British banner. Following the examples of other nations fighting for freedom and getting it; Indian leaders also thought it to be a ripe time to throw out the British. Many leaders of National Congress were jailed, including Mohandas Karamchand Gandhi, but that did not ditter them from carriying out satyagrah and other peace protests when the British realized the seriousness of the situation. Nationwide outrage against Jallianwala Bag massacre(committedby General Dyer) and other repressive policies of the British made matters worse for the British.

During World War-II, Britain again wanted Indian soldiers to fight under their banner, but it was not supported by the Indian leaders. This time was thought to be right time for a call for Quit India movement which was initiated by the Congress even without the support of other parties.This movement was so strong that the Labor Party after wining the elections in Britain decided to hand over the power to the Congress Party with Pandit Jawaharlal Nehru as the first prime minister of the Independent India, but with the bitter truth of partitioning India and Pakistan on religious grounds.

The Indian economy under British rule underwent a phase of constrained development, in spite of having the potential for economic growth; a prosperous agriculture, significant indigenous industry, sizable exports, abundance of minerals and ores, and above all, a surplus which could be invested. In agriculture, the small family farm was predominant. Land was not a commodity and therefore not brought or sold. However, with the British came modern business, technology, capital, and the political institution. The land revenue which amounted to Rs.64.5 lakh in 1762-63, swelled to Rs.1.47 crores in the year 1765-66. The East India Company therefore wanted to manage revenue collection all by itself or its loyalists by giving the right to collect revenue to the highest bidder.

The British introduced three major land revenue and tenurial systems; the Zamindari system, the Mahalwari system, and the Rytwari system. The new agrarian relations stabilized the government revenues but, reduced the peasant to abject poverty. The amount of revenue to be paid by the peasants kept on increasingsubstantially. From initial 10-12% to a high of 80%, moreover, the land became saleable, mortgageable and alienable, which undermined the structure of the rural society. The result was the emergence of money-lenders and thereby, rural indebtedness, sub-infeudation, agricultural labor andcommercialisation of agriculture which had some merits, but at the cost of food grains.[44] The ultimate structure which emerged in the agricultural sector was semi-feudal and semi-colonial in character. It disrupted the traditional structure of Indian village economy. Increase in agricultural productivity as anticipated was not achieved, as the landlords indulged in making quick money (trade and speculation) rather than investing in agriculture, resulting in exploitation and ultimate suffering of the peasants. An ancient peasant culture was subjected to a regime of military feudalism, which achieved its greatest success under the Mughal, whose agrarian state and its revenue base were then captured by the East India Company; a capitalist organization, engrafted on the agrarian state established a parasitical symbiosis, which benefitted the alien and paralyzed the host, who managed to survive under a condition of low equilibrium. The British failed to give an adequate modern banking system to India. The railway network which the British claim to have established was a spillover of their own in Britain. Since they had invested a fortune in their own country, they wanted to give contiguity to the same in India, where this ambitious plan was much ahead of its time as far as India's economic development was concerned, this only disbalanced the Indian economy.[45]

The Emerging Boundaries

Like all boundaries in South Asia, India's boundaries are also man-made. India shares 14,880 kilometers of boundary with other nations; 3323 km with Pakistan, 3488 km with China, 1751 km with Nepal, 699 km with Bhutan, 1643 km with Myanmar 4097.7 km with Bangladesh. The boundary question came into the domain of imperialist China and British India sometimes in 1807 when Napoleon and Alexander concluded a treaty against the British. It was perceived by the British that the eastward expansion of Russia could include India or at least its northern part which was contiguous to the terrain of Afghanistan, Sinkiang, Tibet and Nepal.

Soviets then, were also in quest for a warm water port

and a colonial empire. The British in their wisdom thought to halt the Soviets expansion in line with the Himalayas. This theory pre-empted them to earmark Afghanistan and Tibet as buffer states and therefore demarcate the boundary of India with theirs. Though Jammu and Kashmir was an independent kingdom; the Treaty of Amritsar in 1846 gave the British the responsibility of its security. With the Soviets having started their expansion, the British wanted to keep them thousands of miles away from India.

British-India's foreign and defense policy of a 'united India' rested on the evolution of the buffer state. (The buffer as a concept came into vogue in the 1880s in the aftermath of the Second Afghan War, when Alfred Lyall, the Foreign Secretary, did much to edify the system of alliances that operated at the time. What evolved was a concept of peripheral defense, an arrangement whereby the British adopted a policy of interposing the border of a protected country between the actual possessions they administered, and the possessions of formidable neighbors, whom they desired to keep at arm's length. Curzon later called it a glacis, 'a smooth slope bank' to the Indian fortress; and he maintained that while 'we do not want to occupy it, but we also cannot afford to see it occupied by our foes').

Johnson's Boundary Line came into being when the British, keeping in mind the claims made by Gulab Singh, Maharaja of Jammu and Kashmir, other geographical and historical considerations proposed demarcation of boundary to Lasha and the Chinese central government viceroy in Canton, however no positive response was forthcoming from Chinese. In 1846-87, a boundary was drawn from a little north of the Pangong Lake to the Spiti River; but stopped there and the area further to the north i.e. between the Pongong Lake and the Karakoram Pass was left as *terra incognita,* because of the most inhospitable terrain. At that point of time it was not envisaged that this unmarked inhospitable terrain could became the cause of a bitter war between two most populous countries in the world over a hundred years later. In 1865 a boundary was proposed by W.H. Johnson, which included the unmarked portions well.[46]

This line linked Demchok in the south with 18000 ft high Karakoram pass in the north by taking a circuitous route beyond the Kuen Lun Mountains, covering Aksai Chin. This was sometimes during Dugan revolt, when the Chinese did not control Xinjiang, and therefore probably never presented to them. However, when presented to the Maharaja of Jammu and Kashmir he claimed areas as far as Sanju Pass in the Kun Lun Mountains, including Sahiddula post. This post was occupied by small numbers of Kashmiri troops for nearly twenty years, till 1856. It was 79 miles to the north of Karakoram Pass and the southern foot of Kun Lun. Since Shahidullah, Tagdumbash and Raskam were beyond the Karakoram Range, the next watershed of Kun Lun was considered the natural boundary line.Ney Elias has provided a detailed appreciation of the boundary problem in his memorandum of 23 November 1878. Since Ney felt no necessity of occupying Shahidullah as a defensive post or a border post on the boundary a firm decision was taken by GoI ON 1 September 1885 which requested the Maharaja not to occupy Shahidullah.[47] A memorandum dated 21 May 1887 in this regard was also given by Sir Martimer Durand, Foreign Secretary (Arcitecht of Pakistan-Afghan boundary line) that to keep Shahidullah post beyond Karakoram with the objective of forestalling Soviets when it succeeds Chinese in Yarkhand would be troublesome.

Similarly the area of Demchok was already settled in 1684 Peace Treaty between Ladakh and Tibet at Tinmosgang. This was during the time when King Skyidlda-Ngeema-Gon distributed his kingdom amongst his sons.[48] By this, the frontier ran east of Demchok which even Van Agnew submitted in his memorandum of 13 May 1847. He reported "Demchok as one of the termini".[49] A large stone was placed there after the expulsion of the Mongols as a permanent boundary between Demchokupto the hills of Karbonas.[50] Vans Agnew further reported that the Changchenmovalley was also within the Ladakh region. Lanak La was an accepted border between Ladakh and Tibet. This was confirmed by many travelers. Notable amongst them are:

Captain H.H. Godwin-Austen: A topographical survey officer, had made a sketch of upper Changchenmo and northern border of Pangong district in eastern Ladakh in 1862-1863. He was requested by the governor not to cross the border.[51] Captain M.S Wellby: He wanted to cross Tibet from Leh but was stopped by the Tibetans when he wanted to cross from Wapu La (18,438 ft), a shorter route, but was guided by the Tibetians towards the east of Lanak La, which he has mentioned as Indian border with Tibet.[52]

A.D. Carey: had noted in his diary on 21 August 1885 that the existence of Polu road from India was completely unknown to the Chinese aouthorities.[53] Captain Hamilton Bower: His diary entry of 3 July 1891 reads; "crossed the frontier at Lanak La, and marching 24 miles, which took us nine hours, camped. The pass was easy and there was no snow on it".[54]

(1) Kuen Lun Range

(2) Aksai Chin/ Salt plains

(3) Laktsang ridge

(4) Lanakla

(5) Linzithang plains

(6) Changchemo range

(7) Chinese claim line) dianclaim line1

On many occasions thereafter the boundary kept changing unilaterally without consent of two parties. However, W.H. Johnson's controversial 'advanced boundary line' of 1865, merits some attention, especially since thereafter, the Johnson boundary continued to be shown in one trans-frontier map one after the other, and indeed independent India's claims to the Aksai Chin plateau rests squarely on Johnson's map. The boundary line first found concrete shape in the Survey of India's 1868 map and the Kashmir Atlas. It was based on the Kashmir Maharaja's outpost at Sahiddula, and Colonel F.E. Younghusband, C.I.E.'s claim that a fort in this area was built by Dogras a few years back, which made Johnson opt for the Kuen Lun watershed as the boundary line, and not as some later surveyors were to do, on the main Karakoram.[55]

John Ardagh Boundary line came into existence when in 1897 a British Army officer, Major General Sir John Ardagh, who had earlier been to India and now was the Director of Military Intelligence on the British General Staff, while writing a paper, proposed a boundary along the crest of the Kun Lun Mountains north of the Yarkand River. This line followed almost the same line as Johnson line and came to be known as the "Johnson-Ardagh Line". Sir John Ardagh was adamant, as in his appreciation this line had greater defensibility potential against the Russians and it exemplified the reasoning and apprehensions of the forward school; although it was not accepted at that time, it continued for years to exercise influence in the persistent debate on frontier policy.

Moreover Chinese weakness of controlling outskirts in this region was fast attracting the Russians towards this side. He further elucidated that the approaches to the northern passes should be held by the British for better command and control. Ardagh's memorandum specified that the boundary should be the series of ranges to the north of Karakoram including the Kun Lun which included Aksai Chin and the upper courses of the Yarkand and Karakash river system as well. However,this report was nullified by Viceroy, Lord Elgin.

McCartney- MacDonald was another lineproposed at that point of timewhich was to divide Aksai Chin between both British and China along Lak Tsang range. (a line of hills running roughly east-west, and dividing the Aksai Chin proper, on the northern side, from the Lingzi Tang salt plains, to the south.) This was also proposed to China on March 14th, 1899, by Sir Claude MacDonald who was the British Minister in Pekings, but it was neither negated nor accepted. It is important to know that the aim of China throughout the boundary issue was to extend as far as possible to gain ground for its territorial expansion, but the aim of British was not to let Russian expansion to take place. The aim of both the parties being different, they could have never achieved a fair deal for the future of India.[56] The British note of 14 March 1899 represents, so far as the available records show, the only formal proposal on boundary between India and China in the Karakoram, that is is to say from Wakham to Lanak La pass at the head of the Changchenmo basin, which the British ever made to the Chinese duringh the course of their rule.[57]

Over the years there have been wide variations in the alignments favoured by the British, by one count, eleven different variations, reflecting three basic alignments.[58]

British at this point of time were in a hurry to fix the boundary to avoid Russian expansion but at the same time did not want to antagonize the Chinese, who were claiming the Aksai Chin as their territory. During Qing Dynasty, China reached its largest extent in ruling China proper. However Tibet was not shown as part of China.

The Tibetans did not agree to any Chinese or British interference on their territorial matters and therefore in a hasty and disillusioned attempt the Tibetans occupied some part of Sikkim, claiming it to be theirs, resulted in forced eviction of the Tibetans. An Anglo-Chinese Convention of 1890 thereafter defined the Sikkim- Tibet boundary. There was another agreement in 1893 defining Trade Regulations for opening trade mart at Yatung part of Chumbi valley, just inside Tibet. This convention was between China and British.

During the period of the Boxer crises there were hosts of foreign powers present in China intimidating to break a sovereign state. The Peking Government had realized that over many decades the peripheral regions of China had been neglected and Chinese position weakened to an extent that the present situation would certainly invite presence of Russia and Britain to lay control over Mongolia and Tibet as protectorates. The Great Wall was perhaps the only defensive system extending from Pamirs to the Amur River; that too of a symbolic significance. It was by now clear to the Chinese that loosing Central Asian glacis was like losing the Great Wall.

Russian aspirations appeared to clash with British interest in three main regions; in the Near East, in Central Asia and in the Far East.By 1903 Persia, Afghanistan, Sinkiang and Tibet had become buffer zones along the Indian border into which Russian influence had either penetrated or was about to penetrate. While it had become amply clear that British influence in Tibet was a necessity, the difference of opinion within the British hierarchy never allowed a whole hearted approach towards the problem.

Amongst confusion of deciding the boundary and fate of Tibet in relation to the Russian threat, a mission to Lasha was decided under Colonel F.E.Younghusband, C.I.E. in 1904. Two important factors were necessary to evaluate the relationship with Tibet. Firstly whether there was a real threat from Russia, and secondly what was Chinese intent of Tibet? Both these factors changed with time, in British mindset. It was apparent that, from 1904 to 1911 the Chinese dominated Tibet, but in1912, the Chinese Revolution brought about a Chinese collapse in Lasha which the British endeavored to exploit, in the process obtaining the McMahon line.

Other Political Activities

In the early twentieth century, Lord Curzonhad visualized the Himalayan regions of Ladakh, Sikkim, Bhutan and North East frontier as an 'innerdefence line for India protected by a Tibetan buffer region'. Later China viewed the Himalayas as its outer line of defence, necessary for the protection of its interests in Tibet. However, China considered Tibet with its overwhelming geo-political importance to be the palm of the hand with Ladakh, Nepal, Bhutan, Sikkim and NEFA as the five fingers. China had the palm under its control and now it sought influence over the strategic five fingers.[59]

Lord Curzon had always maintained that any decision concerning Tibet should have the consent of Dalai Lama's government. The connection of Russian Buriat, Dorjiev, thirteenth Dalai Lama and the Manchu ruling circles meanwhile came to the notice of the British, who werealready suspicious of Russian interest in Tibet. Immediately, a proposal to maintain contact with Tibet was felt and a mission under Colonel F.E. Younghusband, C.I.E. was sent to Tibet which subsequently obtained the treaty of 7 September 1904.

This treaty gave some hold to British inside Tibet to consolidate further, but this Convention did not clarify China's status in Tibet, and the Chinese claimed that without their assent as sovereign power, the Lasha Convention was invalid; also certain parts of it were objectionable to the Chinese and the Russian. Meanwhile Dalai Lama's closeness to Soviets and Panchen Lama's closeness to British was becoming more apparent. While they were expressing their closeness to Russians and Britain covertly, both seem to have shown negative attitude towards China. Curzon, who had for several years expressed increasing irritation at the 'fiction' of Chinese authority in Tibet, was determined that Lasha Convention should not lead to a British endorsement of Chinese control on Tibet which the Chinese were themselves unable to make effective.[60]

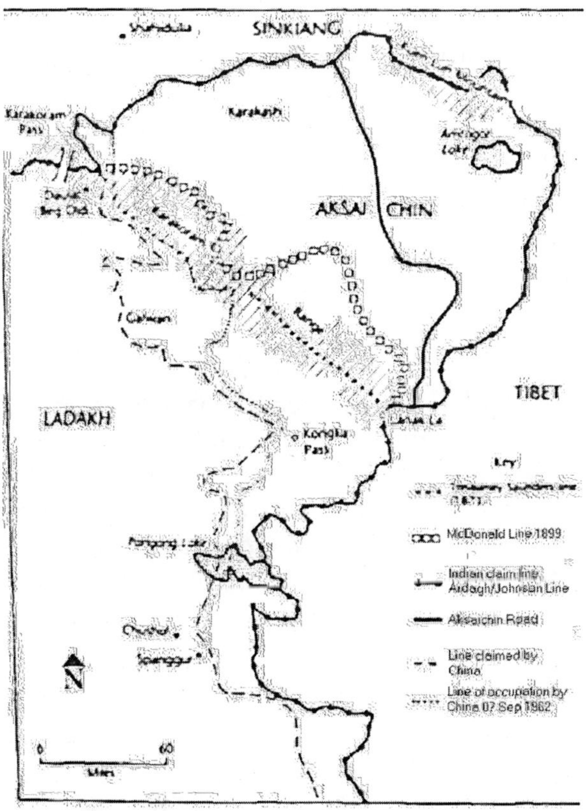

Map 2 BOUNDARY LINES IN AKSAI CHIN

The complexity of the Lasha agreement and the difference of opinion amongst British led to the signing of another Anglo-Chinese Convention on 27 April 1906, with alterations in the earlier Convention, which marked a defeat for those officials of the Government of British India who hoped that Younghusband's mission to Lasha could still provide the basis for maintenance of a significant measure of British influence in Tibet. This time also, while the convention did not declare Tibet to be a part of China; but it certainly implied it.

There was a very complex problem between Russia, Britain, China and the two factions in Tibet which were inclined towards Russia and British. While both Russia and British had cultivated contacts with Dalai Lama and Panchen Lama, respectively; with an aim to use them in their favour at the first opportunity, they always underplayed these contacts as being apolitical thereby creating an atmosphere of suspicion. The Russians wanted the same connectivity with Dalai Lama in so far as religious affinity was concerned as the British had with Panchen Lama. Besides this, the Russians wanted that the British, in return for Russian recognition of British special interests in Tibet, should acknowledge Russian special interests in Mongolia.[61] It was important to know exactly, the boundaries of Tibet to come to any conclusion, however during these discussions it became clear that neither of the parties involved including China knew the exact limit and boundaries of Tibet.[62] An Anglo-Russian Arrangement concerning Tibet was signed under the above circumstances, between Nicolson and Isvolski on 31 August 1907.

Moreover with Soviets, Britain, France and Japan all allied to each other, loss of the frontiers was quite imminent. The Manchu's so far had dominated the frontiers of China with the help of Chinese Imperial Resident, which was also in the case of Tibet. However the present situation warranted a New Dominion status to Tibet, since they were trying to keep every one out of Tibetan affairs. The Chinese were therefore, probably trying to launch a four sided attack to reinforce and consolidate on the problem of their status on Tibet.[63] During this time the fleeing away of Dalai Lama to British India was not exploited by Lord Minto. Tibetans were already irritated with outsiders including the Chinese to have to have destroyed the peace in their territory, and were against any interference in Tibetan affairs. At this juncture Chang Yin-tang (Chinese Special Commissioner) and Henderson's visit to Chumbi valley and other trade mart areas started creating friction since they were expected to enter Tibetonlywithpermission or a valid document; also the Tibetans with some pretext or the other did not allow construction of boundary pillars on the Sikkim-Tibet border which was earlier decided in the convention, resulting in dilution of the British influence. To further aggravate this position, Lord Minto gave orders to the British trade mart at Chumbi Valley to fall back to India on 8 February 1908, thereby almost ending any hold in Tibet, followed by signing of Tibet Trade Regulations between China and British; bringing British in a total state of weakness.

Chang Yin-tang's visit to Tibet was a sign of its intent to patronize Nepal and Bhutan, besides consolidating his position in Tibet. However it did not materialize. The vacuum created in Chumbi by withdrawal of the trade mart was exploited by China to open negotiations with Bhutan and claim their suzerainty, but failed. On the other hand this lead to a stronger bond with between Tibet and British. When Dalai Lama returned from India to Tibet, he asked help fromboth Russians and the British against the Chinese, but being bound by the Convention, no help was forthcoming either separately or jointly.

Having weakened the British position, China started strengthening its own position in Tibet, but was unaware of the de facto boundaries of the small kingdoms that sent their tributes through the Dalai Lama and those directly.

Sovereignty Or Suzerainty: Previous Attempts to Delimit Boundary

The matter of recognision of sovereignty or suzeranity can be determined by the following facts that in the early part of 7th century A.D., the Tibetans overran Upper Burma and Western China and forced the Chinese Emperor to a humiliating peace. As a result of this peace, in 640A.D. the King of Tibet, Srongtsan Gampo, had received a Chinese princess in marriage.[64] Richardson in his book Tibet and its History (London, 1962) has said that although Tibet remained under the Chinese influence for a long time, it was free from actual Chinese rule except during the Manchu regime; Tibet was successfully attacked by China in A.D. 1720 and till 1792 was regarded as Chinese protectorate. Chinese did not show any presence when General Zorawar Singh attacked Tibet in 1841, or when Nepal attacked Tibet in 1856 and when Francis Younghusband led his small force in Tibet in 1904. Moreover in international relations, Tibet had held an independent position. A few instances were; refusal to abide by the Anglo-Chinese Convention of 1890, 1684 Treaty between Ladakh and Tibet, 1842 Treaty between Kashmir and Ladakh on one side and Tibet and China on the other, 1856 Treaty between Nepal and Tibet and lastly the 1914 Convention between Great Britain on one side and Tibet and China on the other side.[65] Governor General Henry Hardinge had set up a Boundary Commission in July 1846 to define "the actual limits of boundaries of Ladakh with Tibet," with two members—P.A. Vans Agnew and Alexander Cunningham. China's refusal to cooperate led the commission to only say that the "ancient boundary of Ladakh and Chanthan and Yarkand is well known and undisputed."

The 'middle kingdom' and mandate of the heaven concept has been known through the ages. Subjugation was ancentral part of the Chinese view of international affairs. The emperor legally was the universal ruler and any territory not under the direct control was unilaterally considered either a tributary or rebellious. Official records of the Qing period –Da Qing Lichao Shilu—, showedsome countries with diverse relationships with the Quin Empire listed as vassal states (-shu2guo2-), which includes Korea, Vietnam, Tibet, Britain and Papacy. Early documents show Tibet as –guo2-(nation), i.e., states equivalent to Korea and Vietnam, however in the later documents, Tibet was referred to as –bu4- (dependency), a term applied to Mongolia. The Qing dynasty for the first time asserted any sovereignity over Tibet in reaction to Younghusbands mission to Tibet in 1904.

An atlas published in Shanghai in 1910 helped publicise this new territorial claim. However, an earlier atlas published in 1879, in a map of Qing Dynasty shows Korea, Manchuria, Taiwan and China proper but not Tibet. In 1876, the British persuaded the Chinese to allow a commercial mission to Lasha under Chefoo Convention; the Tibetans discouraged any Chinese interference in authorizing British to allow taking any decisions on their Foreign policy thereby disapproving of any suzerainty or sovereignty over it by China.

Van Walt van Praag argues that the 1886 and 1890 Conventions help to define the nature of the relationship between the Manchus and Tibet. He argues that both the 1886 and 1890 Convention refer to Tibet as a separate political entity. He bases this argument on the fact that the treaties are headed "Relating to Burmah and Tibet" and "Relating to Sikkim and Tibet". This separation of Tibet, Sikkim and Burmah as distinct from the Chinese or British Empires leads him to conclude that Tibet could not be covered by Chinese sovereignty. Moreover the relationship between the Manchus and the Tibetans was that of "*cho-yon*" i.e., the priest and the patron. Notwithstanding all this, the Chinese slowly increased and stabilized their influence in Tibet and made the Dalai Lama more of a puppet and subsequently started to abolish his authority as an incarnation. China started redefining the extent and the term Tibet, thereby unilaterally modifying the 1904 and 1906 agreements. With the Dalai Lama on the Indian land, things were further embarrassing for the British. The game that started as a threat from Russia ended up with China's somewhat dominating position in Tibet. The Chinese action on Tibet was based on its claim of sovereignty over the latter. Tibet, on the other hand considered itself independent. Tibetan history supports this position, except for a short period during the eighteenth century when Tibet was actually under the forced Manchu rule. Pressure and queer psychology always prompted it to give an impression to the world that China was its master, to keep foreigners out and avoid interference. That gave Lhasa the epithet of the 'Forbidden City'. India's stand has always been that it had no political ambitions in Tibet and that Tibet's autonomy should be maintained within the framework of Chinese suzerainty. If Tibet was a part of China as claimed by it, then there was no requirement to annex it.

In 1910 China having lost territory to Russia began to actively restore its domain on other protectorates and so did it, on Tibet by converting it into a full province. Having done so, China was at India's doorstep; it started demanding taxes from the inhabitants and also ordered its administrative units to cut a road to through the tribal belt to Assam. As compared to the northwest, east was inhabited and full of natural resources and therefore, strongly reacted by Britain. The main aim of Britain was to obtain territory that appeared to commensurate with the Indian culture, keeping in mind the rules and legality of the boundary as far as possible and avert any future threats from China towards India's north-eastern boundary.

With the passage of time the boundaries between all the nation states were becoming more and more complex and important. No nation wanted to lose any territory either to withhold its national pride or to simply keep buffers in-between its boundaries to avoid a conflict between the two. It was also important to have two nations to bilaterally agree and sign the agreement to stand legal acceptance. Lord Hardinge therefore went ahead to establish a boundary which would keep Tibet as a buffer which was earlier accepted in the 1904 Anglo-Chinese Treaty and the 1907 Anglo-Russian Treaty.

The McMohan Line and the Shimla Conference

Keeping all this at the back of their mind Britain, held a conference in Shimla in 1913, between Britain, China and Tibet, to come to a conclusion for a boundary between India and Tibet. Sir Henry Mc Mohan, Foreign Secretary of the Indian Government who was an experienced soldier in demarcating boundaries, such as the Durand Line between India and Afghanistan while being a young captain was the officer in-charge of this mission.[66] He had travelled a lot in the northwestern and northeastern border area of India and new the area like the palm of his hand. The Chinese representative at this conference was Chen I-fan, an experienced diplomat and Lu Hsing-chi, Chinese Council in Calcutta and Chinese viceroy in Lasha, and the Tibetan plenipotentiary was LonchenShatra, the chief minister of Dalai Lama's Government.

The basic aim of Britain in this conference was to divide Tibet into inner and outer zones to enable both Chinese and the Tibetans to establish their supremacy in respective zones, in continuation of the earlier agreements which would also sort out differences in the border issue with India. As it is British-Indian administrative representative and some trade posts had already been established in Tibet vide the British-Chinese convention of 1890 which was primarily to agree on a boundary between Tibet and Sikkim which was the crest of the Himalayas.

The formal opening of the Shimla Conference took place on 6 October and its first working meeting was held on 13 October. It was a matter of coincidence that the conference opened on 6th and Britain recognized the Republic of China on 7th October. Amongst protests and seeking amendments from all sides, the conference did not produce any concrete result. There was a big doubt in all the minds regarding the boundaries of Chinese and the Dalai Lama controlled Tibet. The parties claimed Giamda and Tachienlu which were about 1000 miles apart.

Tibetans were better prepared with their documents, some as old as Sino-Tibetan treaty of 822A.D between Tsan-Po and Hwang Te taken from the inscriptions on the West face of the stone pillar at Lhasa. Impressed with the Russo-Mongol agreement after the Russo-Chinese declaration, McMahon was wanting to redraft some portion of the own agreement on the same lines, i.e., suggest portion of Tibet which the Tibetans were wanting in worst case scenario; inner Tibet, would be under some degree of Chinese sovereignty and the Outer Tibet, would be the autonomous domain of the Dalai Lama under Chinese suzerainty.

The red line showed Tibet as a geographical and political unit nearly as suggested by Tibet and blue line as division between inner and outer Tibet based on Chinese evidence of boundary marker erected by Manchus in eighteen century near Batang. (In 1727 the Chinese Manchu dynasty had erected a boundary stone on Bum La to the West of Batang following the Mekong-Yangtze watershed. The Chinese knew that controlling Tibet would not be easy in absence of a well-connected road communication and therefore started constructing the most important link via Tachienlu which connected Lasha to Szechuan capital at Chengdu, the seat of the provincial Government with the responsibility of Tibetan affairs).

By doing this he would prevent any British territory along the border in Assam Himalayas touching the Inner, or the Chinese-dominated, Tibet, thereby keeping any future possibility of the Chinese to penetrate into the tribal hills. This he thought would also create a buffer between Tibet and Mongolia and keep the Russians also at safe distance.[67] The site of the conference had been shifted to Delhi due to winters. After the new draft was put up post-Christmas, it was not acceptable to either party for their own reasons. With major amendments the draft was reworded and prepared for signatures, but since Chen was getting instructions from China, he was instructed for more changes concerning the boundary and status of Tibet. Now Kokonor territory became a tumbling block, which China did not want to concede. By the end of April 1914, Shimla Conference failed to produce a valid tripartite agreement. No force could be applied on the Chinese since it had now been recognized as a nation state by Britain. Simultaneously the Soviets keeping in mind the Anglo-Russian agreement of 1907 (regarding non-interference in Tibet, on any matter including the special status on trade and trade agent) would interfere and remind the British of quid pro- quoin Mongolia due to the similar situation faced in Mongolia and Afghanistan.

On June 16, Sun Pao-ch'i, the Chinese foreign minister remarked that the real boundary between China and Northern Tibet was not Altyn Tagh range but Kun Lun range. However the end result of the very famous Simla Conference was initialing of the agreement by all three, signing of the map by all three and signing of the convention by Britain and Tibet. As a permanent settlement of the problem the Shimla Conference produced new trade regulations and the McMahon Line. In diplomatic practice, initialing freezes the text; it signifies conclusion of the negotiations, but only signing of the document facilitates its application on ground. China later refused to recognize the document, stating that Tibet had no authority to sign the document, although it initially made no attempt to contest it.[68] The existence of an unsigned Shimla Convention seems to have prevented the Indian Government between 1914 and 1947 from ever expressly recognizing Tibetan independence. Even the British *de facto* dealt with Tibet as a sovereign state, but still were unable to deny Chinese suzerainty *de jure.*

However the negotiated boundary now ran from

eastern border of Bhutan along the crest of the Great Himalayas up to the point of Great Bend in Brahmaputra River where the river emerges from Tibet course to Assam valley.

The Chinese repudiation of this agreement was only in relation to the boundary between Outer and Inner Tibet and not between Tibet and India. This can be amply corroborated by the fact thatthe Chinese had accepted the concept of inner and outer Tibet like in case of Mongolia, which is evident from the memorandum given by the Chinese foreign minister to the British in Peking on 30th May 1919 were he states "In the past the Chinese Government have treated Mongolia and Tibet in the same manner. Outer Mongolia has already been permitted to enjoy autonomy; it follows that no opposition will be placed in the way of Tibetan autonomy".[69] With the change of geopolitical and geostrategic situation and the perceived threat to Tibet and India, the reactionary importance to the boundary was evident. While the boundary at no place was ever marked by any of the kingdoms due to frequent changes in rulers and non-existence of a legal mindset in the olden times; the contemporary times demanded proper demarcation of any territory between two peoples or nation states bilaterally, or trilaterally if a buffer state was also involved, however no boundaries could be fixed unilaterally.

The map in the draft convention showed the alignment of McMohan line that was the boundary with India, earlier agreed with the Tibetans, along with the boundaries of inner and outer Tibet in different colors. The matter of the boundary issue was put in the backburner due to the start of the First World War. The documents of the convention or the maps were not published either.

The boundary issue again surfaced in 1935 when deputy secretary in Delhi, Mr. Olaf Caroc, noted that no publication of the McMohan line documents was done by the government. Amongst twists and turns the boundary issue resurfaced with various suggestions from eminent persons. The publication of this convention was required to be made in the Aitchison's Treaties to authentic record. The British and the Chinese representatives discussed the border incidents at Kashgar. The Chinese representative General Jiang did not accept 1899 as a valid border definition. However, he indicated that the Chinese did not negotiate this proposal because of their refusal to accept British annexation of Hunza and not because they disagreed with the proposed boundary alignment.

It is interesting to note that from 1917 to 1933 the "Postal Atlas of China" published by the Government of China in Beijing had shown Kun Lun as the boundary. Later the boundary was decided at Latsang range not because British felt Chinese had a claim on the region north of it, but was done deliberatly to make China strong in Kashgarh-Yarkkand, so that it becomes an obstacle to Russian advance in the line.

The northern borders of India became live once again with the emergence of Tibetan issue in 1949.

Immediately after coming to be recognized as the People's Republic of China, it turned its attention on Tibet. Heinrich Harrer (a German POW of World War II, who escaped to Tibet and was there till 1949 wrote a book) in his book, 'Seven Years in Tibet' had said: quote, "The threatening attitude of China, though traditional, has now again been intensified. Every Chinese government, whether Imperial, national or Communist, had always professed to regard Tibet as a Chinese province. This pretension was entirely contrary to the wishes of Tibetans, who loved their independence and were clearly entitled to enjoy it", unquote...[70]

Sino-Indian Boundary Dispute: Post Independence

On 7 October 1950, the Chinese troops entered Tibet to annex it. The Tibetans voiced their concern against the

Chinese military action and also fought against the Chinese army in whatever way it could, simultaneously asserting its independence and explaining its view to the world. This was the first instance of diplomatic friction between New Delhi and Beijing.[71] On 29 April 1954 a "Trade and Cultural Intercourse Agreement" was signed between India and China with a view to facilitate pilgrimages and travels to promote trade and cultural relations between "the Tibet region of China" and India. Subsequently India had also unequivocally accepted Chinese sovereignty over Tibet (with the understanding of giving autonomy to Tibetans) to showcase its intent of not having any political ambitions in Tibet; in the bargain giving away whatever her remaining special rights in Tibet in toto.[72] Visits between Jawaharlal Nehru in October 1954 and Zhou En-lai in 1956 were exchanged and it was officially maintained by the Chinese that there was no border problem with India and the McMahon line was believed to be the boundary between both the countries, as in the case of Burma. However, the two faces of the same coin are different; on one side Zhou En-Lai gave an impression of no border dispute and on the other hand, Chinese intrusions into Indian Territory continued unabated. The Chinese started protesting on the Indian troop's presence in Barahoti which they started claiming as theirs.[73] However after the war, in a note dated 3 April 1963, China stated observance of the LAC and that they had vacated the We-Ju(Barahoti) area and would refrain from setting up of civilian check-post there.[74] India reciprocated by sending a note that she had suspended sending civilians to Barahoti region.[75] In 1957, the Chinese violated the boundary in Walong in NEFA area. The most important and a major violation was the construction of Aksai Chin road. In 1957 India was surprised by China when it announced the completion of road connecting Yarkand and Khatang in Sinkiang with Gartok in Tibet. This road was a clear indication of Beijing's intent to accesses her authority over the occupied area in total disregard to Nehru administration.[76]

In 1958 reconnaissance parties of India were attacked and in July 1958 Chinese occupied Khurnak in Ladakh. There were a plethora of Chinese maps showing Indian territory as theirs. On having lodged a formal protest, the Chinese took a U-turn and claimed large parts of the Indian Territory on the pretext of the border not having been delimited. They claimed 36,400, sq.km. In Ladakh and 83,200 sq.km. In NEFA, Punjab, Himachal Pradesh and Uttar Pradesh. Again in 1959 there were intrusions deep into Indian side...[77] Due to Chinese excesses the Dalai Lama in 1959 again fled Lhasa and took refuge in India, followed by about 35000 Tibetans. Surprisingly this was followed by Chou En-lai visit to India in 1960; he proposed withdrawal of both sides by 20km from the McMahon Line in the east, and from the line of actual control in the western sector. This was not agreed by India, since India was within their side already, and China had intruded more than 20km inside India. However Nehru seems to have put the border area line in correct perspective. He had said "There is no sense in the Chinese offer to withdraw 20 km from what they call 'Line of actual control'. Is this the line, they have created by aggression since the beginning of September? Advancing forty to sixty km inside India by blatant military aggression and offering to withdraw twenty kilometers provided both sides do this is a deceptive device which can fool nobody".[78] It is pertinent to make a mention here that, Britain had claimed the area of Aksai Chin in all its official maps for a very long time, but being extremely inhospitable, the area was not administered very regularly. The Chinese knew about it, and they never objected to it, or make any claim to it. When India proclaimed its independence from Britain, it did not proclaim its independence from the British territorial claims and therefore legally inherited all the maps from British which included the Aksai Chin territory, as well as the line demarcated by McMahon as the boundary between China and Tibet. Moreover, all postcolonial countries haveright to interpret the borders within which they achieved independence as legally theirs, and therefore non-negotiable.[79]

The Chinese did their homework well before initiating the process of war. At home, Zhou and Mao strengthened the lost moral of their army and raised the public opinion in favour of nationalism and from outside they obtained reassurances from Russia to favour another communist country going to war under the provisions of the Treaty of Friendship and Alliance of 1950, (although Russia later adopted a posture of neutrality.). US interference by means of unleashing Taiwan against Mainland; American diplomacy seeking to block Hanoi's effort to turn Laos into a base area for war in Vietnam and a subsequent American attack on southern China via Laos were very cunningly and diplomatically resolved. Well prepared militrarily and politicaly China attacked India on 8 September 1962 havingcrossed the international boundary across Thangla Ridge towards Indian post at Dhola, following which Nehru ordered the army to throw out the Chinese from Indian Territory.[80]

After the war, various proposals made in the Colombo and other conferences were rejected by China, and it did not show any resolve to sort out the border dispute thereafter. India reiterated that it was interested in talks only when China reverts back to the positions held on 8 September 1962.[81]

Conclusion

The Indian civilization is an example of a historical continuity, since its facts are so strongly intermingled with the traditions of its culture, that it influences the contemporary social and political behavior, like in the case of present day Chinese connect with their past history. The best and the most effective way to understand the present is to know its past. Similarly to understand the present behavior of China and India towards each other is first to consider the politically charged issue of the role of so-called 'ancient China and India' in understanding the China and India of today.

Although both the countries have equally long and

continuous civilizations, the Chinese civilization offers a sharp contrast to that of India. The Chinese civilization combined and formed one group around 1500 B.C. The establishment of Shang Dynasty at this point of time gave a political expression to combination of civilization. With migration of civilizations from Shang to Zhou in 256B.C. the development of China was enriched and well established which has persisted till today. It is quite evident from the above that the Chinese ideology was traditionally bound by Confucianism by majority of people i.e. Han Chinese which constituted 94 percent of its population, and were socio-political in nature, and contributed in making of a powerful, unified, self-confident and a homogeneous society.

On the other hand, due to the religious affinity, the socio-religious developments in India identify with ideas and practices based on Hinduism. India failed to develop homogeneity and any sense of political or social unity. However it was because of religious philosophy and its unique caste structure that evolved a social system. The evolving mindset of the Chinese therefore was that of community living which inclines them to live as one, thereby giving them a feeling of belonging to one state, where as the Indians have a tendency of separate homeland based on religious affinity.

In the middle of the first millennium B.C.E., the Chinese concerned themselves with theories of kingship and type of governance, prepared themselves for a single state egalitarian society. Indians under the influence of the great philosophers (Buddha and Mahavira) were deep into the transmigration of souls which underplayed the importance of life in this world, thereby dominating religious and not political cord of a human being. Whereas the Chinese philosophy directs people to find fulfillment through socio-political activities, the Indians think world as transitory and unreal and encourages to seek spiritual realization of the absolute by annihilation of ego which bind him to his finite individuality.

The Aryans had their own customs and language and did not emulate anything of the earlier existing scripts or socio-political institutions. The Chinese Zhou dynasty which came after Shang developed the already existing Shang civilization its culture and the writing system and promoted the Chinese ideal of a humanistic, unitary imperial state.

Although the civilization in India arose before the Shang dynasty (c.1600-c.1100 B.C.E.) and was more advanced, but no historical memory of the more urbanized Indus Valley civilization was properly or systematically recorded; the script of this time vanished with the disappearance of the civilization. China provides an increasing number of documents written on bamboo slats and silk cloth reflecting a pervasive concern for political and worldly affairs. Their interest in keeping records led to the quest of inventing paper by the Han dynasty. It took almost 1000 years in India before the Aryan history could be written down; the void during this period produced oral literature embodied in Vedic hymes, prayers and philosophical speculation and the great epics, which were more or less religious in nature.

The emergence of contemporary new empires of Han in China and Maurya in India shows that whereas the Chinese imperial system achieved permanence and stability due to combination of military power with socio-political oriented Confucian ideology of a unitary government, the Indian empire lacked this philosophy and established an imperial system not until the British rule.

Both China and India have been regularly invaded causing breakdown of governance, However China from Han to nineteenth century experienced strengthening of its culture thereby producing a close-knit society, and India from Maurya dynasty to the British rule saw a division facilitating growth of cast and regional culture areas in its own language. Since caste itself is divisive, the "unity in diversity" was indianised.

Buddhism was popular in China during Han period

and it increased its influence throughout the country by seventh century A.D. but because it was antithetical to Confucianism's "this world" ideology soon lost its high position. The loss and gain of popularity of Buddhism and Confucian ideology with the change of dynasties was a common phenomenon. However in the last few years till the Ming, Qing and the Manchu's all adopted and promoted continuity of Confucian state.

Chinese visitors to India, such as Faxian in the fifth century and Xuanzong's and Yi Jing in the seventh century state that their visit was not restricted to religion only. Existence of Indian monks in China dates back to first century CE, when Dharmaraksa and Kashyapa Matanga went to China on invitation of Emperor Mingdi of the Han dynasty and stayed in the 'White Horse Monastery', built for them. Faxian, another scholar from western China came in 401 CE, undertook study of Sanskrit text and took considerable interest in contemporary health arrangements in India. Aryabatta, Varahmihira and Brahmagupta also formed part of exchanges.

Yi Jing, spent ten years at Nalanda, besides other scholars, not only to study Buddhism butalso 'Ayurveda'. Many Indian mathematicians and astronomers, held high positions in China's scientific establishments, and an Indian by the name of Gautama Siddhartha even became the president of the official Board of Astronomy in China in the eighth century. It is pertinent to know in nutshell the historical contacts of a third of the world's population and continuing relevance of this contact, linked as they are with the contemporary strategical concerns. The non-religious consequences of these relations connect with science, mathematics, literature, linguistic, architecture, medicine and music.

Both the invaders in China and India absorbed themselves in their respective socio-political and socio-religious systems but with different outcomes; whereas in China it meant the continuity of a unified, centrally administered state: in India it meant a proliferation of independent kingdoms. Even attempts made by Hindu rulers (Guptas, 320-480; Harsha, 606-647) to repeat the Mauryan experiment resulted only in loosely-knit empires limited to north India. The rulers exercised suzerainty over local dynasties and never established a Chinese-style centralized bureaucratic control system. On governmental basis, China and India were brought closer together during the rule of Kushan Kings in India in the early centuries of the Christian era. Kanishka, with his capital at Peshawar, ruled over a huge empire, which comprised a large part of Northern India and extensive regions in Central Asia reaching up to the border of China.

The diplomatic relations between India and China, according to Dr. R.C. Majumdar, the eminent Indian historian dealing in ancient Indian history lasted for ensuing five or six centuries. Probably between the period 451 and 511 A.D. no less than eight embassies were dispatched from several states in North-west India to China. During Tang Dynasty (618-907A.D.) the whole of China was integrated and unified less than one sovereign and reached its apex of the military zenith and cultural progress. The great Indian monarch, Harshvardhan, sent an Embassy to China in 641 A. D. and approximately three Embassies from China visited India between 643 and 646 A.D.[82]

The barbarian invasion of the fifth and sixth century, although slurred over by the Indian authorities, constitute a turning point in the history of northern and western India, both politically and socially.

Over lordships as a result of wars fought by military castes did not affect the socio-religious system or the lives of the people at large but in twelfth century (before arrival of Muslim)there was a gradual replacement of Buddhism by Hinduism that had become the principle religion of India, giving the country a unifying ethos. The visit of the Chinese traveler to India has himself been witness to his thirteen years of travel in India, covering almost entire sub-continent. Taking a route encompassing Lake IssikKul, Tashkent, Samarqand, Qunduz, Gandhara, Pamir's, Kashgar, Yarkand, Khotanetc not knowing then that some of these places would be a bone of contention between his country and the place visited. The first record of an Indian scholar's visit to China is that of Kashyapa Matanga, who reached China in 67 A.D. in the reign of Emperor Ming Ti.

With the coming of Muslim rulers, there was a radical change in the sub-continent. Islam, a strong, militant religion was wholly opposed to Hinduism and thrust of only one god "Allah" was trying to be propagated, but being few in numbers were clearly unable to attempt the conversion of vast local population to Islam. The Islamic power monopoly was therefore restricted to the bureaucratic center but allowed local Hindu chieftains to continue as tributaries and the socio-religious system to function in the countryside and the villages. The Hindus were treated as second class citizens; Aurangzeb (1658-1707) the last Muslim ruler did try to annihilate Hinduism but failed. The early successes of Islam were against religions which had lost their hold on the minds of the people.

But in India, the Hindu way of life, symbolized by high moral values of tolerance, truthfulness and justice was very much part of the multitude's mental and material being. These eternal and moral values of life which constitute the core of Hinduism were to sustain it in the next five centuries of Muslim and another two centuries of British rule.

India, under the British rule, comprised modern India, Pakistan, Bangladesh and Burma. The consolidation of British rule in India from eighteenth century onward had been met with stiffresistance; especially in 1857, when the first war of independence was launched unsuccessfully. India's struggle for independence gota fillip with the emergence of Indian National Congress in 1885 which provided an organizational and political platform. It was through Indian National Congress, that leaders like Mahatma Gandhi, Motilal Nehru, Madan Mohan Malaviya, Jawaharlal Nehru, C.R. Das and host of others pioneered the cause of India's struggle against British colonialism.[83]

The advent of Muslim League in 1906 and assumption of its leadership by Mohd. Ali Jinnah provided a new turning point to the national freedom struggle in the wake of the fact that the Muslim League demanded a separate State for the Muslims in case India attained independence. The resolution adopted by the Muslim League in 1940 had demanded the division of India into Hindu and Muslim States. Rahmat Ali is generally credited to having coined the term "Pakis'ian"[84] a name which was later adopted by the Muslim League and other protagonists who favored the division of India on communal lines and establishment of a separate state forthe Muslims. By the time, the Second World War ended, the chances of the Indian sub-continent attaining independence had brightened.

They destroyed the domestic industry in India and exploited the village agricultural fabric based on small household type agrarian economy and catapulted it to a capitalist economy for their own gains. They drained the Indian wealth to accommodate their own falling economy due to the war of colonization. India with the highest GDP in the world was reduced to be a third world country, with hunger, poverty and illiteracy on its independence.

The impact of British rule was multifaceted because, the change was followed by the contiguous Islam and Mughal rule which had already made a dent in the social and cultural fabric of the Indians. The visionaries like Raja Ram Mohan Roy, Sir Syed Ahmed Khan, Aruna Asaf Ali and Pandita Ramabai wanted to imbibe new ideas into the Indian culture and were in the forefront of movements to compel the British to bring about the changes.

The British by default undertook introduction of

education, but of a few prominent people, so that they could be used later as clerks or a via media to run their own affairs. They used education as a means to strengthen their political authority in the country by ignoring the masses. However a political awakening also followed and the learned personalities started asking for their rights. Modern education inculcated a habit of a scientific and legal approach to life which was used against the British later.

The Indians were denied political rights and treated with contempt. Higher posts in administration or military were not meant for the Indians. In justice system, attempts were made to separate the judiciary from the executive and establish the 'Rule of Law', but for the British to enjoy the arbitrary powers and interfere with the rights and liberties of the Indians. Being a costly affair, it was discriminative and not assessable to the Indians.

Thus, British rule brought about many changes, mostly for their own good but others that occurred as a byproduct of the interaction with them were molded to suit domestic requirements, which continue to affect our daily lives.

Both China and India were influenced by the British. However, it was difficult for the British to penetrate the Chinese tradition, culture and religious bonding. They were initially not even given right of permanent residence in Canton, the only port open to the west. The influence in China was limited to something like "semi-colony", meaning that though exploited by Western imperialism, technically never lost their independence and met the foreign challenge with their own time-tested socio-political system. Perhaps as a result of this, China proved to be most adept at absorbing and assimilating outside invaders while preserving their own sense of identity, believes and institutions.

India on the other hand, was a colony of Britain and any Indian response could only be within a political framework imposed by the British. The internal identities of Indians draw on different parts of India's diverse traditions.

The observational tilt of Western approaches has had quite a major impact – positively and negatively – on what contributes to the Indian self-image that emerged in the colonial period and survives today.

The conclusion, therefore, seems inescapable that much of the decline in social and moral values of Hindu society is the result and not the cause of their foreign subjugation.

The above historical background of China and India therefore amply prove the following points:-

1. Chinese by nature are assertive, Indians on the other hand are submissive.
2. Chinese are socio-political, Indians are socio-religious in nature.
3. Chinese imperial system achieved permanency and stability, Indian imperial system was not established untill the British rule.
4. Chinese, inspite of having semi-colonial type of environment, took their own decisions, where as India was bound by the political famework imposed by the British.
5. Chinese military is a apart of the political system, Indian military is apolitical.

Thus we can safely say what we had begun with that and what Clausewitzs explained in one of his principles of strategy that historical examples provide impetus to the best kind of proof in the study of war. He cites four key uses of historical examples. First, they may be used as *an illustration* of an idea; second, they serve to show the *best practice* of an idea; third, they can prove the possibility of *an effect*, and finally, they may be used to *develop theory*. At the same times he warns of dangers of putting same template on different situations.Since long time has past, situations changed and maturity gained, we must make useof history to our advantage and national interest.

India - China Relations – Latest Developments

- Army Chief Gen ManojNaravane had taken a review of the situation and announced that further steps will be taken to de-escalate the situation while calling for restrain from personnel of both the Armies.
- A major incident had occurred in the stand-off between India and China in Ladakh on the night of 15th June 2020. One Commanding Officer and two jawans of the Indian Army lost their lives during a violent face-off with Chinese troops in the Galwan area of Eastern Ladakh. These are the first combat deaths on the disputed boundary since 1975. In total, 20 Indian soldiers were martyred in the clashes. Indian Army had given a befitting reply to the Chinese Army and as per different Indian media reports, the Chinese Army lost a substantial number of soldiers in the ensuing conflict.
- Following a high-level visit by commanding officers of both the Indian and Chinese forces, the Chinese army on June 9th, 2020 agreed to withdraw about 2-2.5 km away from the disputed territory, with the Indian army also agreeing to disengage at some locations. Talks for further disengagement are to continue in the coming days.
- In the initial weeks of June 2020, there was a substantial buildup of troops on both sides of the LAC, with both the Indian and Chinese army matching strength for strength.
- On 10 May 2020, Chinese and Indian troops clashed in Nathu La, Sikkim (India). 11 soldiers were injured. Following the skirmishes in Sikkim, tensions between the two countries grew in Ladakh with a buildup of troops at multiple locations.
- On 11 October 2019, Chinese president Xi Jinping met with Indian Prime Minister Narendra Modi at Mahabalipuram, Tamil Nadu, India for a second informal meeting between India and China.

- In 2019, India reiterated that it would not join One Belt One Road initiative, stating that it cannot accept a project that ignores concerns about its territorial integrity.
- In May 2018, the two countries agreed to coordinate their development programs in Afghanistan in the areas of health, education, and food security.
- On 18 June 2017, around 270 Indian troops, with weapons and two bulldozers, entered Doklam to stop the Chinese troops from constructing the road. Among other charges, China accused India of illegal intrusion into its territory, across what is called the mutually agreed China-India boundary, and violation of its territorial sovereignty and United Nations Charter.
- On 28 August 2017, China and India reached a consensus to put an end to the border stand-off. Both of them agreed to disengage from the standoff in Doklam.
- On 16 June 2017 Chinese troops with construction vehicles and road-building equipment began extending an existing road southward in Doklam, a territory which is claimed by both China as well as India's ally Bhutan.
- In September 2014 the relationship became strained as troops of the People's Liberation Army (PLA) reportedly entered two kilometers inside the Line of Actual Control (LAC) in the Chumar sector. The next month, V. K. Singh said that China and India had come to an "agreement of views" on the threat of terrorism emanating from Pakistan.

India's response to the recent India- China Clashes

- **Economically –**
- The government has banned 59 apps of Chinese origin citing the "emergent nature of threats" from

mobile applications.

- Though the tensions on the border, as well as the Covid-19 pandemic, have thrown light on India's economic dependencies on China but India's trade deficit with China fell to $48.66 billion in 2019-20 on account of the decline in imports. The trade deficit stood at $53.56 billion in 2018-19 and $63 billion in 2017-18.
- However, in several critical and strategically sensitive sectors such as pharmaceutical ingredients, semiconductors and the telecom sector, where Chinese vendors are involved not only in India's 4G network but in on-going 5G trials, India remains reliant on Chinese products only.

- **Military** –
  - India has moved in additional divisions, tanks and artillery across the LAC to match Chinese deployments.
  - Further, India has approved the purchase of 33 Russian fighter jets and upgrades to 59 war planes at a cost of Rs. 18,148 crore.
- **Foreign Investment** –
  - Foreign Direct Investment (FDI) from China in India has dipped to $163.78 million in 2019-20 from $229 million in 2018-19. In April 2020, the Indian government tightened FDI norms coming from the countries which share land borders with India. Government approval has been made mandatory.

References

1. The Changing Society of China, Chu Chai and Winberg Chai. Chicago New American Library, 1962, Menter book P. 11.
2. Ibid p 29.
3. China A Global Studies Handbook. Robert Andre LaFleur.

Robert Andre palmer,warrenbrucerapp, John A Robson, Santa Barbara, ABC clio, 2003 Global studie: Asia Pp.11-12.

4. The History of China: David C. Wright. David curtis-westport greenwood press, 2001 P.12.
5. China Emerges: A Concise History of China from Its Origin to the Present, StevenWarshaw 11thRved, Berkdey Diablo press 1988 p. 1.
6. China: A Concise Cultural History. Arthur Cotterell, London Johan Murray 1988 Pp.3-5.
7. A History of China: Wolfram Eberhard, IIIrd rev ed, Berkeley university of California Press 1969 pp 19-22).
8. A Short History of the Chinese People: Carrington Goodrich, Sturgis press 2007 pp16-17.)
9. A Short History of China; M.L.Gupta, New Delhi, Reliance Pub. 1994 p 113.
10. The History of China; David C. Wright, Westport Green wood Press, 2000 pp 39-41.
11. Ibid; pp 42-43.
12. China Emerges; Steven Warshaw, 11th Rev ed, Berkeley Diablo Press, 1998, pp 26-29.
13. Ibid pp 28-31.
14. The History of China; David C Wright, Westport Green wood Press, 2001, pp45-46.
15. China Emerges; Steven Warshaw, 11th Rev ed. Berkeley Diablo Press, 1998, p 34.
16. Ibid pp 36-37.
17. The history of China; David C Wright' Westport Green wood Press 2001 pp 64-66.
18. Ibid pp 60-61.
19. China Emerges; Steven Warshaw, 11th Rev ed. Berkeley Diablo Press, 1998 pp. 46-47.
20. Sen Amartya, (2005), The Argumentative Indian; Writings

on Indian History, Culture and Identity, Penguin Books Ltd, England pp. 161-189

21. China Emerges; Steven Warshaw, 11th Rev ed. Berkeley Diablo Press, 1998 pp 53-57.
22. Michael Franz, (1986), China, through the Ages: History of Civilization, USA, and West view Press p124.
23. Ibid, pp. 135-140.
24. Py Ho and S.P. Lisowski,1997, 2ndedition; A Brief History of Chinese Medicine, World Sciencetific Publication Pvt. Ltd., Singapore, p. 38.
25. Dreyer Edward L (1982), Early Ming China-A Political History 1355-1435, Stanford University Press, California.
26. Ibid, pp. 5-8
27. Kissinger Henry, (2011), On China, Penguin Group, USA. pp 89-90.
28. Ibid, pp181-197.
29. Smith A.Vincen, C.I.E. (1958) The Oxford History of India, Oxford University Press, Oxford. pp45-55.
30. Sinha N.K & Ray Nitish R, (1973), A History of India, Orient Longman Ltd., Calcutta. pg. 59-60.
31. Stein Burton (1998) A History of India, Blackwell Publishers Ltd., UK.
32. Chakavarti Prithwis Chandra, The Indian Historical Quarterly, vol 4, No4, 1930.12, pp 645- 664. Assessed on 02 April 2013.
33. Nehru Jawaharlal (1960), The Discovery of India, Meridian Books Ltd, London, pg113.
34. Ibid, pg113.
35. Sinha N.K. and Ray N.R. (1973), A History of India, Orient Longman Ltd., 1973, Calcutta, p 117.
36. Ibid, pp 206-209.
37. Smith A.Vincen, C.I.E. (1958) The Oxford History of India, Oxford University Press, Oxford. p.266.

38. Sinha N.K.and Ray N.R. (1973), A History of India, Orient Longman Ltd., 1973, Calcutta, pg 303-323.

39. Smith A.Vincen, C.I.E. (1958) The Oxford History of India, Oxford University Press, Oxford. pg. 449.

40. Ibid, pp363-374.

41. Ibid, pp377-400.

42. Stein Burton (1998) A History of India, Blackwell Publishers Ltd., UK.pp-146.

43. Nehru Jawaharlal (1960), The Discovery of India, Meridian Books Ltd, London, p. 294.

44. IOSR Journal of Humanities & Social Sciences(JHSS), Vol. 2, 4 Sep-Oct 2012, pp16-26.

45. Rothermund Dietmar (1988), an Economic History of India, From Pre-Colonial Times to 1986, Croom Helm with Methuen, Inc. New York's 32

46. Maxwell Neville (1970), reprinted 2010, India's China War, Naraj Publishers, Dehradun, p26.

47. A.G. Noorani, 2011, India-China Boundary Problem 1846-1947, History and Diplomacy, New Delhi: Oxford University Press, p., 48.

48. M L Sali ,1998, India China Border Dispute, New Delhi, APH Publishing, Details of Peace Treaty between Ladakh and Tibet at Tingmosgang at Appendix 1, pp.,255-257.

49. Vans Agnew. A Few Remarks on Maharaja Gulab Singh's Boundary with China. Enclosures to the secret letters from India, vol.110, No. 39, 8 June 1847. Reproduced by Dorothy Woodman, p. 354.

50. M L Sali ,1998, India China Border Dispute, New Delhi, APH Publishing, Details of Peace Treaty between Ladakh and Tibet at Tingmosgang at Appendix 1, p 46.

51. H.H. Goodwin- Austin, 1867, Proceedings of R.G.S.J., vol. 37, p., 347." Notes on the Pongong Lake District of Ladakh," from a journol made during a survey in 1863. Quoted in Dorothy Woodman. P., 325.

52. Lippincott, 1898, Through Unknown Tibet, p.47. Quoted in Dorothy Woodman, p. 325.
53. A.D. Carey, 1887, A Journey Round Chinese Turkistan and Along the Northern Fronteirs of Tibet, Proceedings of R.G.S.J, vol. 9, Quoted in Dorothy Woodman. P. 62.
54. Bower Hamilton, 1894, A Journey Across Tibet, London, p.1, Quoted in Dorothy Woodman, p. 64.
55. Mohan Guruswamy and Zorawar Daulet Singh, India China Relations: The Border Issue and Beyond, Viva Books, New Delhi, 2009. ISBN: 8130911957 HB.
56. Maxwell Neville (1970), reprinted 2010, India's China War, Natraj Publishers, Dehradun, pp30-34.
57. Alaister Lamb, 1973, The Sino-Indian Border in Ladakh, Canberra, Australia, National University Press, p. 50.
58. Maxwell Neville, 1971, India's China war, Mumbai, Pantheon Books, p. 81.
59. K. Warikoo,(ed), Himalayan Frontiers of India: Historical, geo-political and strategic perspectives, 2009, Routledge, Oxon. Preface)
60. Lamb Alastair,(1966), The McMahon Line, A Study in the Relations between India, China and Tibet, 1904 to 1914, Vol-1; Morley, Minto and Non- Interference in Tibet, Routledge & Kegan Paul Ltd, Great Britain, p.45.
61. Ibid, p.88.
62. Ibid, 98-99.
63. Ibid p.121.
64. Waddell Austin. L, Lhasa and its Mysteries, With a Record of British Tibetan Expedition of 1903-1904 p.24.
65. Chaterjee RK, (1978), India's Land Borders: Problems and Challenges, Srerling Publishers (P) Ltd, New Delhi pp.76-77.
66. Maxwell Neville (1970), reprinted 2010, Indi's China War; Naraj Publishers, Dehradun, p.47.

67. Lamb Alastair, (1966), The McMahon Line, A Study in the Relations between India, China and Tibet, 1904 to 1914, Vol-2; Morley, Minto and Non- Interference in Tibet, Routledge & Kegan Paul Ltd, Great Britain, pp.490-491).

68. Kissinger Henry, (2011), On China, Penguin Group, Usurp 186) also read the Geneva Convention on the Law of Treaties 1969, article 12(2).

69. Guruswamy Mohan, (2006), Emerging Trends in India-China Relations, Hope India Publications, and Gurgaon. p.47.

70. Chaterjee RK,(1978), India's Land Borders: Problems and Challenges, Sterling Publishers (P) Ltd, New Delhi p.75.

71. Sudhakar Bhatt, India and China, New Delhi: Popular Books Service, 1967, p.11.

72. White Paper-I, Ministry of External affairs, Government of India, pp 98-107.

73. Shankar Bhatt, India and China New Delhi: Popular Book Service, 1967, p.17.

74. White Paper, IX, p.37.

75. White Paper, p. 29.

76. Lorene's Kavic, India's Quest for Security, Defense Policies, 1947-65 (California, 1967), p.63.

77. Chaterjee RK, (1978), India's Land Borders: Problems and Challenges, Srerling Publishers (P) Ltd, New Delhi pg. 85

78. Saraf Pushp, April- June, 2013' Borders Affairs, Vol. 14 No.3. p. 2.

79. Kissinger Henry, (2011), On China, Penguin Group, USA. p.186.

80. Times of India, 13 October 1962.

81. India, Lok Sabha Debates, vol XII, No. 29, Col. 5996.

82. A Short History of China; M.L. Gupta. preface.

83. Tara Chand, History of the Freedom Movement in India New Delhi, 1972, pp.22-23.

84. Sangat Singh, Pakistan's Foreign Policy (Bombay, 1970), p.4

2

Border Dispute

Boundary disputes are sui generis and unlike other types of international disputes. India has border disputes with almost all its neighbors (Pakistan, Nepal, Sri Lanka and Myanmar) but none of these have led to major wars. However, China's border disputes have led to war with India in1962, with Vietnam in 1969 and with the Soviet Union in 1979. Before discussing the issue per- se, let's be clear of some terms that would be used in the course of this chapter. Firstly, the difference between a boundary and a frontier since they are unintentionally referred to as synonymous, while they are not; 'boundary' denotes a line where as a 'frontier' is more properly a region or zone having width as well as length and, therefore merely indicates, without fixing the exact limit, were one state ends and other begins.

Another term which is used rather loosely is delimitation and demarcation. The 'delimitation' of a boundary refers to the proceedings connected with the determination of a boundary line in a treaty, an arbitral award or a boundary commission's report as the case may be; either the watershed or the crest or mid channel of river or something alike. However delimitation alone, will not, in every case give a boundary of finality and it will be necessary to fix its position more definitely on the ground to supplement it on ground by fixing pillars or monuments or fence etc. as on paper, only then will it be called as demarcated.[1]

Line of Actual Control (LAC) is often used whenever reference is made to the Sino-Indian border; it is the line up to which troops of the two sides exercise effective control. It has not been demarcated, but the term was first used by the then Chinese Premier Zhou Enlai, in a letter to the Indian Prime Minister in 1959.[2] It is necessary to conceptually clarify the line of actual control. The Sino-Indian LAC was created as a result of the confrontations of the 1959-1962 periods between the two countries. Line of actual control is the de-facto Border. It generally means the line where the control of each side sharply ends. This line divides the territories and frontiers actually under the control of the two belligerent parties and more precisely it separates the armed forces of the two sides. It is a notional line neither demarcated on the ground nor delineated on the map. Nor is there, any agreement between the two sides where exactly the line runs. The LAC in this sense differs from the Line of Control (LOC). In case of LOC the separating line between the two parties are known to both countries and there may be delineation of the boundary on a map or demarcation on the ground except formal recognition as the international border. Both LAC and LOC are thus different from border. Border connotes a sense of permanence (although not ever permanent) characterised by formalisation, mutual acceptance and recognition either byvirtue of traditional, customary, distinctive natural features or by mutually agreed artificial agreement. It depicts a line that seperates one country, state, province from another or a frontier line; you cannot cross the border without a visa. LAC and LOC on the other hand connote a sense of transition which may get altered at any moment as they are neither recognised nor formalised. In short, LAC when delineated onmap and demarcated on the ground becomes LOC and when LOC gets the seal of formalisation on the basis of mutual acceptance and settlement, it becomes border. In case of India and China there is no agreement between the two countries as to where do the line actually lie. Both countries use different names for the same features and frontiers along the border. The desolateregion devoid of inhabitants makes it difficult to know each other's actual control. More interestingly, there were three different LACs between the two countries - one thatexisted in November 1959, one before 8th September 1962 andone where the Chinese reached after the massive invasion on 20th, October 1962. The agreement signed on 7th September1993 does not define the LAC. "The Chinese official sources maintain that there is an LAC well known to both sideswhile Indian officials claim there is an LAC which existsobjectively and is known to both sides.[3]

It was seen from the historical background of both China and India that for much of the history, boundaries were not as firm or as immutable as they have now become. China and India's boundaries kept changing on the rise or fall of the state of its neighbours'. Boundaries were not marked or demarcated with precision or else on the ground or map. Going by history Indian empires extended much beyond what it is actually today. The more powerful Mauryan and Mughal Empires extended well beyond the geographical limits of the Indian sub-continent.It extended beyond the Himalayas to include large parts of Afghanistan. Similarly the Chola dynasty in south had taken Straits of Malacca under them. In early days therefore, there were no mutually predetermined international boundaries but rather separate zones, which usually occurred without plan or consciousness on the part of the tribal, ethnic or national groups that were separated. The necessity for lines of partition only rose, as Holdich points out, when men turned from the lordly enjoyment of agriculture and tillage of the soil. The need for fixed boundaries was aggravated when the modern States of

Western Europe began to develop on the ruins of the Holy Roman Empire.

1648 is generally accepted as the date of establishment of the modern state system by the Peace of Westphalia. The first known formal conference for demarcation of boundaries is known to have been held in Vienna in 1815 following the defeat of Napoleon, to redraw and demarcate the boundaries of the European states.[4] It is imperativetofirst understand the strategic importance of the area of dispute which will by itself dictate the causesof indecision on the issue till date.

The Importance of Himalayas

The Himalayas were a stabilising factor in the geology of the subcontinent; it checked the tide of great population movements from Central Asia which overran large parts of Europe. The Himalayas were a unique factor, not only in the sub-continent but also in Asian continent. Himalayas gave the land route to the people who have carried the torch of religion, spirituality and commercial activity over a long time. To a Hindu, Himalaya is his spiritual home. Most of the religious places of the Hindus are located in these mighty mountains and connected to centuries old beliefs which can be read in Vedas and other religious history text of epics like Mahabharata and Ramayana.Places like Badrinath, Kedarnath, Kailash, Mansarovar, and Amaranth and rivers those are so sacred to a Hindu like Ganges and Yamuna are all engraved in the Himalayas. They not only affect the climate of India but also other parts of Asia in its proximity. It is a major water source for not only India and China but also other neighbouring countries. It harnesses in its fold about 15,000 glaciers and huge amount of water which is soon becoming a most sort after strategic resource, including the 70 km long Siachin Glacier, on the India – Pakistan border which is the second largest glacier in the world. India shares its borders with TAR of China, Pakistan, Nepal and Burma, all in the Himalayas.

The Himalayas and the regions south of it have been the cradle of Buddhism which reached Ladakh region of these mountains, during the reign of Emperor Ashoka. Ladakh along with Baltistan and Hunza was conquered and annexed to Kashmir valley by Maharaja Gulab Singh in the early nineteenth century.[5]

Strategic Importance of Aksai-Chin and Ladakh Region

The Aksai Chin region lies towards western side of Ladakh, which is about the area of the size of Switzerland, situated between the Chinese self-governing regions of Xinjiang and Tibet" This "barren plateau has been claimed by India as part of Ladakh section of the state of Jammu and Kashmir" "The high-altitude wasteland of Aksai Chin is almost unpopulated and has a small number of natural resources"

Aksai Chin in the past was travelled only by the residents of neighboring territories in search of salt and by infrequent hunters. In "1717, however, it was crossed by the Tsungar invaders of Tibet and 233 years later it was used for the same intention by the Chinese."[6] At present, Aksai Chin is administered by China as part of Hotan County in the Hotan Prefecture of Xinjiang Autonomous Region. "The line that divides the Indian occupiedareas of Jammu and Kashmir from Aksai Chin is known as the LAC and is synchronized with the Chinese Aksai Chin claim line"

"Topographically, Aksai Chin is a high altitude desert. In the southwest, the Karakoram Range makes the de facto border LAC between Aksai Chin and Indian occupied Kashmir. Glaciated peaks in the middle part of this boundary reach heights of 6,950 meters. In the north, the Kun Lun Range splits Aksai Chin from the Tarim Basin, where the rest of Hotan County is located. The northern piece of Aksai Chin is known as the Soda Plain and contains Aksai Chin's main river, the Karakosh". The river, which "gets melted water from several glaciers, crosses the Kun Lun farther northwest, in Pishan County and penetrates in to the Tarim Basin, where it acts as one of the chief sources of water. For Karakash and Hotan Counties."

"The eastern branch of the area contains a number of small endorheic basins. The biggest of them is that of the Aksai Chin Lake, which is fed by the Aksai Chin River. The region is more or less uninhabited", has "no stable settlement, and receives modest precipitation as the Himalayas and the Karakoram obstruct the rains from the Indian monsoon. At 17,000 feet elevation, Aksai Chin has no human significance other than an early trade route that crossed over it, providing a short pass during summer for convoys of yaks between Xinjiang and Tibet". At present, "China National Highway 219 runs through Aksai Chin linking Xinjiang and Lazi in Tibet". Despite this "region being virtually not fit to live in and having little resources, it remains strategically significant for China as it links Tibet and Xinjiang" It is easy to defend but difficult to attack. It is observed from the satellite pictures that Aksai Chin is divided into two unequal portions by a ridge called Laktsang, or LakTsung, which runs southeast, towards a little north of Lanak La, and is about 15 miles across. The northern Plateau, from Laktsang Ridge to the source of the Karakash River in extreme north is the proper Aksai Chin. The southern Plateau between Laktsang and Changchenmo Ridge is called the Lingzithang plains or the white plains. The western highway from Kashgarh to Lasha passing through Aksai Chin is a strategic lifeline for western Tibet, with huge convoys seen during the fair season.

The Kashgarh-Aksai chin road has major halting places at Yarkhand Mazar(at 241 km stone), Tielong (at 672 km stone), and Sumxi (at 730 km stone). Rudok is 933 km from Kashgarh and Sumxi is the first Tibetan inhabited place on the road. At km marker 518 begin the soda plains and km marker 670, near Tielong Aksai Chin plains end to enter Tibet. The study of the satellite images available on the internet confirms existence of Laktsang Ridge. In the past attempts have been made to deny this landmark, saying "there is no such thing as a 'LakTsung range'.[7]

Post 1962 War: Chinese Withdrawal in East, Status Quo in Aksai Chin

Chinese after the war withdrew to the McMahon line in the eastern sector but retained the ground position in the western sector i.e., the area of Aksai Chin. It is evident that Chinese had already war-gamed the importance of both the areas and therefore acted as pre-planed. Tawang being closer to the Indian plains can be reinforced in a much quicker time frame than China could do in case of an extended war. Chinese reinforcement trail would be much longer from its mainlandand therefore difficult to sustain and defend. Moreover she was at that point of time interested in consolidating its rear i.e. strengthen Eastern China against US and Japan and Western China with Central Asia. By having a long drawn war in its rear it would have perforce opened a rear front which was against her strategic interest and would engage her into a prolonged expenditure of her national comprehensive power and depleting her economic resources thereby causing instability and liability.

On the other hand Aksai Chin was a high altitude, barren land with extremely cold weather conditions, and absolutely no vegetation and habitation. Economically, this area per-se was of no value except of the fact that an historic old silk route existed in that part of the country which had lost its economic relevance at that point of time. However, it overlooked central Asia and could be used to tame the central Asian region. China had constructed a highway through Aksai Chin connecting Tibet and Xinjiang with the aim of shifting more of Han Chinese in Tibet to influence and dilute the Tibetan monopoly in that region and evoke itsall time ally Pakistan. Some lateral roads had also been planned at that point of time as a long term strategy. (latter connected from the Aksai Chin road to the Line of Actual control to enable quick built-up of Chinese troops and reinforcements whenever required.) Having already built this road unilaterally, without India's knowledge, and knowing its strategic importance, it was imperative for China to safeguard its longtime national interest first and foremost. Moreover India tended to play down the issue of Aksai Chin because it was a remote area and of little strategic interest to India. Indeed, according to John W. Garver, it was "essential to Chinese control of western Tibet" In other words, in contrast to India's legalistic and nationalistic claims over the region, for China, control over Aksai Chin had a geopolitical imperative.[8]

Importance of Gilgit-Baltistan and KKH

KKH is the highest paved international road in the world. It connects China and Pakistan across the Karakoram mountain range through the Khunjerab Pass at an elevation 4,693 meters. It connects Pakistan's Gilzit-Baltistan and Khyber-Pakhtunkhna region to China's Xinjiang.[9] It is also referred to as the eighth wonder of the world due to the difficult conditions in which it was build. In Pakistan it is called as N-35 and in China as China National Highway 314 (G-314). It was built by Pakistan and China together, starting from 1959; completed in 1979 and opened to the public in 1986. The route of the KKH traces one of the many paths of the ancient Silk Road. It runs from Kashgar in China to Abottabadin Pakistan for 1300km. An extension to southwest meets the Grand Trunk Road, at Hassanabdal, Pakistan. It is being connected to Gwadar port and the city of Rawalpindi in Pakistan. In case of hostilities between India and China, the PLA Navy would find Gwadar port most convenient logistic location on the Indian Ocean. The strategic use of this highway in prior stocking of the port to avoid interdiction by air during active operations would help both China and Pakistan. This road remains closed from January to June due to heavy snowfall. The region of

Gilzit-Baltistan has a geo-political importantance. The Chinese were faster than the Indians to understand the strategic importance of this region and grabbed the opportunity to take away whatever territory that was being ceded by Pakistan in friendly overtures.

With the strategic equations taking twists and turns in South Asia, the importance of the region is beginning to effect the Indian strategic health. Illegal occupation of a portion of the Indian state of Jammu and Kashmir (J&K) which Pakistan calls as PoK, since the first war between India and Pakistan, sizes up to approximately 85,793 sq km. This was further divided in 1970, into two separate administrative divisions, namely, Mirpur-Muzaffarabad (commonly referred to as Azad Jammu and Kashmir, by Pakistan) and the Federally Administered Gilgit-Baltistan. Being the northernmost part of PoK, Gilgit-Baltistan was earlier referred to as the "Northern Areas" in Pakistan.

After the Sino-Indian conflict of 1962, the government of Pakistan illegally ceded a huge portion of territory of the Shaksgam Valley of PoK, (5,180sq km) to China in a border agreement of 1963. However, Article 6 clearly stated that "the two Parties have agreed that after the settlement of the Kashmir dispute between Pakistan and India, the sovereign authority concerned will reopen negotiations with the Government of the People's Republic of China, on the boundary as described in Article Two of the present Agreement, so as to sign a formal Boundary Treaty to replace the present agreement."The Shaksgam Valley or the Trans Karakoram Tract is part of Hunza-Gilgit region of POK, and is a disputed territory claimed by India but controlled by Pakistan. It borders Xinjiang Province of the People's Republic of China (PRC) to the north, the Northern Areas of POK to the south and west, and the Siachen Glacier region to the east. Situated between the Hindu Kush and Karakoram Range of mountains in the north and western Himalayas in the south, the geo-strategic placement of Gilgit-

Baltistan makes it ever more significant for the country occupying it.

The region borders Pakistan's Dir, Swat, Kohistan and Kaghan districts of Khyber Pakhtunkhwa in the west, the Wakhan Corridor of Afghanistan in its northwest, Xinjiang Province of China to its east and northeast, Azad Jammu and Kashmir under control of Pakistan to the southwest, and a 480 km-long LoC running alongside India in the southeast covering a total area of 74,600 sqkm. Gilgit-Baltistan is an intersection of Asia's massive landmass; it connects parts of West Asia, Central Asia, South Asia and China. The economic linkages and benefits established through this region are visible especially to Pakistan, China, Tajikistan and Afghanistan. The region provides for a passage to the critical trading routes stretching from West Asia and Africa through to China.

In order to access the mineral and energy-rich markets of Central Asian countries including Uzbekistan, Turkmenistan and Kazakhstan, Gilgit-Baltistan has established itself as a focal point. Pakistan and for that matter, even China, have underscored the consequence of this steep corridor to further their geo-strategic objectives in the region. Making it more lucrative and communicable, China's western highway, known as the Lhasa-Kashgar or Xinjiang Highway which connects Xinjiang to Tibet, by linking Kashgar and Lhasa (3,105 km), from Quilanaldi, branches off to the Khunjerab Pass and, subsequently, becomes the KKH right up to Gilgit.[10] Comprehending the long-term importance of the highway, the Pakistan Highway Administration and China's state-owned Assets Supervision and Administration Commission (SASAC) signed an agreement in 2006 to upgrade and widen the width of the highway from 10 to 30 meters. Besides this, the Pakistan and Chinese Railways has proposed Karakoram Rail Corridor. The reported linkage will be provided by the Khunjerab Pass in the Karakoram Range through a 700 km rail corridor. This corridor shall link Kashgar in Xinjiang to

Havelian (adjoining Abbottabad) near Rawalpindi in northern Pakistan.

In order to curtail the continuing revolts against political suppression and long-standing alienation, the Pakistan government granted what it termed as "self-rule" to the Northern Areas in August 2009. Pakistan approved the "Gilgit-Baltistan Empowerment and Self Governance Order" which makes way for provisions for an elected Legislative Assembly and elected government. However, the Ordinance has failed to bring about any legitimate political reform toa region which has no politico-constitutional status or fundamental rights. Although, currently Pakistan seems focused to enhance and benefit from the geo-strategic placing of Gilgit-Baltistan, it might just be a matter of time when the region's political subjugation shall become its Achilles' heel. There are unconfirmed reports of Pakistan most likely leasing this area to China in the garb of constructing the rail network, since this arrangement would meet the requirements of both the countries.

The KKH, it is believed has been used for the transfer of nuclear and missile equipment to Pakistan.[11] Oflate,China is also discovering that expansion beyond its boundaries is a two-way street. China not only exports influence, but is influenced in turn and not always for the best – Islamic fundamentalism, terrorism and separatism are problems that China has begun to contend with increasingly following the opening of its overland links to Pakistan and other Central Asian countries. China will, therefore, be increasingly interested in how Pakistan and by extension, Afghanistan deal with rising Islamic sectarianism and fundamentalism, in order to safeguard its own domestic interests.

The ominously rising strategic salience of the Gilgit–Baltistan region was made sharply apparent by Selig Harrison's startling disclosure in 2010 that some 7,000–11,000 Chinese troops had entered the Gilgit–Baltistan area, ostensibly for flood control. The Chinese version claimed it was for repair of the KKH. Indian military sources later reported that some 3,000–4,000 Chinese military engineering personnel were engaged in repair/widening of the KKH, construction of hydroelectric projects and building of tunnels (which could serve to hide missiles).

A Chinese civil company (China Mobile) is also constructing cell towers for mobile networks in this region. However, some people are of the view that Pakistan is handing over de-facto control of the strategic Gilgit-Baltistan region in the Occupied Kashmir to China because of the simmering rebellion of the people against Islamabad. *The New York Times* in a report said that there were two important new developments in Gilgit-Baltistan; a simmering rebellion against the Pakistani rule and the influx of an estimated 7,000 to 11,000 soldiers of the Chinese People's Liberation Army in the area which is closed to the world.

"China wants a control on the strategic area to assure unfettered road and rail access to the Gulf through Pakistan", for which it is building high-speed rail and road link. The link up would enable Beijing to transport cargo and oil tankers from eastern China to the new Chinese built Pakistani Naval base at Gwadar, Pasni and Ormara in Baluchistan, just east of the Gulf in 48 hours. Many of the PLA soldiers entering Gilgit-Baltistan are expected to work on the railroad. Some are extending the Karakoram Highway, built to link China's Xinjiang province with Pakistan. Others are working on dams, expressways and other projects. There are unconfirmed reports of the construction of 22 tunnels in secret locations, where even Pakistanis are barred. Tunnels would be necessary for a projected gas pipeline from Iran to China that would cross the Karakoram through Gilgit. "But they could be also used for missiles storage sites," stated The New York Times.

Strategic Importance of Arunachal Pradesh

The land is mostly mountainous with Himalayan ranges along the northern borders criss-crossed with mountain ranges running north-south. These divide the state into five river valleys: the Kameng, the Subansiri, the Siang, the Lohit and the Tirap. High mountains and dense forests have prevented intercommunication between tribes living in different river valleys. It is rich in minerals and natural resources.

The geographical isolation thus imposed, led different tribes to evolve their own dialects and grow with their distinct identities. Nature has endowed the Arunachal people with a deep sense of beauty which finds delightful expression in their songs, dances and crafts.

It provides strategic depth to Brahmaputra valley and other Northeastern states of India. It has all weather communication system for any military purpose as compared to Aksai Chin.

It provides security to Bhutan's Eastern flank by virtue of being contiguous to India. Tawang which is an important religious monastery is located on the periphery and is a sensitive issue between China and India. In case Tawang is exposed, Bhutan would be then in a pincer group of china on both its flanks. This would also be detrimental to India's security, since in that scenario China's borders would rest on the plains of Assam; posing a threat to the other North Eastern states of India. The Chinese obsession with the Tawang Region is totally strategic in its aims. In any future conflict with China this region offers the shortest cut to China proper and to Tibet. India's communications infrastructure in this region was developed in World War II for US military aid to China and isstill existent and can be further improved.

In terms of any air operations in this region Arunachal Pradesh would provide multi-layered air defense deployments on the ground as deterrence. Veiled references in the past were made by Indian official spokesmen that progress in this area could not be made as China was constantly pressurising India to accept a swap of Tawang in lieu of Aksai-Chin. China claims about 90,000 sq km (55,900 square miles) of Arunachal Pradesh along the border as part of its territory, that it sees as "southern" Tibet. Arunachal Pradesh strategically worries China most because it is from this region that India's missile ranges cover most of the Chinese heartland targets.

Indian Perspective of Sino-Indian Boundary

India and China have over 4000 kms[12] of common frontier. The boundary between India and China runs along the arc of the KuenLun and the great Himalayan ranges forming perhaps the most impressive natural boundary in the world. The authenticity of this can be gauged from the limits of administration on either side during the past so many years through valid international agreements. The alignment of the frontier lies, from West to East, along the Mastagh range and the Aghil range; across the Karakoram pass; along the main KuenLun range and the Chumesang river; between the two halves of the Pangong Lake; along the Kailash range and the Zanskar range; across the Shipki pass, the Manna pass, the Niti pass, the Kungri Bingri pass, the Darma pass and the Lipu Lekh Pass; and thereafter along the great Himalayan range of the Sikkim, Bhutan and the Arunachal Pradesh.

In the western Sector, the Chinese in 1959 claimed 22,400sq kms. In July 1980 once again displaying in consistency of their claims, the chairman of the Foreign Relations Committee, Wang Bingh had claimed 40,000 sqkms of territory in this sector.[13] Today China is in occupation of 38,000 sq- kms of Indian territory in the Aksai-chin area of Ladakh region in Western Sector.[14]

In the Western Sector, the Jammu & Kashmir boundary of India extents to about 1700 kmsalong Sinkiang & Tibet. Starting from the tri-junction of the boundaries of India, China and Afghanistan, it runs eastward through the Kilik pass, Mintaka pass, Kharchanai pass, Parpik pass and the Khunjerab pass. It thereafter goes towards north-western bend of Shaksgam or Muztagh River ascending the Aghil Mountains. Further running through the Aghil pass, Marpo pass and then to the Karakoram pass. From the Korakaram pass, the boundary lies along the water shed between the Shyok and the Yarkand River and runs through the Qara Tagh Pass to cross the eastern bend of the Qara Qash River and to ascend the main Kun Lun Mountains. Running along the crest of Kun Lun descends in a south-westerly direction down to Lanak Pass.

South of the Lanak Pass, the boundary passes through the Kone Pass and Kepsang Pass which lie along the watershed between the Chang Chenmo and Chumesang in India and the streams flowing into DyapTso in Tibet. Thereafter, the boundary runs along the southern bank of the Chumesang and the eastern bank of the Chang-lung Lungpa, skirts the western extremity of the eastern half of Pangong Lake, cuts across the eastern part of Spanggur Lake and follows the northern and eastern watershed of the Indus River through Chang Pass upto the Jara Pass. Subsequently, it turns south-west, crosses the Indus about 8 kms southeast of Demchok, and following the watershed between Hanle River and the tributaries of Sutlej River, it passes through the Charding Pass, Imis Pass and the Kyungzing Pass. Thereafter, it turns westwards and crosses the Pare river about 8 kms south of Chumar to reach Gya peak.[15] The boundary in this sector had been sanctified by custom and tradition. After a war between Tibet and Ladakh, this was confirmed in the treaty of Tingmsgang in 1684.[16] This was reconfirmed when a treaty was again signed by the representatives of Dogra ruler of Kashmir on one hand

and of Dalai Lama of Lasha and the Emperor of China on the other. In 1842 Chinese referedthe boundary in this treaty as having been fixed from ancient times.[17] Therefore it was proved that Demchok and Imis Pass were part of Ladakh.

After the treaty of Amritsar in 1847, Lord Harding, Governor General of India, wrote to both Tibet and China to formally fix the Ladakh – Tibet boundary but Chinese did not feel the necessecityof doing so.[18]

The agreement signed between Dewan Basti Ram on behalf of the Kashmir state and ManguaIIslae on behalf of Tibet[19] had also confirmed of the border.

One can see the uniqueness of this alignment; it being along continuous watersheds ranging in height from 14,000 ft. to 25,000 ft., forming a formidable wall of snow and stone. For the sake of division of boundaries, the actual watershed is acknowledged as the central ridge or the crest line of the Himalayas which divide the rivers flowing southward into India and northward to Tibet. By international norms this is called as the 'watershed principle' of demarcating the boundaries.

There are numerous examples, such as; between France and Spain along the Pyrenees, [20] between Chile and Argentina along the Andes, between Sudan and Congo, between China and Sikkim and Nepal. China had agreed to this principle with Great Britain in 1894 and 1897 to lay down watershed between the Mekong and the Salween as boundaries between Burma and China.[21] Also available at-In the north, the Indian boundary follows the watershed between the Indus system in India and the Yarkand and YurungQash systems in China.

Chinese Emperor Kang Hi, between 1711 and 1717 had maps compiled by Jesuit missionaries and Lamas, which showed the southern boundary of Tibet along the Himalayan range. The map published by Peking University in November 1925, depicts the maximum extent of China in the days of the Ching dynasty, and also shows the Indian frontier along the present Indian alignment. Besides this, there are records of the civil administration and revenue collection to prove that the area claimed by India is de Jure theirs. Aksai Chin and Chang Chenmo Valley formed part of Ladakh Hazrat of Kashmir and the locals collected salt from here. The revenue records and the tour and census reports of Kashmir from 1862 to 1908 mention Tanktse, Demchok and Khuranak on the Indian side of border, as parts of Ladakh. The history of Ladakh's control over Gartok and Rudok in western Tibet is a matter of importance. Minsar, an enclave of Dogras within western Tibet, used to pay revenue to the Dogras until the early twentieth century. The British used Gilgit, Skardo, Hunza and Chitral as 'frontier listning posts' to monitor developments in Central Asia and Xinjiang throughout the Dograperiod. The area is rich in minerals and natural resources.[22]

Central Sector or the middle sector stretches from the GyaPeakat the north-eastern tip of Himachal Pradesh to the tri-junction of Bhutan, Arunachal Pradesh and Tibet. The 225 km long northern and eastern border of the Indian state of Sikkim with southern Tibet.[23] In March 1890, the Anglo-Chinese Convention signed at Calcutta defined and confirmed the boundary of Sikkim, (then a protectorate of India)and Tibet. The boundary alignment was jointly demarcated on the ground- the eastern portion in 1895-96 and the northern in 1902-30. and the 482 km long Bhutan-Tibet border[24] (This is also a natural, traditional, customary border, following the crest of the Himalyas, recognised by the Chinese Government. constitute the East Central sector of the northern border, which the Chinese have never questioned. However it lays claim on the portions of the West Central section from time to time.

The West Central boundary of the central sector constitutes the Indian states of Himachal and Uttar Pradesh with the Ari district of Tibet. Starting from the Gya Peak the boundary follows the watershed between the Spiti and

Pare rivers and crosses the Pare River about 1.6 kms south of the village of Kauirik. It connects to the Leo Pargial peak, crosses the Sutlej at its bend, along the Zaskar range lies through the Shipki Pass, Raniso Pass and Shimdang Pass. Following the Sutlej and the Ganges basins lies through Thaga Pass, Tsang Chok Pass, Muling Pass, Mana Pass, Niti Pass, Tun Jun Pass, Kungri Bingri Pass and the Lipu Lekh Pass to join the tri-junction of India, Nepal and Tibet boundaries.[25] This boundary is also traditional and the delineation is confirmed by old revenue records and maps of the Indian administration for centuries.[26] In this sector the boundary follows the watershed between the Tibetan portion of the Sutlej and the Ganges in India.

In Spiti, the area up to the watershed was included in the British Indian revenue settlements from 1851 onwards and Hindustan- Tibet Road up to Shipki Pass was maintained by the Government of India. Same was the case of frontier areas of Garhwal up to the Sutlej-Ganges watershed. Article-IV of the 1954 Agreement between Tibet Region of China and India confirms that the areas in the Central Sector have been under Indian control. The Sikkim and Bhutan part of the borders have been agreed on the watershed principle and the McMahon line. As also all the passes mentioned above were used for traders and pilgrims.[27] The memoirs of Yuan Chawang who visited India in 640 A.D. and the inscriptions on the copper plate of the Katyuri Kings of Garhwal and Kumaon indicate the Hindu Kingdom of Garhwal extended up to Ganga-Sutlej watershed. The Vishnu Purana and Yogini Purana prove Himalayas to be the Indian boundary. The ninth and thirteenth century writings (political Geography of the Assam Valley) states Akas, Daflas and Bhotias as tributaries of the Ahom Kings.

Eastern Sector like other sector is also a natural, traditional and administrative dividing line. It runs east from the eastern extremity of Bhutan to the tri-junction of China-Burma-India borders near the Diphu Pass. In 1913-

1914, Captain Bailey had carried out extensive survey of the area to determine the line separating the territorial jurisdiction of southern Tibet and India which was known as North East Frontier Tract. Starting from the tri-junction of India-Bhutan-Tibet, it follows on to the Mela Ridge and runs along the crest of Thang La.

East of Nepal, it is the crest of the Himalayan range forming the watershed between the northern tributaries of Brahmaputra, like the Teesta, Senkosh, Raidak, Manas, Kameng, Khru, Kamla, Dihang and Dipang, in Sikkim, Bhutan, and Arunachal Pradesh and the southern tributaries of Tsang Po in Tibet.

Desideri, an Italian traveler who had visited Tibet in the early eighteenth century depicts that Tibetans had no dealings with the tribal people. Horace Della Penna, another French traveler in Tibet in 1730, states that Tibet was bounded in the south by Lhoba i.e., the tribal territory. Captain John F. Mitchell, in his report on the North East Frontier of India had mentioned that the northern boundary of the Abhors (one of the tribes of modern Arunachal Pradesh) is the Nainphala, i.e., the Himalayas. All these facts can also be corroborated with the writings of the Chinese travelers in India during that time such as, Wei Tsang Tu Chic, Hisi-Tsang Tu Kao.

Moreover, northern boundary of Burma which was a part of India during the 1914 Simla Conference which had been left undefined was bridged by extending the McMahon Line from the tri-junction of India, Burma and Tibet along the northern watershed of Irrawaddy to the IsuRuzi Pass, where it met the northern extremity of the previously settled boundary between Burma and China. In 1950 and 1954 during Sino- Indian interactions there was no objections raised by China on the boundary, on the other hand they gave solemn undertaking to respect the existing arrangement.[28]

The Sino-Indian Border : Post 1962

Nations avoid war, to grow economically and grow economically to fight a war. Both China and India has overtly shown resolve to sort out the boundary issue but covertly there seems to be a status quo. Although a yearly meeting on the boundary took place after the 1962 conflict, there were frequent intrusions and stand offs along the border, due to different perceptions of the boundary. India and China restored ambassadorial relations in August 1976.

The rapprochement between the two countries in 1976 enabled India and China to initiate High level border talks in 1981 to find a solution to the vexed problem. On 20 June 1980, Eric Gonsalves, one of the secretaries in Ministry of External Affairs was in Beijing, reportedly to prepare the grounds for Hwang Hwa's visit. On 21 June 1980, vice Premier Deng Xiapengissueda settlement saying that the border problem with India should be settledon present line of actual control in a "package deal". China could recognize the present line of actual control in the eastern sector and India should recognize the status-quo in the Western sector.

Reacting coolly to the proposal, Indian Foreign Minister, P.V. Narasimha Rao submitted in the Lok Sabha on July 1980 that ways other than the package solution could prove more "effective". India, on its part hoped to settle the borderquestion in a spirit consistent with national honor and interests of both sides on a basis of equality.[29] The Indian believed that the Deng-package was "based on the fruits of military gains" of the 1962 conflict since it entailed a recognition of the post- 1662 border.[30] The next high-level contact came at Cancun in Mexico on 28 October 1981, where Mrs. Gandhi met the new Chinese Premier, Zhao Ziyang during the North-South dialogue.[31] It was Indira Gandhi who took the initiative of starting the official-level talks in 1981.India suggested that the Colombo proposals, formulated by six non-aligned Asian and African nations in 1962, should be the basis of the negotiations.

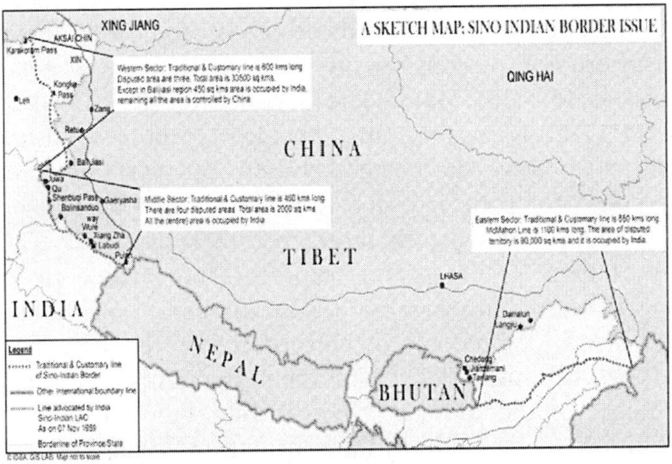

http://indiatoday.intoday.in/story/indian-army-war-readiness-against-china/ 1/157763.html assessed on 21 july 2013.

The proposals contained the following basic elements; China should withdraw from the Western sector which, pending a final solution, would become a demilitarized zone; inthe eastern sector, Indian and Chinese forces could be positioned along the McMahon Line, except the Tangla ridge and Longju areas, where the line of control could be settled latter. When China characterised these recommendations as out dated, India urged that the various issues be treated as separateentities. This approach entailed an initial focus on more amenable issues, intended to create a positive atmosphere for discussion on more contentious ones. But China rejected this plan.[32] The Second Round of talks was held on 17-21 May 1982 at New Delhi, again without any further push towards border solution, but certainly created more space for future discussions. The Third Round of the talks held in Beijing from January 29-2 February 1983, was equally barren so far as the "central issue" was concerned. Beijing saw an "inseparable" link between these talks and theincrease in exchanges in various fields between the two countries, although Beijing felt that the talks had gone to the "heart of the matter."[33] The Indian view was that the settlement of the boundary question was central to normalization of relations, whereas the Chinese position was that although China would continue to "seek a way for a fair and reasonable settlement of the boundary question", it was equally if not more important to establish a greater of mutual understanding through trade, exchanges, communication and so forth, on a bilateral basis.[34] Fu Haq, believed that they had an "arduous task" but they would try not only to further develop bilateral relation but seek a fair andreasonable settlement of the boundary question. This became the standard Chinese phrase for tackling the boundary issue, year after year and meeting after meeting.[35] The Fourth Round of talks was held in New Delhi on 24-28 October 1983. The Indian delegation was led by K.S. Bajpai, Secretary (East) in the External Affairs Ministry and the Chinese delegation was led by Gong Dafei, Vice Foreign Minister. Government of India had repeatedly opposed a status-quo on the border issue from the very beginning. This time it bore fruits and the Chinese agreed to a sector by sector discussion, to facilitate agreement and India accepted the Chinese view that this should later be tied up in an overall solution.[36] India believed that it had a strong case in the eastern sector and Beijing hinted that it was willing to accept the McMahon Line without conceding the name. The Fifth, Round of the Sino-Indian talks was held in Beijing from 17-22 September 1984. Indian delegation was led by Natwar Singh, Secretary in the Ministry of External Affairs and the Chinese delegation was ledby Gong Dafoi, adviser to the Foreign Ministry. It appeared that there was a real likelihood of a breakthrough and that the Chinese position had softened somewhat and according to an Indian official connected with the talks, the Chinese appeared amenable to settling the dispute along the McMahon Line in the eastern sector with minor Indian concessions including certain pieces of Indian Territory in the Aksai-Chin area.[37] However this proposal did not materialize due to the Indian domestic politics during an election year. Five rounds of the talks had been completed before Indira Gandhi met with her untimely death in October 1984. Rajiv Gandhi took over from where his mother had left, and this time with more enthusiasm. Rajiv Gandhi's first personal encounter with Chinese Premier, Zhao Ziyang was in New York, in October 1985, where both had gone to participate in the 40th anniversary meeting of United Nations. The Sixth Round of the official level meeting was held in New Delhi on November 4-10, 1985; the substantive discussions, however, did not yield much result. The Indian delegation was led by A.P. Venkatateshwaran, Secretary of External Affairs. The Chinese delegation was led byVice-Foreign Minister, Liu Shuqing.

A resultant difference in opinion remained as wide as ever both in approach and substance. This round was significant only to the extent that both India and China got down to discussing substantive issues after having devoted attention during the earlier round to guiding principles.[38] Various statements made by Parliamentarians in the Indian parliament arouse the Chinese to reciprocate in a similar manner, giving statements favorable to them. Xinhua circulated on 8 May 1986; "Introduction to the Sino-Indian border issue," outlining the Chinese views of the history of the border dispute asserting that "China had never occupied a single inch of Indian territory", while more than 90,000 Sqkm. of Chinese territory was under Indian occupation.

Despite this, China had continued its efforts to achieve a settlement and had in the official talks "forwarded a number of reasonable proposals." It did not spell out the proposal and merely reiterated the principles mentioned by HaungHau during his visit to India in 1981.[39] A major intrusion by the Chinese, starting from 16 June 1986 took place in Thandrong pasture area of Somdurong Chu Valley under Zimithang circle of Tawang district. This was as usual, just days before a Sino-Indian event i.e., 7th round of boundary talks were to begin. This event is also referred to as Wangdung incident. At a hurried called press conference on 15 July 1986, a senior official of the Indian Ministry of External Affairs revealed that Chinese troops and civilians had intruded about seven kilometers into the Indian side of the McMahon Line in the vicinity of the Somdurong Chu Valley.

The intrusion, according to him, took place sometime in June and 40 Chinese, some of them in uniform and some in mufti were stillcamping on the Thandrong grazing ground. India had made no efforts to throw the intruders out, as the area was, in the words of the official, "very inhospitable and placed unfavorably from our side." The Government of India, he said, had lodged a strong protest with Beijing against the intrusion.[40] The Chief Minister of Arunachal Pradesh, Gegog Apang, on his return from New Delhi, told the News persons at Itanagar that Chinese had entered into Somdurong and Wangdung villages on the Indian side and were still camping there. These villages were six-km. and three- km. respectively inside the Indian Territory from the Line of Actual control, which had been the grazing land of Arunachal Pradesh since time immemorial.[41]

This incident again led to an eyeball to eyeball situation but with a difference this time. Massive built-up of armed forces on both sides ended up in two major exercise by India simultaneously on northern and western borders showing its resolve to fight on both fronts if the situation warranted. Later, political and diplomatic interaction between China and India eased out the tensions of a war. Despite this episode, the Seventh Round of border talks was heldas planned from 21-25 July 1986 in Beijing. The talks could not resolve the issue of China's recent intrusion into Indian Territory and neither was any effort made to make any progress on the boundary question. Exchange of views on the Chinese intrusion into Wangdung in the Somdurong Chu Valley area of Arunachal Pradesh, was brought up by India, but the Chinese maintained that they were north of the Line of Actual control and within their territory. Thus, the intrusion issue remained unresolved, and though Indian sources described the atmosphere of the talks as "Calm and Business like", apparently not much progress was made on theboundary dispute.[42]

On 1 August 1986, Shiv Shankar Menon, during a 'call attention motion' in the Indian Parliament gave a statement that the intrusions were "violation of the agreement of 1984", but India was keen on ensuring a negotiated settlement.[43] The minister further said, "from the McMahon line, the extent of the intrusion was two to three kilometers inside India" as the crow flies. The Government in an inquiry found that the Chinese as on that day had not built a helipad in the area into which they had intruded, as was being reported.[44] He also explained that there was some confusion regarding McMahon Line "which weconsider the boundary but they call as the actual line of control". On the issue of the border negotiations the Foreign Minister promised the house that, "we shall continue to strive for a peaceful settlement of the boundary question and also make efforts to resolve through peaceful negotiations, the question of Chinese intrusion". He hoped that peace and tranquility will prevail on the border and that pending a final solution;

the status quo will be maintained. Before the eighth round of talks, on 8-9 December 1986, the Indian Parliament Conferred full statehood on Arunachal Pradesh. From the Indian point of view, this was simply a logical evolution of the Administrative process.

The Chinese, however, saw it as a possible legal erosionof their claims in eastern sector. As expected, there was a strong criticism from Beijing, on 11 December blaming India for derailing the process and charged India, that their action, "seriously violated China's territorial integrity". The Chinese Government "Solemnly" declared that "the bill passed by the Indian Parliament was entirely illegal and that, China would never recognize the so-called Arunachal Pradesh.[45] In 1982, the Chinese in order to pressurise India protested vigorously when Arunachal Pradesh sent a company of dancers to perform at New Delhi ASIAD Games Ceremony.

Prime Minister, Rajiv Gandhi, however ruled out the possibility of India making territorial concession to China as was being suggested by the spokesman of the Chinese Foreign Ministry in Beijing under the plea of "mutual understanding and mutual accommodation". He reiterated that our stand on the border was very clear and that question of any concessions does not arise.[46] He underplayed the latest incident in the eastern sector. He said that there were a few problems in some areas in making the McMahon Line in the eastern sectors of Sino-Indian border; these problems also exist in the Western sector; these could be solved with the help of modern methods of thesurvey which were not available earlier.

Speaking to the officers of the National Defense College, Rajiv Gandhi stated that efforts were on, for an early solution, but with caution.[47] Chinese news agency Xinhua, reported that, "India stressed that timewas needed to find a settlement due to the complexity of the issue, andboth sides desired that joint efforts be made to create a favorable atmosphere for a solution.[48] Meanwhile India opined that the level of talks must be raised from official to a political level. Both China and India agreed to hold Eight Round of talks sometime in late 1987. Chinese Minister of Foreign Affairs expressed that before the talks on delineating the border began, both India and China should strictly observe the "Line of Actual Control," which was drawn in the border region in 1959, to avoid unpleasant incidents. The withdrawal of troops by China and India began on 14 August 1987. It was, part of an agreement reached with the army commanders on ground.[49] The Eighth Round of negotiations on Sino-Indian border dispute finally resumed on 13-18 November 1987, in New Delhi. Although, no breakthrough was expected, but, as a result of own initiative, the stage now seemed to be set for the talks being picked up at the political level. Like every time, not much progress was made on the boundary issue per-se, but the Chinese did invite Rajiv Gandhi to visit China, which he did, to improve overall relationship in Sino-Indian relations. Time and again the Chinese kept giving signals in various meetings and forums that the boundary issue could be resolved only if there was a give and take of territories and mutual exchange. However, the Indian side was always adamant to solve the issue in a more receptive and harmonious atmosphere. Rajiv Gandhi also kept reiterating this in various forums. During a visit to Budapest, he stated that India wanted peace with China and that all possible steps were being taken to understand the national interest of both the nations to come to an just and satisfactory solution to the boundary dispute.

Both, New Delhi and Beijing had agreed that the talks must be raised to political level if a breakthrough has to be achieved. Beijing also insisted that the initiative in this respect should come from the Government of India. Addressing the Krishnan Menon Society, on 31October 1988, Chinese Ambassador to India, TuGuowei said that "since China's disengagement proposal for the solution of border problem had not yet been reciprocated in real actions by Indian side, the border situation was not so stable and was even marked with certain hidden dangers." Tu, sounded the warning, "We therefore should not neglect the gravity and urgency of this reality. This statement of the boundary issue does require political wisdom and statesmanship from the both sides, at the same time both sides also reiterated the point of maintaining peace and tranquility.[50] The Phrase-Mutual Understanding and mutual accommodation was taken in diplomatic circles as the usual Chinese way to suggesting that only territorial concession from India could lead to a solution of the long standing boundary questions.

The talks again resumed in 1988, following the visit of Indian Prime Minister Rajiv Gandhi to China; a JWG was set up to look into the border problem. President R. Venkataraman paid a state visit to China in May 1992. This was the first Head of State-level visit from India to China. In 1993, during the visit of Prime Minister P.V. Narasimha Rao an Agreement on the Maintenance of Peace and Tranquility along the Line of Actual Control was signed on 7 September, and the India-China diplomatic and Military Officers group was set up to assist the JWG. The agreement facilitated the following.[51]

(a) Firstly, the agreement reiterated that the Sino-Indian boundary issue must be resolved through peaceful and friendly consultations and that neither side shall use or threaten to use force against the other by any means. Also pending an ultimate solution of the boundary question, both the sides shall strictly observe the LAC between the two and that no activities of either side shall overstep the LAC. In case of being cautioned by the opposite side of crossing the LAC, they shall immediately pull back to their own side of the LAC. Difference of views as to the alignment of the LAC can be determined later by both sides.

(b) Secondly, the strength of military forces by both the sides along the LAC should be kept to a minimum level, compatible with the friendly and good neighbourly relations between the two countries. It further reiterated that the two sides agree to reduce their military forces along the LAC in conformity with the requirements of the principle of mutual and equal security to ceilings, and that the reduction of military forces shall be carried out in stages in mutually agreed geographical locations, sector wise, within the area along the line of control.

(c) Thirdly, in case of a military exercise being carried out by any side, each side shall give the other prior notification of the military exercises of specified levels near the LAC permitted under the agreement.

(d) Fourthly, in case of contingency or other problems arising in the area of LAC, the two sides shall deal with them through meetings and friendly consultations between the border personals of the two countries.

(e) Fifthly, the two sides also agreed to take adequate measures to ensure that air intrusions across the LAC do not take place and that the two sides shall undertake mutual consultations in case intrusions occur.

Defining LAC is not quite a simple task. There are physical difficulties of the terrain as well as those related to differing versions of where the notional line lies and above all the complicated political issues involved. According to the plan envisaged by the two sides, the local commanders of both sides will work on defining their respective locations on the ground through joint surveys. The work will be undertaken first on areas where there is little contention and then having gained experience and trust in working together, more difficult ones will be undertaken. The most contentious issues, as reported, will however be referred to higher bodies like the expert committee in the JWG. The Indian official sources have however clarified two aspects.[52] First, the delineation of the LAC will not be the final basis for the settlement of the disputes. This is just an attempt to maintain peace and tranquility along the LAC as it exists on the ground today. It is the consolidation of the existing position on the ground, not final settlement. Second, the agreement will no way weaken the Indian stand and its original claim over the Chinese occupied territories which still stand intact, subject to further negotiations. The agreement according to diplomatic sources in both the countries is a major step towards eventually resolving the tangled border dispute. The agreement has been termed by the press not only "as a key to the confidence building measures but the corner stone of the solution to the dispute."[53] The major achievement of a mutually accepted LAC will be to prevent inadvertent confrontations which will destabilise the Sino-Indian relations and detract from the process of negotiating the final settlement. The epoch making agreement effects many profound changes in the existing situation and is beneficial to both countries in many ways.

1. It would settle the confusion with regard to the actual existence of the LAC.
2. It will create a long desired ground for the final settlement of the conflict.
3. By initiating confidence building measures like reduction of military forces on both sides, prior notification of military exercises and halting of air intrusions, it would enhance the security of both the countries.
4. Such measures also ease the financial burden of maintaining a sizable military presence in the mountain areas. Both the countries can now use their armed forces for more positive and urgent causes.
5. The atmosphere created by the agreement could lead

to greater economic cooperation, and enhance border trade.

6. The agreement sends a signal to the world that the two Asian giants are capable of resolving their problems without the involvement of other countries.

It conveys a message to Pakistan about the futility of internationalising a bilateral issue. The agreement was therefore extensively welcomed in both India and China. The Chinese official news agency Xinhua described the agreement as a landmark in the bilateral relations. The Indian press termed it as an impressive 'triumph of Indian diplomacy'. The Times ofIndia wrote, "It will mark the beginning of a new phase in bilateral relations based on mutual confidence and better political understanding."[54] The Hindustan Times in its editorial wrote, "The agreement confirms that the two Asian giants have decided to stay on a positive course."[55]

Dutta, an eminent defense analyst in an article described the agreement as "a product of a new context of post-cold war thinking and conditions, of post war reforms, of a liberalising and increasingly open India. The agreement reiterates the faith of both nations to the Panchsheel or five principles and buttresses it with other security enhancing and conflict avoidance measures.[56]

President Jiang Zemin's state visit to India in November 1996 was the first by a PRC Head of State to India. One of the four agreements signed on 29 November during his visit included the CBMs in the Military Field along the LAC, covering adoption ofconcrete measures between the two militaries to enhance exchanges and to promote cooperation and trust.[57] This agreement reaffirmed the intent and spirit of 1993 agreement, inter-alias, laid down the limiting of lethal armaments along the border, which would help in preventing any tension in the border area. Some of the important articles of the agreement are as follows:

Article IV of the agreement provides that both sides shall avoid holding large-scale military exercises of more than one Division, in close proximity of the LAC in the India- China border area. If in case such exercises are to be conducted, the strategic direction of the main force involved shall not be towards the other side. If either side conducts a military exercise involving more than a Brigade Group in the close proximity of the LAC in the India-China Border area, it shall give the other side prior notification with regard to type, level, planned duration and the area of the exercise, to include numbers and type of units participating in the exercise.The date of completion of the exercise and the de-induction of troops from the area of the exercise, also to be intimated to the other side, within five days of the completion of the de-induction.

Adequate mechanism for prevention of air intrusions on the India-China border, and facilitating flights and landings by military aircrafts, was also worked out. However if , in spite of the preventive measures , the intrusion takes, it should cease as soon as detected and the incident shall be promptly investigated by the side operating the aircraft. The results of the investigation shall be immediately communicated, through diplomatic channels or at border meetings, to the other side. It further provided that combat aircraft of any category shall not fly within ten kilometers of the LAC. However, the agreement permitted the flying of unarmed transport aircraft, survey aircraft and helicopters up to the LAC. Military aircrafts of either side may fly across the LAC or over the airspace of the other side or land on the other side only after obtaining prior permission of the latter after providing detailed information in accordance with the international practice in this regard. In order to ensure flight safety in emergency situations, the authorities designated by the two sides may contact each other by the quickest means of communication available.

Article VI stipulated that neither side shall open fire, cause bio-degradation, use hazardous chemicals, conduct blast operations or hunt with guns or explosives within two kilometers from the LAC, leaving aside routine firing practice in the small arms firing ranges. Requirement of blast operations for developmental activities shall be informed through diplomatic channels to the other side or by convening a border personnel meeting, preferably, five days in advance. If the border personnel of the two sides come in a face-to-face situation due to differences on the alignment of the LAC for any other reason, they shall exercise self-restraint and take all necessary action to avoid an escalation of the situation.

Article VII of the agreement provided for the flag meetings between their border representatives at designated places along the LAC and for maintaining and expanding telecommunication links between the border meeting points at designated places along the LAC and to establish systematic medium and high-level contacts between the border authorities of the two sides.

Article VIII of the agreement provided that if the personnel of one side cross the LAC and enter the other side because of unavoidable circumstances like natural disasters, the other side shall extent all assistance to them and inform their side, as soon as possible regarding the forced or inadvertent entry across the LAC. The return of the personal to their own side shall be settled through mutual consultations. It also provides that two sides shall at the earliest, provide, information pertaining to natural disasters and epidemic diseases in contiguous border areas.

Article X mentioned that recognizing the full implementation of some of the provisions of the present agreement will depend on the two sides arriving at a common understanding of the alignment of the line of actual control in the India-China border areas; the two sides agree to speed up the process of clarification and confirmation of the LAC. As an initial step in this process, the authorities clarified the alignment of the LAC in those segments where they have different perceptions. They also agreed to exchange maps indicating their respective perceptions of the entire alignment of the LAC as soon as possible. It had provisioned that pending the completion of the process of clarification and confirmation of the LAC, the two sides shall work out modalities for implementing confidence-building measures envisaged under this agreement on an interim basis, without prejudice to their respective positions on the alignment of the LAC as well as on the boundary question.

These above measures built more confidence on both the sides to come closer. The JWG has held 14 rounds of talks between 1988 and 2003. In 2003, two special representatives, oneeach from India and China were appointed to find a political solution to the border dispute.

At the invitation of Wen Jiabao, Prime Minister Atal Bihari Vajpayee paid an official visit to the People's Republic of China from 22 to 27 June 2003.On June 23, 2003, China and India signed the Declaration on Principles for Relations and Comprehensive Cooperation between the People's Republic of China and the Republic of India.

Leaders from both countries noted with satisfaction the progress made over recent years in bilateral relations.Both noted that the sustained economic and social development in the two countries, representing one third of humanity is vital for ensuring peace, stability and prosperity not only in Asia but also in the whole world.The two sides agreed that China and India have a mutual desire for good neighbourly relations and have broad common interests. They agreed to fully utilize the substantial potential and opportunities for deepening mutually beneficial cooperation. Highlights of the agreement are appended below:

The two sides agreed that India and China have a mutual desire for good neighbourly relations and have broad common interests. They agreed to fully utilize the substantial potential and opportunities for deepening mutually beneficial cooperation.

Friendship and cooperation between the two countries meets the need to:

- promote the socio-economic development and prosperity of both India and China;
- maintain peace and stability regionally and globally;
- strengthen multipolarity at the international level; and
- enhance the positive factors of globalization.

Both sides affirmed that they would abide by the following principles, promote a long-term constructive and cooperative partnership and, on this basis, build a qualitatively new relationship:

- Both sides are committed to developing their long-term constructive and cooperative partnership on the basis of the principles of Panchsheel, mutual respect and sensitivity for each other's concerns and equality;
- As two major developing countries, India and China have a broad mutual interest in the maintenance of peace, stability and prosperity in Asia and the world, and a mutual desire in developing wider and closer cooperation and understanding in regional and international affairs;
- The common interests of the two sides outweigh their differences. The two countries are not a threat to each other. Neither side shall use or threaten to use force against the other; and
- Both sides agree to qualitatively enhancing the bilateral relationship at all levels and in all areas while addressing differences through peaceful means in a fair, reasonable and mutually acceptable manner. The differences should not be allowed to affect the overall development of bilateral relations.

Both sides agreed to hold regular high-level exchanges between the two countries. This will greatly enhance mutual understanding and expand bilateral relations. With a view to deepening their coordination and dialogues on bilateral, regional and international issues, both sides agreed on the need for annual meetings between Foreign Ministers of the two countries. They also agreed that personnel exchanges and friendly contacts between ministries, parliaments and political parties of the two countries should be further enhanced.

The two sides welcomed the positive momentum of bilateral trade and economic cooperation in recent years and shared the belief that continued expansion and intensification of India-China economic cooperation is essential for strengthening bilateral relations.

Both sides shared the view that existing complementarities between their two economies provide an important foundation and offer broad prospects for further enhancing their economic relations. In order to promote trade and economic cooperation, both sides will take necessary measures consistent with their national laws and rules and international obligations to remove impediments to bilateral trade and investment. They reaffirmed the importance of the ministerial meeting of the Joint Economic Group (JEG) and agreed to hold the next (seventh) JEG meeting within the year.

The two sides will set up a compact Joint Study Group (JSG) composed of officials and economists to examine the potential complementarities between the two countries in expanded trade and economic cooperation. The JSG would also draw up a programme for the development of India-China trade and economic cooperation for the next five years, aimed at encouraging greater cooperation between the business communities of both sides. The Group should present a study report and recommendations to the two Governments on measures for comprehensive trade and economic cooperation by the end of June 2004.

The two countries will launch a financial dialogue and cooperation mechanism to strengthen their dialogue and coordination in this sector.

The two sides agreed to enhance cooperation at the World Trade Organization, which is not only to mutual benefit but also in the broader interest of developing countries. The two sides will hold dialogues on a regular basis in this regard.

Historical and cultural links between India and China will be strengthened, inter-alia, through the promotion of exchanges in culture, education, science and technology, media, youth and people-to-people relations. They agreed to set up Cultural Centers in each other's capitals and facilitate their establishment.

Both sides will work towards the enhancement of direct air and shipping links, tourism, exchange hydrological data in flood season on common rivers as agreed, cooperation in agriculture, dairy, food processing, health and other sectors.

They agreed on the need to broaden and deepen defence exchanges between the two countries, which will help enhance and deepen the mutual understanding and trust between the two armed forces. They confirmed that the exchange of visits by their Defence Ministers and of military officials at various levels should be strengthened.

The two sides agreed to appoint a Special Representative each to explore from the political perspective of the overall bilateral relationship the framework of a boundary settlement.

The Indian side recognises that the Tibet Autonomous Region is part of the territory of the People's Republic of China and reiterates that it does not allow Tibetans to engage in anti-China political activities in India. The Chinese side expresses its appreciation for the Indian position and reiterates that it is firmly opposed to any attempt and action aimed at splitting China and bringing about "independence of Tibet".

The Indian side recalled that India was among the first countries to recognize that there is one China and its one China policy remains unaltered. The Chinese side expressed its appreciation of the Indian position.

India and China recognised the primacy of maintaining international peace. This is a prerequisite for the socio-economic development of all developing countries, including India and China. The world is marked by diversity. Every country has the right to choose its own political system and path to development. As two major developing countries, India and China acknowledged the importance of their respective roles in the shaping of a new international political and economic order. The international community must help the developing countries to eliminate poverty and narrow the gap between the North and the South through dialogue and cooperation so as to achieve common prosperity.

The two sides acknowledged the vital importance of the role of the United Nations in world peace, stability and development. They are determined to continue their efforts in strengthening the UN system. They reaffirmed their readiness to work together to promote reform of the UN. In reform of the UN Security Council, priority should be given to enhancing representation of the developing countries.

Both sides stood for continued multilateral arms control and disarmament process, undiminished and equal security for all at progressively lower levels of armament and for multilateral negotiations aimed at nuclear disarmament and elimination of nuclear weapons. They are firmly opposed to introduction of weapons in outer space, use or threat of force against space-based objects and support cooperation in development of space technology for peaceful purposes.

The two sides recognised the threat posed by terrorism to them and to global peace and security. They resolutely condemned terrorism in any form. The struggle between the international community and global terrorism is a comprehensive and sustained one, with the ultimate objective of eradication of terrorism in all regions. This requires strengthening the global legal framework against terrorism. Both sides shall also promote cooperation on counter-terrorism through their bilateral dialogue mechanism.

India and China face special and similar challenges in their efforts to protect the environment while simultaneously forging ahead with rapid social and economic development of their countries. In this context, the two sides agreed to work together in a practical manner to cooperate on preserving the environment and ensuring sustainable development and to coordinate positions on climate change, biodiversity and other issues in relevant multilateral fora.

The two sides supported multilateral cooperation in Asia, believing that such cooperation promotes mutually beneficial exchanges, economic growth as well as greater cohesion among Asian countries. The two sides viewed positively each other's participation in regional and sub-regional multilateral cooperation processes in Asia.

The two sides stated that the improvement and development of India-China relations is not targeted at any third country and does not affect either country's existing friendly relations and cooperation with other countries.

The two sides agreed that the official visit of the Prime Minister of India to the People's Republic of China has been a success, has contributed to enhancing mutual understanding and trust between the Governments, leaders and peoples of the two countries, and marks a new step forward in strengthening the all-round cooperation between India and China in the new century.

In 2005 an agreement between the Government of China and Government of India on the political parameters and guiding principles for the Settlements of the boundary was signed by Dai Bingguo of China and M.K. Narayanan of India, in New Delhi on 11 April 2005. Also further impetus was provided during the visit of Wen Jiabao in April 2005 in the protocol between India and China on modalities for implementation of confidence building measures in the Military field along the LAC in the border areas. This protocol more or less reiterated the earlier points of 1986 agreement. However some important amplification of earlier points was as follows.

a. Article III of the Protocol explained the following

i. In the event of alleged air intrusion of its controlled air space by the military aircraft of the other side, either side may seek a flag meeting within 48 hours of the alleged air intrusion, in order to seek a clarification. The results of the investigation after completion may be communicated to the other side through a flag meeting within a period of four weeks.

ii. If a military aircraft of either side is required to fly across the LAC or to overfly the air space of the other side, prior permission shall be sought from the other side according to the procedures and formats to be mutually agreed upon.

iii. If a military or a civilian aircraft of either side is required to fly across the LAC or to land on other side of the line of the LAC in an emergency situation, the two sides will ensure flight safety in such situations by adhering to procedures to be mutually agreed upon.

b. Article V provided for the followings

i. Both sides shall hold two additional borders meetings each year at Spanggur Gap in the Western Sector, Nathula Pass in the Sikkim Sector and BumLa in the Eastern Sector respectively in celebration of the National Day or Army Day of either side.

ii. Both sides are, in principle, to expand the mechanism

of border meeting points to include Kibithu-Damai in the Eastern Sector and Lipulekh Pass or Qiang La in the Middle sector. The precise location of these border meeting points will be decided through mutual consultations.

iii. Both sides shall conduct exchanges between the relevant Military Regions of China and Army Commands of India. Specific arrangements shall be decided upon through mutual consultations between the relevant agencies under the Ministry of Defense of both sides.

Certain important steps were taken as a follow- up of the CBM's, like holding of a cordial meeting at a new border point in Arunachal Pradesh, on November 18, 2006, during President HuJintao's visit to India. The two sides met at Kibithu in Anjwa district of Arunachal Pradesh, to discuss the modalities for the conduct of troops along the border. The border meetings between personnel of two countries have traditionally been held at Chusul in Ladakh, Nathula in Sikkim and Bum La in Arunachal Pradesh. (Warm meeting at New Border Point, The Hindu, November 21, 2006, also see, The salient points of the 2005 agreement signed on 11 April are as follows. Article I says the differences on the boundary question should not be allowed to affect the overall development of bilateral relations. The two sides will resolve the boundary question through peaceful and friendly consultations. Neither shall use or threaten to use force against the other by any means. The final solution of the boundary question will significantly promote good neighbourly and friendly relations between India and China.

Article II The two sides should, in accordance to the principles of peaceful coexistence, seek a fair, reasonable and mutually acceptable solution to the boundary question through consultations on an equal footing, proceeding from the political perspective of overall bilateral relations.

Article III Both sides should, in the spirit of mutual respect and mutual understanding, make meaningful and mutually acceptable adjustments to their respective positions on the boundary question, so as to arrive at a package settlement to the boundary question. The boundary settlement must be final and covering all sectors of the India-China boundary.

Article IV The two sides will give due consideration to each other's strategic and reasonable interests, and the principle of mutual and equal security.

Article V The two sides will take into account, inter alia, historical evidence, national sentiments, practical difficulties and reasonable concerns and sensitivities of both sides, and the actual state of border areas.

Article VI The boundary should be along well-defined and easily identifiable natural geographical features to be mutually agreed upon between the two sides.

Article VII in reaching a boundary settlement, the two sides shall safegurad due interests of their settled population in the border areas.

Article VIII Within the agreed framework of the final boundary settlement, the delineation of the boundary will be carried out utilising means such as modern cartographic and surveying practises and joint surveys.

Article IX Pending an ultimate settlement of the boundary question, the two sidesshould strictly respect and observe the line actual control and work together to maintainpeace and tranquillity in the border areas. The India-China Joint Working Group and the India-China Diplomatic and Military Expert Group shall continue their work under the Agreements of 7 September 1993 and 29 November 1996, including the clarification of the line of actual control and the implementation of confidence building measures.

Article X The Special Representatives on the boundary

question shall continue their consultations in an earnest manner with the objectives of arriving at an agreed framework for a boundary settlement, which will provide the basis for the delineation and demarcation of the India-China boundary to be subsequently undertaken by civil and military officials and surveyors of the two sides.

In September 2005 as a boost to the CBM's the militaries of India and China conducted a friendly Volley ball match along the Line of Actual Control in Nathula in Sikkim so as to keep the border areas incident-free. A high-level Indian Armydelegation led by the GOC-in-C Eastern Command, Lt Gen Arvind Sharma held constructive talks with senior officers of the Chinese People's Liberation Army (PLA), including the Commander of the Beijing Military Region, Zhang Li in Feb 2006. General Sharma said that more such sporting events would be organised to enhance mutual trust between the defence forces of the two countries.[58]

After 2005, there was nearly no significant progress on the boundary talks," as per Hu Shisheng, a South Asia scholar at the China Institutes of Contemporary International Relations (CICIR). He feels that any future talk at the most could be just "accepting and respecting each other's LAC claim." He further recommends, both sides could "put aside the sovereignty issue" and leave the boundary question for next generations to solve. Mr. Hu's sentiment was taken at face value in an article published in the Liberation Daily, a voice of the CPC in Shanghai, which seconded his suggestion.

In 2007 the Special Representatives Mr. M.K. Narayanan of India and Dai Bugguo from China met in Hydrabad house, New Delhi for the ninth round of consultations on the border issue. At the end of the talks they only stated that they had reached an agreement in April 2005 on "political parameters" and "guiding principles" on the basis of which a detailed settlement would be negotiated.[59] Same year they again met at Coonoor, Tamil Nadu for the tenth round of talks. Media reports indicated that as per Narayanan the talks were 'good', while Bingguo was oblique in stating that the talks were useful as part of 'achieving the goal of common development for the benefit of people of both the countries`. The response of the Chinese Foreign Ministry spokesman, Liu Jianchao was, "They had in-depth exchange of views and the two sides are committed to make joint efforts to promote the process." Fu Xiaoqiang, a researcher with the Institute of South Asia, under the China Institute of Contemporary International Relations, said "Through several rounds of talks, China and India both have adopted a more realistic and self-restrained attitude."

In 2007 the 11th Round of the Special Representatives Talks on India-China boundary question, held useful and positive discussions on the framework for the settlement of the India-China boundary question. The two sides agreed that the next round of talks would be held in Beijing. The specific dates would be decided through diplomatic channels".[60] Therewas an apparent change in the Indian government policy on the Boundary issue with China with adoption of the principle of, "give and take" as opposed to 1962 Resolution of the Parliament.

The linkage between this flexibility and Chinese support in the NSG may not be a mere coincidence but irony of realpolitik. Chinese statements over the past some time also indicated that Beijing is keen to resolve the issue based on a compromise formula. Use of phrases such as, "positive direction, mutual adjustment and give and take principles", by the Chinese denote the possibility of greater progress in Sino Indian border talks in the subsequent rounds.

The rational approach taken at that time is questionable but it surely indicated that the government was willing to be more open about the proposals for adjustments with China on the boundary issue. Nevertheless this may also have been a tactical stand given that it preceded important political visits to China later that year. As also the prospects of mid term polls over the Indo US nuclear deal may even lead to the proposals remaining in cold storage for some time to come. However the great words spoken after each agreement did not correspond to any action on the ground, bacauseat the tactical level there was an ongoing dispute between India and China on construction of bunkers by India on the Sikkim-Bhutan-Tibet trijunction, at Batang La and Dokala. The 12th round of talks also between M.K. Narayanan and Dai Bugguo were again nothing but repeat of the previous ones. However in September the Chinese had for the first time opened fire on the ITBP jawans in the Kerang in North Sikkim. Till 2009, the special representatives had held 13 rounds of talks, without making any headway. Meanwhile, China had become more assertive in the recent past, and started laying claims on areas that were thought to be settled for example the finger area in Sikkim.[61]

The 14th round of talks were held in China on 29 November 2010 this time between Shivshankar Menon from India and same old Dai Bugguo from China. The talks were held amongst the explosive news from wikileaks that China has been involved in Internet hacking since 2002. But it was yet to come up with evidence on earlier charges that Chinese agencies have hacked Indian military sites.[62]

China sought to give a new twist to its border dispute with India. A news report filed by the Chinese official news agency Xinhua described the Sino-Indian border as 2,000 km, taking away almost same length from the existing border between the two countries. The claim caught India by surprise, which always claimed that its border with China is more than 4000km. Xinhua's reference to the border issue was based on an official briefing by Chinese Assistant Foreign Minister Hu Zhengyue on Premier Wen's visit to India.[63] The new angle to the dispute given by a Minister suggested that China no longer considered the boundary of nearly 1,600 km of the 2000 km separating Jammu and Kashmir from Xinjiang and Tibet as a border with India. Besides this development, China also referred to Arunachal Pradesh as

"South Tibet" and continued to issue stapled visa to residents of Jammu and Kashmir.[64]

The geopolitical rivals, India and China face each other over a highly disputed border. The purity of virtually the entire 4,057 km border - one of the longest in the world - The amount of Indian land China occupies or openly covets tops 135,000 sq km, or approximately the size of Costa Rica. China currently has unresolved land and sea border disputes with 11 other neighbours. But in comparison with China's territorial disputes with other neighbours now or even in the past, its land disputes with India stand out for their sheer size and importance.

Both countries seem to have overcome the second step towards solving the problem; agreeing on the framework under which to settle the boundary. However, unless the boundary is demarcated bilaterally, intrusions are likely to be an ugly certainty besides continuation of growing trust deficit between the two Asian giants. In all its possibility, China has in hand to look after itsinternal development, issues such as relations with the United States, current territorial disputes with Japan and the situation in the South China Sea in terms of China's pressing priorities. "In urgency, it is true that China-India relations are secondary to those more urgent issues," however, in China's present foreign policy, India is regarded as one country that China has confidence in, as for issues such as... the regional order in the Asia-Pacific region in particular, climate change and trade regime talks.

State Councilor Dai Bingguo was the Special Representative and the chief negotiator on the boundary issue since 2003 and has worked as China's point man for India, Dai, so far negotiated with four top Indian officials — Brajesh Mishra, J N Dixit, M K Narayanan and present National Security Advisor Shivshankar Menon — on the border issue and normalisation of relations. He is about to retire and his successor will probably be Mr. Yang Jiechi.

India and China have been friends for 99.9 per cent of the time in over 2,000 years of exchanges between them, says Dai Bingguo, underlining that the two sides should "cast off" the shadow of the 1962 war and build a bright future together.[65]

In relation to the BDCA, (Border Defense Cooperation Agreement) the Chinese side is reported to have put forward 16 proposals. China is particularly keen on India signing the BDCA proposed by them. In response, India is said to have agreed to consider the proposal and had given some counter suggestions from their side including reiteration of the need for clarification and confirmation of the LAC pending final settlement, so as to eliminate grey areas or differing perceptions of the LAC. This has been the long standing demand of India which China has been stone walling.

Conclusion

The developments in early 1959 deepened suspicions about China's intents. One was Zhou Enlai's letter of January 1959 written to Nehru, affirming that a border dispute did exist between the two countries, thereby taking a complete U-turn from his earlier confirmations;, other being uncalled-for and illegal quelling of rebellion in Tibet and accusing India of interfering in Tibetan affairs. Nehru's understanding of promises made by Zhou Enlai on China's willingness to accept the McMahon Line and preservation of Tibetan autonomy got a jolt and viewed by Nehru as signs of betrayal by China, and a hostile step towards India.

Couple of other anti Indian activities carried out by China in the region to downgrade India's image, raised serious apprehensions. China settled its boundary dispute with Burma on the basis of 1941 line drawn by the then British authority, without keeping India informed of the same. Moreover China concluded with Nepal, the Kathmandu-Tibet highway agreement in 1961 without knowledge of Indian authorities. Nehru, a man of vision also observed a most possible alliance between China and Pakistan in view of their common dislike of India; which came out to be true later. The strategic perception of Nehru was based on knowledge of individual Chinese and their national character. He had visualized that China would entangle India one day and that has come true and known as the "The String of Pearls" in contemporary world.

The Chinese have changed the very status of the border between India and China. While India maintains that the border dispute covered 4,057km along LAC, China now states that the dispute was confined to 2,000km, that is Arunachal Pradesh, and discounting western sector altogether. There are areas where both sides have overlapping ideas of where the LAC is. To strive for the settlement of the China-India boundary question and to make greater progress in the China-India strategic and cooperative partnership in the contemporary world, where the events take place in lightning speed, standard operating procedures of both sides have to show restraint. In the last few decades, focus has been on establishing channels of communication between the two governments to deal with crisis situations and improve border management as a whole.

Many such groups and committees have been formed by the mutual understanding of both countries, but it gives an impression that the Chinese are creating situations to compel both to take or at least show to take steps towards solving the border issue, palatable to them. The drafts and meetings of repetitive nature, time and again reiterating the same points all over again on one side and regularly violating the LAC to show the difference in perception of the boundary line, on the other proves the disregard to handle the issue.

Surely Pakistan's ceding Indian Territory (PoK) to China in 1963 may have been more due to the enmity between India and Pakistan and for having a lasting friendship with China since both needed each other in playing the game of hegemony than having any geopolitical vision at that point of time. But slowly the area has gained geo-political dimensions and interests.

It seems that both China and India are strategically unprepared for war. The two Asian giants are presently on the Catchup-curve from developing to developed countries. While they are simultaneously modernising the militaries, the over-all national strategies appear to be to maintain the status quo till comprehensive national power reaches a level where surplus can be invested in war making, Says Brig. (Retd) Rahul Bhonsle a defense analyst.

Twenty Indian soldiers lost their lives in the recent border skirmishes with China, in the Galwan Valley. This was the fiercest border conflict with China to have occurred after the 1962 war. This is an important topic for the UPSC International Relations segment. In this article, you can read all about the India-China conflict, its repercussions, what it means for India in terms of relations with China, and also the way forward.

Context

- Violence in the Galwan Valley on the India-China border has claimed the lives of 20 Indian soldiers.

Where is Galwan Valley?

- The valley refers to the land that sits between steep mountains that buffet the Galwan River.
- The River has its source in Aksai Chin, on China's side of the LAC, and it flows from the east to Ladakh, where it meets the Shyok River on India's side of the LAC.
- The valley is strategically located between Ladakh in the west and Aksai Chin in the east, which is currently controlled by China as part of its Xinjiang Uyghur Autonomous Region.
- At its western end are the Shyok River and the

Darbuk-Shyok-Daulet Beg Oldie (DSDBO) road. Its eastern mouth lies not far from China's vital Xinjiang Tibet road, now called the G219 highway.

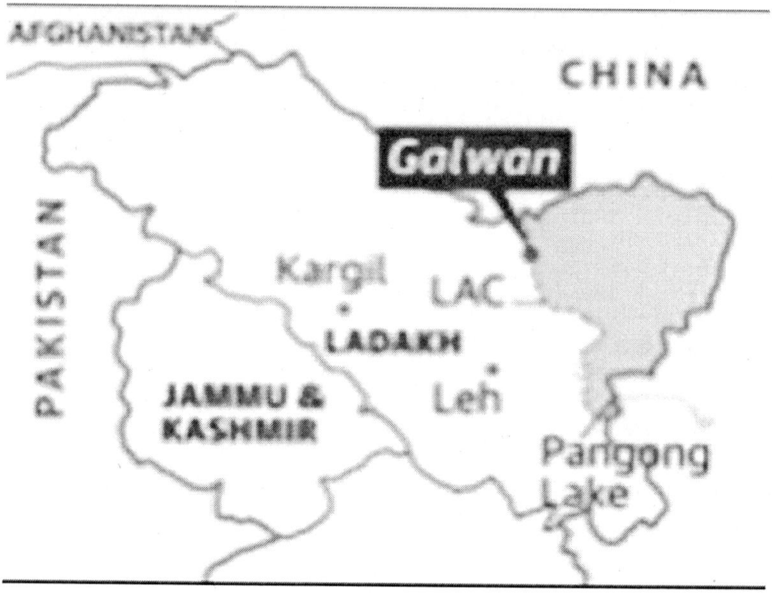

Where does the Line of Actual Control lie?

- The LAC lies east of the confluence of the Galwan and Shyok rivers in the valley, up to which both India and China have been patrolling in recent years.
- After the June 15 clash, however, China has claimed that the entire valley lies on its side of the LAC.

Territorial claims and LAC claims

- They are not the same. The distinction between territorial claims and LAC claims is sometimes blurred.
- The LAC refers to territory under the effective control of each side, not to their entire territorial claim. For instance, India's territorial claims extend 38,000 sq km on the other side of the LAC across all

of Aksai Chin, but the LAC India observes runs through the valley.

It is true that the LAC has never been demarcated and there are differences in perception of where it lies in more than a dozen spots, but there have not been previous incidents in the valley.

Background

- Indian troops were armed. All troops on border duty always carry arms, especially when leaving the post.
- Those at Galwan too did carry arms. But, long-standing practice (as per 1996 & 2005 agreements) did not allow the use of firearms during faceoffs.

1996 Agreement

- The 1996 agreement is on Confidence-Building Measures in the Military Field along the Line of Actual Control in the India-China Border Areas.
- **Article VI (1) of the 1996 agreement** says "With a view to preventing dangerous military activities along the line of actual control in the India-China border areas... Neither side shall open fire, cause bio-degradation, use hazardous chemicals, conduct blast operations or hunt with guns or explosives within two kilometres from the line of actual control. This prohibition shall not apply to routine firing activities in small arms firing ranges."
- However, it is Article VI (4) that is more applicable in the current instance: "If the border personnel of the two sides come in a face-to-face situation due to differences on the alignment of the line of actual control or any other reason, they shall exercise self-restraint and take all necessary steps to avoid an escalation of the situation. Both sides shall also enter into immediate consultations through diplomatic

and/or other available channels to review the situation and prevent any escalation of tension."

2005 Agreement

- **In Article 1:** "the two sides will resolve the boundary question through peaceful and friendly consultations. Neither side shall use or threaten to use force against the other by any means".
- The 2013 Agreement on Border Defence Cooperation also stated that neither side shall use its military capability against the other.

Since no round has been fired on the Sino-India border in Ladakh after 1962 and with a view to preventing any escalation, these routines of not firing have been drilled into the soldiers.

Possible Factors for Chinese Aggresion

India's border infrastructure

- India has been strengthening its border infrastructure along the LAC.
- The strengthening of the Darbuk-Shyok-Daulat Beg Oldi road may have angered the Chinese. The Chinese demand in the ongoing negotiations is also premised on India stopping its infrastructure development.

Change in the status of J&K

- One popular argument is that China's move is driven by local factors such as India's decision to change the status of Jammu and Kashmir and Ladakh. Read more on this in the article, Article 370.

Bilateral tensions

- The relations between the two countries have been steadily deteriorating.

- India has been against China's Belt and Road Initiative (BRI) and the China-Pakistan Economic Corridor (CPEC). China further views India's assertions regarding Gilgit-Baltistan as an implicit attack on the CPEC.
- India has put curbs and restrictions on Chinese foreign direct investment.

China's internal dynamics

- The internal pressures that have been generated within China – in part due to the COVID-19 pandemic, are also influencing Chinese behaviour.
- The COVID-19 pandemic is the most serious health crisis that China has faced since the founding of the People's Republic of China in 1949. The Chinese economy has been on the downslide which is also contributing to increasing political pressure on the country's leadership.
- The coupling of political and economic tensions has greatly aggravated pressures on Chinese leadership and the rising tide of anti-China sentiment the world over has further worsened matters.
- Chinese aggression has been observed not only along the LAC but also in the South China Sea. This might indicate a deliberate planning on the part of the Chinese leadership to divert attention from domestic issues.

India's alignment with the U.S.

- While India professes to be non-aligned, it is increasingly perceived as having aligned with the U.S.
- India's United States tilt is perhaps most pronounced in the domain of U.S.-China relations. Recent instances are often highlighted to confirm

the perception that India tends to side with the U.S. and against China whenever there is a conflict of interest between the two.

- An evident degree of geopolitical convergence also exists between the U.S. and India in the Indo-Pacific, again directed against China.
- India is a member of the Quad (the U.S., Japan, Australia and India) which has a definite anti-China connotation.
- The U.S. President's proposal of redesigning the G-7, including countries such as India (India has conveyed its acceptance), but excluding China, provides China yet another instance of India and China being in opposite camps.

India is being increasingly projected as an alternative model to China, and being co-opted into a wider anti-China alliance which China clearly perceives as a provocation.

India's traditional clout in its neighbourhood was slipping

- For India, tensions with Pakistan have been high keeping the troops occupied in the border areas.
- Nepal raised boundary issues with India.
- Sri Lanka is diversifying its foreign policy and China is making deep inroads into that region.
- Bangladesh was deeply miffed with the Citizenship Amendment Act.
- Even in Afghanistan, where Pakistan, China, Russia and the U.S. are involved in the transition process, India is out.

A confluence of all these factors, which point to a decline in the country's smart power, allowed China to make aggressive moves on the LAC.

Concerns

- Though the LAC has never been demarcated there had not been previous incidents in the valley. By now staking a claim to the entire Galwan Valley and up to the confluence of the rivers, China is, in India's view, unilaterally altering the LAC.
- This goes against the 1993 Border Peace and Tranquility Agreement (BPTA), under which India and China agreed to strictly respect and observe the LAC between the two sides.

Undemarcated borders

- The alignment of the LAC has never been agreed upon, and it has neither been delineated nor demarcated.
- There is no official map in the public domain that depicts the LAC. The current understanding of the LAC reflects the territories that are, at present, under the control of each side, pending a resolution of the boundary dispute.

Difference in claims

- For the most part, in the western sector, the LAC broadly corresponds with the border as China sees it. However, India and China do not agree on the alignment of the LAC everywhere.
- Differences in perception, particularly in 13 spots in the western, middle and eastern sectors of the border, often lead to what are called "face-offs", when patrols encounter each other in these grey zones that lie in between the different alignments. Some of these areas are Chumar, Demchok and the north bank of the Pangong Lake in the western sector, Barahoti in the middle sector, and Sumdorong Chu in the east.

Chinese tactics

- China has in several territorial disputes, intentionally left its claims ambiguous.
- The Chinese haven't stuck to their previously agreed positions. China's alignments of the LAC have kept changing.
- The border skirmishes along the Line of Actual Control seem to be indicative of the Chinese approach to use the border problem to pressurize India on other issues.

Points of Discussion

- The principal responsibility for intelligence assessment and analysis concerning China rests with the National Security Council Secretariat (NSCS) and India's external intelligence agency, the Research and Analysis Wing (R&AW), and to a lesser extent, the Defence Intelligence Agency.

Summit diplomacy

- "Summit conferences apply to the meeting of heads of government of the leading powers in an effort to reach broad measures of agreement".

Why are there more summits?

- The rise of summitry is a consequence of the paucity of resources of smaller nations who are less able to finance and sustain a vast diplomatic service and thus rely on summits for representation and negotiation.
- It will speed up the process as heads of countries are directly negotiating.

Concerns

- The preference given recently to summit diplomacy over traditional foreign policy-making structures proved to be a severe handicap.

- Summit diplomacy cannot be a substitute for carefully structured foreign office policymaking.
- Summits put professional diplomats briefly into the shade.
- India believed the tensions between India and China were diffused after the Doklam crisis as we had meetings at the highest level in Wuhan and Mamallapuram.
- Personal bonhomie with leaders will not result in friendly ties with countries.
- Prime Minister Nehru had a good equation with Premier Zhou En-lai.

What's next?

- Bilateral relations in other areas will be under considerable strain. Soft landings cannot be expected.
- No leadership-level contact between the top leaders of the two countries can be anticipated in the near term.
- Indian businesses in China and Chinese business operations in India can expect the going to be tougher than before. The scenario of trade and investments could encounter similar obstacles.
- In areas that impinge on national security, as in the cyber field and in telecommunications, and in technologies that enable spying and surveillance (5G, for instance), stringent controls, exclusions and clampdowns can be expected in the treatment and the entry of Chinese companies in India.

Should India Remain Non-Aligned?

Yes

- The circumstances that led to the India-China war of 1962 offers an analysis of the Chinese approach.

- Faced with the disaster of the Great Leap Forward and increasing isolation globally, the Chinese chose to strike at India rather than confront Russia or the West.
- This is not the time for India to be seen as the front end of a belligerent coalition of forces seeking to put China in its place.
- India has consistently followed a different policy in the past, and it is advisable that it remains truly non-aligned and not become part of any coalition that would not be in India's long-term interest.

No

- It will be in India's economic and strategic interests to align with the US and the Western world which will remain together despite the fissures under Trump. India needs investments, technology, and a manufacturing ecosystem to employ millions of its young population and improve its living standards.
- It requires advanced weapons and technologies for its military.
- India is ambitious and wants to be a great power and the US and the Western world recognise this and are willing to partner India.
- The US is in talks with India to restructure Global Supply Chains. The US is encouraging its companies to look at India as an alternative to China.
- This presents a big opportunity for India whose continental size, large market, young and skilled labour, and shared values with the West makes it an attractive destination. In fact, an alliance of democracies could crystallise with economic cooperation at its core.

Defence ties between the two have been cemented with increasing weapons sales and important defence agreements.

- There are regular bilateral and multilateral military exercises and dialogues on economic and strategic cooperation.

On the other hand, Beijing wants to keep India boxed into South Asia, and tries to keep it off balance using Pakistan to which it supplies arms and supports. It has made inroads into the region using the Belt and Road Initiative (BRI).

- It continues to block India's membership in the Nuclear Suppliers Group (NSG) and continues to needle New Delhi in the UNSC over Kashmir.

Much of India's diplomacy in the last few years has been to counter China and its influence. India faces China as a competitor in Africa, West Asia, Central Asia and the Indo-Pacific. Indo-US ties are complementary, and a formal alliance will help realise the full potential of these relations.

Conclusion

- Non-alignment or being a swing state makes sense if the gains to be derived from either side are equal. China will not be to India, what the Soviet Union was.
- In the post-COVID-19 world, India will have to make a disruptive choice — of alignment.

Way Forward

Given the current circumstances, India should strategize an action plan aimed towards protecting its sovereign interests.

Prepare militarily

- India needs to be prepared, continue to build roads and improve the infrastructure along the border, to keep itself ready to deal with any contingency.
- India must improve the military capacity of the tri-service Andaman and Nicobar Command

given its immense geostrategic value, as it overlooks Asia's maritime strategic lifeline and the world's most important global sea lane.

Pressure points

- India could choose to leverage the sensitivity of the Chinese to the one-China policy and other vulnerabilities like the Tibet issue and Hong Kong protests, to force a change in China's attitude.
- This would allow India to signal to China that it has options, and that China would be wise not to escalate these situations too far.

Shifting focus

- To counter China India must look for options beyond LAC.
- The South China Sea/Indian Ocean Region maritime domain presents India with the best options where the regional geopolitical context is favourable.
- India should demonstrate that it is willing and capable of influencing the maritime balance in East Asia, where China faces off a combination of the United States, Vietnam, Australia, Indonesia and sometimes Malaysia and the Philippines as well.
- China perceives a vulnerability in the Malacca strait given its marked dependence on the sea lines of communication for its vast trade and energy imports.

Going global

- India should go global to defend against China. India's counter to Chinese power in the Himalayas should be to assume a more global role of its own.
- In Asia and Africa, debt-traps induced by the BRI are gradually stoking discontent. If India focuses

on leveraging its advantages as a development partner, particularly in the post-COVID-19 era, it can use its newfound influence as a bargaining chip against Chinese interests in these countries.

Building alliances

- India must build power-balancing alliances.
- Many countries are seeking leadership from other quarters to counter-balance Chinese influence. In Southeast Asia, countries are pushing back against Chinese aggression in the South China Sea.
- This provides an opportunity to build partnerships with such countries to balance China's growing influence.

India can give itself leverage against China by improving its bilateral relationships with other countries that are similarly worried about China's growing influence – such as Australia, Vietnam, Japan, and even the U.K.

Several foreign policy experts argue that India's strategic dealing with China has to begin with South Asia. In this regard, it is important to reinvigorate SAARC.

- One way to reinvigorate SAARC is to revive the process of South Asian economic integration.

Aligning with the United States

- This is also an opportunity for India to align its interests much more strongly and unequivocally with the U.S. as a principal strategic partner.
- A closer alignment with the U.S. represents India's opportunity to counter China, while efforts to foster regional partnerships and cultivate domestic military capabilities, although insufficient by themselves, could play a complementary role.
- Moving into a closer partnership with the US would allow India an opportunity to rebalance

the Indo-Pacific region.

- India should also infuse more energy into its relations with Japan, Australia, and the ASEAN.

Taking the long view

- India's leverage and balancing power within the Indo-Pacific and the world beyond stems from its strong democratic credentials, the dynamism of its economy, its leading role in multilateral institutions, and the strategic advantage of its maritime geography — an asset possessed by few other nations, and which must be deployed much more effectively to counterbalance the Chinese ingress into this oceanic space that surrounds us.
- The events in Galwan Valley should be a wake-up call to many of India's Asian friends and partners enabling a high-resolution envisioning of Chinese aggressiveness.

Conclusion

- Good neighbourhood relations are crucial for national stability and well-being.
- If India is to disengage from economic involvement with China and build the capacities and capabilities it needs in manufacturing, and in supply chain networks closer home, it cannot be a prisoner of the short term.
- It is time for India to boldly take the long view in this area as also on its South Asia policy.
- India cannot continue to remain in a "reactive mode" to Chinese provocations 2+and it is time to take an active stand. Since India's choices vis-à-vis China are circumscribed by the asymmetry in military power, resort must be sought in realpolitik.
- This would force China to reconsider its tactics and force it towards negotiations with India.

References

1. Cukwurah A.O. (1967), The Settlement of Boundary Disputes in International Law, University of Manchester, Manchester. pp. 11-28.
2. Saraf Pushp, April- June, 2013' Borders Affairs, Vol. 14 No.3. p. 2.
3. Times of India, New Delhi, 4 September 1993.
4. Guruswamy Mohan (2006) Emerging Trends in India- China Relations, Hope India Publications, Gurgaon.
5. Chaterjee RK, (1978), India's Land Borders: Problems and Challenges, Sterling Publishers (P) Ltd, New Delhi pp. 35-51.
6. R.A. Huttenback, 1964: 201-207.
7. Gondker Narayan Rao, 1968, The India-China Boundary: AReapprisal, Asia Publishing House, London, p. 56.
8. The Hindu, April 27, 2013.
9. Zulfiquar Khalid, Pakistan in The Pamir Knot, Geostrategic imperatives (Lahor: Vanguard, 1987), p 115.
10. Virender Sahai Verma, "Geo- strategy and the Karakoram Highway", as given in "Sino-Pakistani Strategic Co-operation", Peace Initiatives, Vol.V, Nos. III-V1, May - December 1999, p.l16.
11. B. Raman, "Gilgit & Baltistan, China & North Korea," *SAAG Paper*, No. 289, South Asia Analysis Group, 7 August 2001,).
12. Surrender Chopra, ed., Sino- Indian Relations, (Amritsar: Guru Nanak Dev University, 1985), p. 31 and Bankok Post (Bankok), 8 September, 1993.
13. Indian Express (New Delhi), 27 July 1980.
14. Patriot (New Delhi), 10 December 1988.
15. For more details, refer to the Report of the Officials of the Governments of India and the People's Republic of China on

the Boundary Question, (MEA, GoI,February 1961), pp. 1-2. Henceforth to be referedas, REPORT.

16. The Sino-Indian Boundary, Texts of Notes relating to the Sino-Indian Boundary, published by the Indian Society of International Law, New Delhi-1, pp.1-2.

17. Ibid, p.3, also see A.G.Noorani, 2011, India-China Boundary Problem 1846-1947, History and Diplomacy. New Delhi, Oxford University Press, p. 22

18. Quoted in a letter dated 26 September 1959 from Prime Minister of India to the Chinese Premier, Chou En-Lai, para7, White Paper No. II, p.36 and A G Noorani, ibid, p.29

19. Bajpai. S.P., India- China Boundary: Central Sector, in S.P. Sen(ed): The Sini- Indian Border Question—A Gistorical view, Calcutta, 1971, p. 92.

20. Peter Sahlins,1989, Boundareis: The Making of France and Spainin the Pyrenees, University of California Press, California. P.188

21. International Boundary Study No.-42,Nov. 30 1964: Burma –China Boundary, by the Office of the Geographer, Bureau of Intelligence and Research, USA.

22. K. Warikoo,2009, Himalayan Frontiers of India: Historical, geo-political and strategic perspectives, Routledge, Oxon preface.

23. Report, p. 101.

24. See Chinese note of 26 December 1959. Cited in White Paper III, p. 79

25. Report, P.2

26. Letter of Prime Minister Jawaharlal Nehru to Chou En- Lai,, 22 March 1959, quoted in China's Betrayel of India—Background to to the invasion, Publication Division, Ministry of Information and Broadcasting, GoI, November 1962), p.20.

27. Report, P. 85

28. Chaterjee RK, (1978), India's Land Borders: Problems and Challenges, Sterling Publishers (P) Ltd, New Delhi pp 109-116

29. T.S. Murthy, Paths of Peace, (New Delhi: A.B. C. Publishing House,1983), p.126.and Dilara Choudhary, "Sino-Indian Border Disputes: Same recent Developments, Biss Journal, January 1988, p. 31

30. Parshotam Mehra, Negotiating with the Chinese 1946- 1987: Problems and Perspective (New Delhi: Reliance Publishing House, 1980), p. 110

31. The Statesman (New Delhi), 29 October 1981

32. India Today 31 January 1982.

33. Indian Express, 5 February 1983.

34. Anil Rai, "Skirting the Border Line", Financial Express, New Delhi, 7 February 1983.

35. Telegraph, Calcutta, 31 January 1983.

36. Times of India 31 October 1983.

37. Sumit Ganguly, "The Sino-Indian Border Talks, 1981- 1989:- A view from New Delhi", Asian Survey, Vol. XXIX, No.12, December 1989, p. 1128.

38. Times of India, 12 November 1985.

39. Xinhua, (English), 8 May, 1986.

40. Times of India, 16 July 1986. The Statesman, New Delhi, 16 July 1986.

41. The Hindu, 18 July, 1986.

42. Times of India, 24 July, 1986.

43. Times of India, 2 August 1986.

44. Indian Express, 2 August, 1986

45. China Daily 17 December, 1986.

46. Times of India, 19 December, 1986

47. Hindustan Times, 15 November, 1986.

48. Xinhua, English, 18 November 1986.

49. The News Nation, 15 August 1987.

50. The Statesman, (New Delhi), 1 February 1988).

51. Brahma Chellaney, Asia Jugergrnaut, Harper Collins, 2010, pp. 296-300.

52. Hindustan Times, New Delhi, 7 September 1993.

53. The Times of India, New Delhi, 4 September 1993.

54. Times of India, New Delhi. 8 September 1993.

55. Hindustan Times, New Delhi, 8 September 1993.

56. Surjit Dutta, "Sino-Indian Relations in Post Cold War", Strategic Analysis, New Delhi, Feb. 1994, p-1426.).

57. Rasgotra M & Chopra V.D.(1997), India's Relations with Russia and China: A New Phase, Gyan Publishing House p. 31

58. India, China to interact more on borders, Hindustan Times,(Beijing), PTI, Feb22 2006.

59. The Hindu (on line edition) Jan 18 2007.

60. MEA India Press Release.

61. Das Pushpita, (2010), India's Border Management; Select Documents, Institute of Defense Studies and Analysis, New Delhi, p. 12.

62. Times of India, 29 Nov. 2010.

63. The Tribune, 20 Dec. 2010 (Chandigarh) "China fires fresh salvo in border dispute".

64. Asia News Agency , 12 Dec. 2010.

65. The Economic Times,12 Dec. 2012

3

China in Kashmir

The present chapter analyses the critical role and the increasing influence of China both in Indian Administered Kashmir and Pakistan administered Kashmir. It would also highlight Chinese interests in Kashmir and its policy approach towards the Kashmir dispute that has remained the bone of contention between India and Pakistan. Further, the chapter discusses the emerging strategic relations between Pakistan and China. It also make an assessment of the growing Chinese influence in Pakistan occupied Kashmir (PoK) in the recent past and its security concerns for India.

Kashmir is a region where India, China, and Pakistan all have territorial claims.[1] China's role and involvement in Kashmir issue is getting complicated with every passing years. China has over the years developed keen strategic interests in the Kashmir dispute between India and Pakistan. In fact, it is quite well known that the occupation of Kashmir is divided amidst three states, India, Pakistan, and China. As against the general understanding that Kashmir problem is related to India and Pakistan, but China is equally a part of the problem. It is due to the fact that China at present occupies 42,685 sq. kms of J&K.[2]

Beijing's interests lies in both Indian occupied Kashmir as well as Pakistan occupied Kashmir (PoK). Given the rich natural resources present in Kashmir, Beijing seeks the exploitation of rich resources particularly energy and also to upset India's military superiority over the arch rival Pakistan.[3] Chinese interests and involvement in Kashmir will definitely have spill over implications on India from the short to the long-term perspective.

The state of Jammu and Kashmir at the time when India got independent from British has a total area of about 2,22,236 sq. Km. However, in 1949 when a cease fire line was drawn, Pakistan went on to occupy about one third of the area i.e. 78932 sq. km (comprising of the whole of Gilgit, Mirpur, Kotli and a part of Poonch). In the post 1962 war with India, China occupied about 64000 sq. kms in Ladakh known as Aksai Chin. Besides, 5,180 sq. km. of Jammu and Kashmir was illegally ceded to China by Pakistan under the March 1963 Sino-Pak Boundary agreement. As of now, only 101,437 sq. km is with India. China deny Aksai Chin to be a part of Kashmir.[4]

By virtue of the occupation of one-fifth of territory, China shares border with Kashmir.[5] Chinese interests in Kashmir have started to flourish in the post 1962 war. Since then, China has been calling for self-determination in Kashmir. Such a China's policy has to be seen in the context of Pakistan's continued relevance in China's strategic calculus in South Asia. China shares positive sentiments with Kashmiri people.[6] By refusing to issue visa to Lt. Gen B.S. Jaswal serving in Indian Occupied Kashmir, Beijing has sent a clear message that Kashmir is a disputed territory left over from history. China invested heavily on energy and power generation projects on both sides of Azad Jammu and Kashmir and in Gilgit-Baltistan region. If on the one side China refused to accept Indian side of Kashmir, then, on the other side, it is continued to be actively involved in Pakistan occupied Kashmir.[7] In fact, prior to official meeting between

India's Prime Minister Manmohan Singh and his Chinese counterpart Wen Jiabao in Hanoi on 29 October 2010, China's Foreign Ministry Spokesperson Ma Zhaoxu has affirmed that, "China's visa policy toward residents of the India-held Kashmir is consistent and remains unchanged."[8]

China looms large on India's unfriendly relations with Pakistan. It seeks to exploit the lack of political misunderstanding between the two South Asian neighbours to its advantage. Seeing the security scenario in the South Asian region, China has improved engagement with Pakistan thereby making strategic and economic investments in the latter. The idea is to keep the common enemy under strategic pressure for strategic purpose.[9] The last one decade has seen India gaining significant weight on the international stage by virtue of its growing economic and military prowess, which is never in the interests of China and Pakistan. Pakistan and China share a very strong desire to halt India's progress in this direction. In fact, India has been the main factor that has influenced China and Pakistan policies toward each other. The two sides have a close understanding on the need to enhance strategic coordination, advance pragmatic cooperation and work together to meet challenges in pursuit of common development. Pakistan in particular viewed India as a potential challenger leading to use China to counter Indian power in the region.

The close strategic partnership between the two countries has been based on the principles of mutual respect, mutual trust and mutual benefit. Pakistan's search for a country that can help sustain a sufficient military capacity for itself against India coalesces with China's intention that "a militarily strong Pakistan would serve their objective of keeping India preoccupied on two fronts, thereby safeguard their national security interests."[10]

Beijing is fuelling that arms race between the two South Asian rivals. It has in the past and even today helped

Pakistan maintain conventional military balance between India and Pakistan by equipping the latter with JF-17 aircraft and JF-17 production facilities, F-22P frigates with helicopters, K-8 jet trainers, T-85 tanks, F-7 aircraft, small arms and ammunition. It has also built a turnkey ballistic missile manufacturing facility near Rawalpindi and helped Pakistan develop the 750-km-range, solid-fuel Shaheen-1 ballistic missile.[11] China's strategy of providing advanced arms and equipment requirements for Pakistan will continue to remain a case of serious national security concerns for India. Pakistan continues to be the major beneficiary of China's unending support to acquire nuclear materials and technology. Arms-control analysts, Gary Milhollin has very rightly pointed out that,

> "If you subtract China's help from Pakistan's nuclear program, there is no nuclear program."[12]

In the same line, another strategic affairs analysts, Robert Ross is of the perception that,

> "China continues its support for Pakistan by supplying nuclear and missile technology because China views a credible Pakistani deterrent as the most effective way to guarantee the security of its sole ally in Southern Asia against Indian power."[13]

The chapter argues that although relations between China and Pakistan may be getting stronger, but when it comes to Kashmir dispute between India and Pakistan, China is never interested in the resolution of one of the oldest disputes that exists in the world today. China's interest lies in keeping the issue intact so that India, its strategic rivalry is tied down in a long-term rivalry with Pakistan.[14]

Map 1

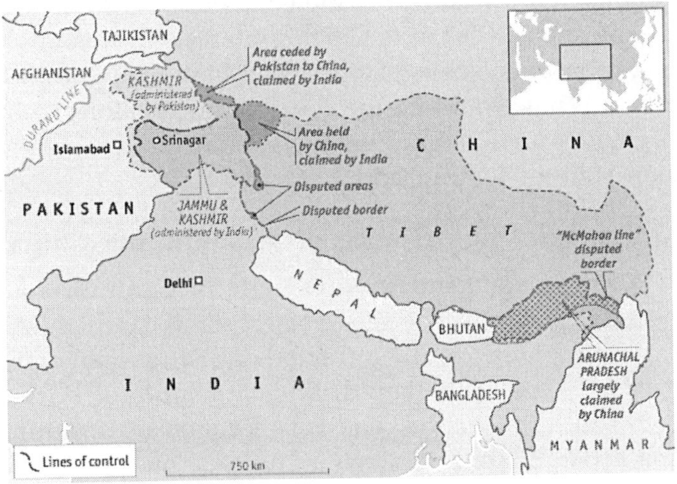

In response to China's stance on Jammu and Kashmir, Pakistan has allowed China's People's Liberation Army (PLA) to enter into Pakistan-controlled Kashmir. Lt Gen KT Parnaik, heading the Northern Command has warned that China's military presence in Pakistan-controlled Kashmir was too close for India's comfort. "It poses military challenges to India and not only along the Sino-Indian border but also along the LoC." He further added that "We hear many people who are concerned about the fact that if there were to be hostilities between us and Pakistan what would be the complicity of the Chinese. Not only because they are in the neighbourhood but the fact that they are actually stationed and present on the LoC." Besides, "The Chinese Links with Pakistan through PoK lend strength to the China-Pakistan nexus which has been of great security concern for us. It jeopardises our regional and strategic interest in the long run...the Chinese footprints are too close for comfort."[15]

The present chapter seeks to make a critical analysis on the role and influence of China in Kashmir. The last over five decades has seen change and continuity in Beijing's policy approach toward the Kashmir dispute between India and Pakistan. It would also throw light on the more recent developments. In doing so, the chapter seeks to answer for these questions – What is China's interests in Kashmir from a long-term perspective? How does China view the Kashmir conflict? What would be the possible implications to India's sovereignty on Kashmir vis-à-vis Chinese involvement in Indian state of Jammu and Kashmir?

Geo-Strategic Significance of Kashmir for China

China's role and involvement in Kashmir has not occurred in vacuum. The geo-strategic significance of Kashmir has without any doubt attracted the attention of China towards it. One of the key distinctive feature of Kashmir is its geo-strategic location. The very location of Kashmir give China economic and strategic advantage over its long-term strategic rival India. Silk Route holds immense significance for China for it helps to maintain dominant military position over India. Silk Route connects China with Pakistan and passes through Kashmir. Through Gilgit, China can infiltrate deeply into the Kashmir valley of our country. Besides Gilgit, China and Pakistan together can pose a serious threat to the security of our country via Siachen Glacier.[16]

Another significance for Kashmir lies in the fact that it shares borders with Afghanistan, a country where acts as a bridge between South Asia and Central Asia.[17]

China's Kashmir Policy: Historical Perspective

It is quite pertinent to understand the factors that shaped the China's Kashmir policy in the past decades prior to post cold war era. According to B. Raman, China's Kashmir policy has been consistent with a change in its stance on Indian-held Kashmir. It has diluted its past acceptance of J&K as a de facto part of India.[18] In the immediate years of the independence of India and Pakistan, Chinese stance has been neutral. It hesitated to taking side between India and Pakistan over Kashmir issue. Chinese hesitation were further strengthened when Pakistan joined western alliances. By remaining neutral, Chinese Premier had in 1957 gave a statement that both sides should resolve the issue bilaterally through peaceful means.[19]

The situation in which India's relations with China was at its historic low in the 1960s, Chinese leaders and people were supportive to the Kashmiri people in their claim for right to self- determination. In a piece that was published in the People's Daily on 5 September 1965, it was highlighted that,

> "...the Chinese people deeply sympathize with the just struggle of the people of Kashmir for their right to self-determination... the Chinese government and people... resolutely support... the Kashmir people's struggle for national self determination... the Kashmir people will surely realize their desire for national self-determination."[20]

The Sino-Indian war of 1962 brought about a shift in Chinese policy towards the Kashmir issue. In the post Sino-Indian war, there witnessed a perceptible shift in the Chinese position from maintaining neutral to inclination towards Pakistan's position on the Kashmir issue. This was the time when the relations between India and China started to deteriorate. Beijing supported Islamabad's position on the Kashmir issue to demonstrate solidarity with an "all weather" ally during periods of Sino-Indian estrangement and hostility.

During the visit to Pakistan in 1964, China's Prime Minister Zhou Enlai declared its commitment to support for the resolution of Kashmir dispute in accordance with the wishes of people of Kashmir as pledged to them by India and Pakistan. The very next year, President Ayub visited China and entered into a joint statement that declares the support for self-determination of Kashmiri people. In a message received from China on 16 September 1965, it is clearly mentioned that the Kashmir dispute between India and Pakistan should be settled on the basis of respect for Kashmiri people's right of self determination, as pledged by both countries. It is also stated that by China's non-involvement in the Kashmir dispute between India and Pakistan would mean allowing both sides to peacefully resolving the problem. But, non-involvement absolutely doesn't mean failure to distinguish between right and wrong; it absolutely does not mean that China can approve of depriving the Kashmiri people of their right of self determination.

Till the early 1980s, China's Kashmir policy has seen constant call for the right of self-determination for Kashmir people.[21] However, with China seeking to maintain close relations with India for the mutual benefit, Beijing seems to have changed its mind. And as the relations with India got normalised, China shifted its approach from a policy of inclination to neutrality to avoid needless alienation of India, coupled with running the risk of entrapment. For that matter, the Chinese policy got reflected in Deng Xiaoping's June 1980 statement that, "... Kashmir ... was a bilateral issue left over from history between India and Pakistan, and should be resolved peacefully..." This carried forward to the decade of the early 1990s, when China's position became unequivocal that the Kashmir issue is a bilateral matter.[22]

In the past, Pakistan took Chinese protection on the issue of Kashmir, be it in UN or giving moral support. However in the early 90's there was a change in Chinese approach, when it advocated peaceful negotiations between the two sides over the Kashmir dispute.[23] The major concern for Pakistan is in regard to China adopting a neutral position on Kashmir.[24] During Chinese President Jiang Zemin visit to India and Pakistan in late 1996, he advocated a direct dialogue between the two countries on Kashmir as well as progress towards better bilateral relations.[25] Speaking at a press conference, Mr. Zhu, said, 'China had neither any intention nor will it play any mediatory role between the two countries.'[26] Seeking to maintain a balance between India and Pakistan, Chinese Premier, Zhou Enlai had in an interview stated that, "We were on friendly terms with India; we took an attitude of non-involvement in the Kashmir issue. We... hope that India and Pakistan would settle the Kashmir issue and other problems in a friendly manner, with Pakistan. Despite, friendly terms with Pakistan, we have not given up our desire for friendship with India."[27] The neutral stand taken by China on the Kashmir issue is a result of the fear psychosis of spill over implications of ongoing terrorist violence in Kashmir into its Muslim dominated province of Xinjiang.[28]

China's Kashmir Policy in the 21st Century

From the beginning of the Kashmir problem to the end of twentieth century, China's Kashmir policy have seen four different forms. The decade of 1950s saw China remained neutral, but, the following decades of 1960s to 1970s, witnessed inclination towards Pakistan's position over Kashmir issue owing to the unhealthy relations between India and China. However, by 1980s, the policy of China return to the previous position of neutrality due to normalization in China-India relations. In the post Cold War period it changed its position and said that Kashmir is a bilateral issue between India and Pakistan and it should be resolved through peaceful means.

China's Ministry of Foreign Affairs had in 2002 declared its official position on Kashmir issue that,

> "China's position on the issue of Kashmir has been clear cut. We have always maintained that the Kashmir issue is one between India and Pakistan left over by history. China hopes that the two sides should seek new ways to appropriately solve the problem through peaceful exchanges and negotiations and refrain from military conflicts".[29]

In regard to China's stand on Kashmir and the expanding relations between China and Pakistan, John Garver, has very rightly said that, from the very beginning, China started supporting the Kashmiri people's war of self-determination, a support that was translated in the following years to material support to launch an insurgency inside the state of Jammu and Kashmir (J&K).[30]

China's involvement in Kashmir is getting stronger and deeper with every passing years. China's sympathy for Pakistan over the Kashmir issue, and for secessionists in the territory itself, are extremely unwelcome for India. China's Kashmir policy has to be seen within the broader contexts of its South Asia policy. It has adopted a policy seeking to serve its regional and global interests. On the Kashmir issue, seeing the nature of engagement and the understanding it has with both Islamabad and New Delhi, Beijing have supported the former's positions to demonstrate solidarity with it. India's long-term strategic rivalry with both China and Pakistan really influenced Beijing to be supportive towards Islamabad in its dealing with new Delhi over the Kashmir issue. However, when relations with New Delhi gets normalized, Beijing adopted a policy of neutrality to avoid unnecessarily alienating India and running the risk of entrapment.[31] Overall, China's policy towards Kashmir has ranged between support to Islamabad and maintaining neutrality between the two South Asian rivals.

By virtue of the fact that China shares border with Kashmir, the policy adopted has in one way or another supported the case of Pakistan in Kashmir. China's generous support is based on the rationale that a strong Pakistan in the region of South Asia which is of no threat to Beijing but is necessary to balance India from the long-term point of view. China shares some sentiments with Kashmiri people. As part of its evolving policy, China invited Mirwaiz Umer Farooq, the president of All-Parties Hurriyat Conference in 2009 to showcase its support for the people of Kashmir. To further make the matter really worse, Beijing has invested billions of dollars on different energy and power generation projects on both sides of Azad Jammu and Kashmir and similarly in Gilgit-Baltistan region. While, on the other side, it has refused to accept Indian control of Kashmir and considers it as disputed territory.[32]

For strategic reasons, China has so far maintained that Kashmir is a disputed territory between India and Pakistan and rejects Indian claim over Kashmir as an integral part of it. There witnessed change and continuity in Beijing's policy towards Kashmir from time to time and offered different methods of resolving it. Under the so-called China's Kashmir policy, Beijing offer military assistance to Pakistan in its dealing with India which also serves its long-term interests of containing New Delhi from gaining international leverage.

Chinese Involvement in Pakistan Occupied Kashmir (PoK): Security and Strategic Concerns for India

Pakistan occupied Kashmir (PoK) comprised of both Azad Jammu and Kashmir and Gilgit-Baltistan. India's official stand has been made clear to the Pakistanis and the international community that PoK is part of the state of Jammu and Kashmir (J&K), and hence an integral part of India. It has been under the illegitimate control of Pakistan since 22 October 1947.[33] The geo-political and geo-strategic significance of PoK has increased manifold after the establishment of the Karakoram highway (KKH) that connect Pakistan with China via PoK. What makes PoK really significant for China can be reflected from the fact that it shares border with Xinjiang province of the People's Republic of China to the north.[34] The KKH offers tremendous opportunities for both countries in terms of trade and transfer of arms and equipment needs including nuclear and missile material from China to Pakistan.[35]

From the Islamabad point of view, China is the most reliable and capable partners to dealing with the threat of

India. Chinese involvement in PoK is quite usual when the former provide the necessary support to the latter's need whether it may be in the case of Kashmir or providing arms and equipment needs to deal with a much stronger Indian side.

Whatever may be the reasons, the Chinese presence in PoK has opened a new chapter to the prolonged strategic rivalry between India and Pakistan over the state of Jammu and Kashmir. The growing Chinese presence in the region is a case of serious concerns for our country.[36] In 2009 and 2010, India responded sharply to reports of the presence of Chinese soldiers and workers in the region. India's External Affairs Minister, Sushma Swaraj had termed the CPEC project "unacceptable" for it pass through PoK. National Security Advisor Ajit Doval raised eyebrows when he reminded an audience of BSF officers to factor in 106-km-long non-contiguous border with Afghanistan in a clear reference to Gilgit-Baltistan's Afghan frontier. She has unequivocally emphasised that entire state of J & K including Gilgit-Baltistan as an integral part of India in recent press releases. With the recent up-gradation of Karakorum Highway through Gilgit-Baltistan, the collousivity of China and Pakistan and likelihood of two front war especially along PoK and Aksai Chin increases.

The vast improvement in communication infrastructure especially in Giligit-Baltistan will enable Pakistan to sidestep forces in a much faster rate and quantum compared to India, hampered by external and poorly developed lines-of-communication. This implies that Pakistan will effectively be able to increase force-ratios in theatres to her advantage in a much reduced timeframe.[37]

By way of increasing its influence in Pakistan occupied Kashmir, China desires to secure access to the Arabian Sea and Indian Ocean. This would hold the key for its commercial, energy, and military supplies with other countries via the CPEC corridor. Gaining foothold in PoK would bring Chinese naval forces close to India's south-western waters that can prove to be effective in times of crisis with India. That's the reason why India's Ambassador to China, Gautam Bambawale has said that the CPEC corridor 'violates our territorial integrity.' Most importantly, the CPEC project undermines Indian sovereignty as it passes through a Pakistan-administered part of Kashmir.[38]

India expressed deep concern and reservation over the US$42 billion China-Pakistan Economic Corridor (CPEC) which passes through Pak-Occupied Kashmir.[39] China's growing involvement in PoK through the CPEC not only pose setback to India's sovereign claim over PoK, but, also, its role and presence distorts the balance of position in the dispute.[40] However, against the rising voice of India, China has compared its developments effort in PoK to that of India's developmental projects in Arunachal Pradesh, which according to the former is not part of India. China in cooperation with Pakistan is undergoing the transit and transport project that passes through PoK. They are of the argument that if India can carry out all sort of political, economic and military developmental projects in Arunachal Pradesh, China can do the same in PoK.[41]

The matter of concern for India is that China in the name of development efforts in PoK is carrying out its military activities in the region. Beijing has stationed its PLA troops in the region, and in particular to the 772-km-long Line of Control (LoC) running between India and Pakistan. Besides, it is also being reported that a unit of PLA soldiers is placed near the Khunjerab Pass with the negative intent of establishing its military edge in India's northern sector is pretty clear.[42] Pakistan welcomed Chinese involvement in the infrastructure and development activities in the region which serve Beijing interests of putting a pressure on India. On the other hand, by way of opening to China, Pakistan seeks to capitalize on it to counterbalance India in a crisis situation with India.[43]

India's External Affairs Minister, Sushma Swaraj had stated in response to a question raised in Lok Sabha in December 2014 that,

> '... Government has seen reports with regard to China and Pakistan being involved in infrastructure building activities in Pakistan Occupied Kashmir (POK), including construction of China-Pakistan Economic Corridor. Government has conveyed its concerns to China about their activities in Pakistan Occupied Kashmir, and asked them to cease such activities.'[44]

China-Pakistan Engagement: Historical Perspective

Pakistan's decision to develop close relations with China was influenced by the former's self-interest because 'in view of Pakistan sponsored militancy in India and passive hostility of the Afghan Government, Pakistan doesn't want another great neighbour to be its enemy. Until the late 1950s, Pakistan's relations with China was nothing special. However, with the Sino-Indian relations started declining in 1959, Pakistan was driven closer to Beijing. The Sino-Indian War proved a watershed in the Sino-Pakistan relations. In the aftermath of 1962 war, Pakistan was convinced that split between New Delhi and Beijing had come full circle. Hence the circumstances allowed 'Enemy's enemy is my friend' to perpetuate as the mode of discourse and decks cleared for future Sino-Pakistani entente-cordiale. Taking advantage of this discourse, Pakistan under a border agreement on 2 March 1963 ceded a portion of "Azad Kashmir" to China. India protested to both China and Pakistan stating its position that it would not agree to any arrangements or agreements on Indian territory which was under 'illegal occupation of Pakistan.' The Indian Government alleged that Pakistan had not given away 2050 square miles but 11,000 square miles of territory according to the data of the Survey of Pakistan. The agreement signified serious strategic implications for India and helped China to have a direct access and attack capability on Kashmir by land via the Karakoram pass and by air via direct Chinese air link to the Gilgit airfield. Islamabad presumed that any attack by India on Pakistan would bring China to its rescue. Pakistan's then Foreign Minister, Z.A. Bhutto declared on 17 July 1963 that, "An attack from India on Pakistan is no longer confined to the security and territorial integrity of Pakistan~ it now involves the territorial integrity and security of the largest state in the Asia as well."

However in the 1965 Indo-Pakistan war, despite assurances to help Pakistan, China did not offer any physical moves and only gave verbal warnings to India. Between 1965 and 1971, Pakistan received USD 200 million worth arms aid from China. Of which, USD 45 million worth of arms were supplied in 1971 alone.

Chinese cultivated relations with Pakistan for two reasons - one, Pakistan was looked upon as a link to the Middle East and two, in the regional initiatives, Chinese strategy was to forge closer links with South Asian countries to create a sub-regional balance to counter the Indian pre-eminence in South Asia. Pakistan sought precisely the kind of countervailing authority that China had willingly provided i.e, convince its special friends, that despite its potential resources, China would never behave like a superpower and within the regional context it was able to project an image of a weighty neighbour, particularly in South Asia.[45]

To strengthen the strategic part of the relations between China and Pakistan, both concluded a comprehensive nuclear cooperation agreement in 1986. Under the agreement, China has committed to support Pakistan in the design, construction, and operation of nuclear reactors and even assist the latter with the enrichment of weapons grade uranium. Besides, it also transferred tritium gas to

Pakistan specifically meant to advance the yield of atomic bombs.[46]

In 1989 China built a 27 MW nuclear research reactor in Pakistan and Pakistani scientists were being trained in China. In the early 1990's China built an un-safeguarded plutonium reprocessing facility at Chashma, which was the chief source of Pakistan's weapon grade Plutonium. In 1995 China build another un-safeguarded reactor at Khushab. The same year China transferred 5000 ring magnets to Pakistan, after which it got exposed and there was a worldwide condemnation of China. In 1996, China transferred an industrial furnace with a casting surface in which the bomb core is cast and helps Pakistani engineers install it in Khushab. The commitment and involvement of China in Pakistan's nuclear programme leads one to believe that in the event of an Indo-Pak conflict, Chinese would align with Pakistan, so long as it remained convinced that neither the US nor the USSR would intervene.[47]

In the aftermath of the end of the cold war, if on the one side, there witnessed sharp reduction in Pakistan's strategic relevance for the United States, but on the other sides, Pakistan move closer to China to compensate for this loss. The post-Cold War global strategic developments have its impact on the relationship between China and Pakistan. Both countries enjoy a multifaceted partnership which ranges from political to economic and trade and from defence and security to nuclear cooperation. In 1996, during the state visit of President Jiang Zemin to Pakistan, the two countries decided to establish a comprehensive friendship. They signed a Treaty of Friendship and Cooperation, to the effect that "neither party will join any alliance or bloc which infringes upon the sovereignty, security and territorial integrity" of either nation or "would not conclude treaties of this nature with any third party." However, the suitable environment was created when China had equipped Pakistan Air Force with F-7P fighter in 1992. On the very same year, China also supplied to Pakistan 34 M-11 battlefield missiles, a solid-fuel variant of the Soviet Scud-B missile.[48]

The growing significance of relations between the two sides can be acknowledged from the historic speech made by Chinese President Jiang Zemin to the Pakistan Senate on December 1996 that underlines that,

> 'Our two peoples have regarded each other as friends in need and brothers bound by common fate, always sympathizing with and supporting each other. The Chinese Government .... stand ready to join the Pakistani side in further solidifying this friendly and cooperative relationship.'[49]

As the relationship gets stronger with every passing year and the Beijing's ensuring security guarantee for Islamabad has only brought significant change in the latter perception towards the former. Pakistan gives strategic importance to its partnership with China. This was very well reflected in the words of Dr Shireen Mazari, "The Peking has not only repudiated to back down on its defence pledges to Islamabad, in spite of Western pressure, but has been about especially responsible for permitting Pakistan a modicum of sufficient defence ability and nuclear development clearly makes China absolutely essential for Pakistan's survival., Pakistan has become extremely casual about its relations with China." Despite U.S. imposition of Pressler Amendment upon Islamabad, China continue to extend support to Islamabad nuclear weapons programme. China was closely working with Pakistan over the development of 9300 Mw power plant at Chasma. Moreover, China has been accused for transferring 500 ring magnets for Pakistan's nuclear facilities.[50]

Pakistan is in no way behind China when it comes to cementing this close strategic partnership. Pakistan is making every effort to ensure that the relationship with China continue to progress unhindered. Pakistan has clout in controlling the Islamic separatist movement in China's Xinjiang Autonomous Region.[51] To show its commitment in this aspect, Pakistan not only killed Hasan Mahsum, the leader of the East Turkestan Islamic Movement (ETIM) in October 2003 but also agreed to conduct a joint anti-terrorism exercise in the province in August 2004.[52]

Pakistan attaches significant importance to its expanding relations with China from the futuristic perspective. As was very rightly pointed out by Lt. Gen. Talat Masood in a way that, "China concluded defence cooperation agreement; supplies were subject to almost no limitations, and Beijing does not look for commercial but for strategic gains from this partnership."[53] In support of what the army general has said, Shen Chun Chuan, an analysts from China is of the view that, "The partnership not only benefited Pakistan military .... China's continued cooperation has greatly contributed towards enhancing the morale of Pakistan's military establishment as also expanding military's influence and role in Pakistan's polity."[54] In fact, Pakistan believes that China provided the much needed force that is crucial to achieving its long cherished aim of capturing Kashmir by pressurising India and if necessary to contain it.[55]

Where the Kashmir issue between India and Pakistan is concerned, it serves China's interest to keep the Kashmir pot boiling, by diverting India's attention from other issues. Beijing has also equipped Islamabad with JF-17 aircraft and JF-17 production facilities, F-22P frigates with helicopters, K-8 jet trainers, T-85 tanks, F-7 aircraft, small arms and ammunition. It has also built a turnkey ballistic missile manufacturing facility near Rawalpindi and helped Pakistan develop the 750-km-range, solid-fuel Shaheen-1 ballistic missile.[56] China's strategy of providing advanced arms and equipment requirements for Pakistan will continue to remain a case of serious national security concerns for India. Details of China's major arms supplies to Pakistan:

Table

China's Major Arms Supplies to Pakistan

Sl. No.	Years of Delivery	Weapon Designation	Weapon Description	No. Ordered/ Delivered
1	–	F-6	Fighter aircraft	100
2	–	A-5-Fantan A	Fighter/ground attack	98
3	1993	F-7M Airguard	Fighter	40
4	–	F-7P Skybolt	Fighter	40
5	2005	FC-1	Fighter	150
6	–	Super 7	Fighter	–
7	1986-90	F7	Fighter	75
8	2002	F7MG	Fighter	57
9	1986	Q5- Fantan-A	Fighter/ground attack	100
10	–	FT-7P	Fighter trainer	15
11	–	K8	Trainer aircraft	–
12	–	Hong Ying-5	Portable surface-to-air missile	300
13	–	Anza	Portable surface-to-air missile	450
14	1994-2000	QW-1 Vanguard	Portable surface-to-air missile	560
15	–	HN-5A	Portable surface-to-air missile	–
16	–	Al-Khalid (P90)	Main battle tank-2000	–
17	1978-90	T-59	Main battle tank	975
18	1991-93	T-69II	Main battle tank	450
19	1993	T-85III	Main battle tank	12
20	1990-2002	Red Arrows 8	Anti-tank missile	200
21	–	Type-56	Towed gun 85 mm	190
22	–	Romeo	Submarine	2
23	–	Hainan-Class	Fast attack craft patrol	3
24	–	Huzhun	Hydrofoil	3

25	–	Huangfen	Fast attack craft patrol	-
26	–	Shanghai	Fast attack craft gun	12
27	–	Hegu	Fast attack craft	4
28	–	Huangfen	Fast attack craft	4
29	–	Hainan	Fast attack craft patrol	4
30	–	Huzhuan	Fast attack craft torpedo	4
31	1997	C-801/802	Ship-to-ship missile system	4
32	1997	C-802	Ship-to-ship missile system	32

Source: Srikanth Kondapalli, "Pakistan in China's Security Perceptions", in Swaran Singh (ed.), *China-Pakistan Strategic Cooperation: Indian Perspectives* (New Delhi: Manohar, 2007), pp. 74-75.

China-Pakistan Strategic Engagement at the Dawn of 21st Century

President Pervez Musharraf during his visit to China in November 2003 said that the China- Pakistan strategic partnership was "deeper than the oceans, higher than the mountains."[57] The China's relations with Pakistan are no more bilateral, but possesses multi-dimensional character.[58] The deepness of the bilateral engagement between the two sides can be reflected from what Pakistan Prime Minister, Shaukat Aziz had said at Islamabad's Institute of Strategic Studies on 27 September 2005 that,

> 'Pakistan and China enjoy all-weather friendship based on complete trust and confidence. Our friendship is rooted in the psyche and ethos of our people. From Khunjrab to Gwadar, the symbols of Pakistan-China friendship dot the landscape. The mega projects that we have undertaken with China's help are like anchors that hold two countries together in trusted friendship.'[59]

Continuing in the two countries' anti-India stance, Pakistan's Foreign Minister Shah Mehmood Qureshi said in 2010 that "Pakistan and China strongly feel that India should not become a permanent member of the United Nations Security Council, as it would disturb the balance of power in the region."[60] Out of the deepening relations, Islamabad expect China to support in its political and military dealing with India and its position on Kashmir. As committed China is providing Pakistan with the much needed help for its national security needs by way of aid and investment. That's the key reason as to why Islamabad attaches significant importance to its engagement with its closeally China.[61]

The events of 11 September 2001 were, however, a turning point in India-United States relations. Since then, the security understanding between the world's two largest democracies has improved significantly. The United States offered civil nuclear cooperation to India and rejected similar cooperation with Pakistan. It has also encouraged India to play a significant role in the reconstruction of Afghanistan, which detracts from Pakistan's objective of gaining strategic depth in that country. For Pakistan, this increases the value of the Chinese friendship that today Islamabad considers China to be the cornerstone of its foreign policy.[62]

In April 2005 China and Pakistan signed a Treaty of Friendship, Cooperation, and Good Neighbourly Relations. The agreement binds the two countries to desist from joining "any alliance or bloc which infringes upon the sovereignty, security, and territorial integrity of the other side."[63] Pakistan's Information Minister Sheikh Rashid Ahmad stated in a TV interview that Pakistan would stand behind China if the United States ever tried to "besiege" it. From Pakistan's perspective, China is a far more reliable partner than the United States, given that the latter in the recent past has been much more committed to strengthening its ties with India.

During President Pervez Musharraf's visit to China in

2006, Beijing committed itself to equip Pakistan with JF-17 (Thunder) aircraft. On 23 May 2006, Pakistan clinched a $600 million defence deal with China, which included the construction of four F-22P frigates for the Pakistan Navy (three to be built in Shanghai and the fourth at the Karachi dockyard), upgrading of the Karachi dockyard, and transfer of technology for the indigenous production of a modern surface fleet.[64] In a move that would further strengthen the already stronger ties with Pakistan, China during the visit of Pakistan's Prime Minister Yousuf Raza Gilani in May this year, has agreed to provide 50 JF-17 thunder aircraft equipped with more sophisticated avionics on easy loan terms.[65]

Since the dawn of the current century, the two countries have committed themselves to further strengthening their economic ties. The visit of Pakistan's Prime Minister Shaukat Aziz in December 2004 and the subsequent visit by the Chinese Premier in April 2005 to Pakistan paved the way for future cooperation. The two sides signed a number of agreements and memoranda of understanding (MoU), after which China provided Pakistan a preferential credit of $500 million, out of which $150 million was for Phase II of the Chashma nuclear power plant. Also, a new Pakistan consulate was opened in Shanghai. The two sides have also taken initial steps towards establishing a free trade area, by cancelling tariffs on 767 items. China-Pakistan trade has expanded rapidly from $1.4 billion in 2001 to $5 billion in 2006.[66] China is engaged in 120 projects with Pakistan such as heavy engineering, power generation, mining and telecommunications, and expects its investment in Pakistan to grow from $4 billion in 2007 to $15 billion by 2010.[67] During the visit of Premier Wen Jiabao to Pakistan in 2011 the two sides signed agreements for thirty-five new pacts. These pacts may bring $30 billion investment to Pakistan over the next five years from China.[68]

On the other side, India-China trade volume has improved significantly, from $2.9 billion in 2000 to $61 billion in 2010, compared to $1.16 billion to $7 billion over the same period with Pakistan.[69] Nevertheless, China's long-term interest of restraining India from gaining international space is certain to prevail over the short-term interest of expanding trade and other ties with India.

Chinese Nuclear Cooperation with Pakistan and Proliferation Concerns

By entering into a civilian nuclear agreement, the United States has not strengthened India's missile and nuclear programmes because India has agreed to separation of civilian facilities from that of the military facilities, thereby voluntarily placing all the civilian facilities under the IAEA safeguards. By entering into the civilian nuclear initiative, India's interests do not lies in undermining the non-proliferation regime, but to strengthen the regime. India's commitment to preventing the proliferation of Weapons of Mass Destructions (WMDs) is justified by its impeccable record of not transferring any of its nuclear related technology and materials to the third countries.[70] Regardless, China supported Pakistan in its ambitions of acquiring nuclear and missile programmes by violating international commitments. Even after joining the Nuclear Non-Proliferation Treaty (NPT) in 1992 China has engaged in nuclear and missile cooperation with Pakistan.[71] Pakistan continues to be the major beneficiary of China's unending support to acquire nuclear materials and technology. Arms-control advocate Gary Milhollin has very rightly pointed out that, "If you subtract China's help from Pakistan's nuclear program, there is no nuclear program."[72]

By supporting Islamabad in its nuclear weapons programme, Beijing has sent an indirect message to Washington that if you can do this for your partner (India) then why I should desist from doing the same for my long time ally (Pakistan). Shen Dingli, a nuclear security expert and Vice President of Institute of International Studies at Fudan University accused Washington of "contributing to nuclear proliferation" as "New Delhi can now devote its resources and energy to the research and development of nuclear weapons...Wouldn't it be possible for other nuclear states to cooperate with Pakistan in the development of nuclear energy? Pakistan...has a need to develop civil nuclear energy and the right to do so..."[73]

Pakistan, it may be noted, has an execrable record of nuclear proliferation. China's Foreign Ministry spokesman Qin Gang has repeatedly dismissed such concerns by claiming that "Civilian nuclear energy cooperation between China and Pakistan is completely in line with international obligations of non-proliferation, and is completely meant for peaceful purposes."[74]

It was during his visit to India, retired Israeli Army General, Shalom Harari has alleged Pakistan for nuclear proliferation in the Arab World. He said that,

> "Israel recently got information that Pakistan was supporting the nuclear weapons program of Syria by supplying it some of the key components." He further added that "Pakistani and its nuclear scientist A Q Khan were involved in Libyan nuclear program. Khan was involved in the Uranium program by supplying them atomic detonators. Pakistan is actually the main proliferators of atomic bombs in the Middle East to Islamic states."[75]

In future too, the possibility of Pakistan proliferating nuclear components and technological know-how cannot be ruled out. Therefore, China should think twice before moving ahead for any kind of nuclear cooperation with Pakistan, because it would face a serious threat to international peace and security.

Conclusion

China looms large on India's relations with Pakistan. India has in recent years gained significant weight on the international stage by virtue of its growing economic and military prowess, but Pakistan and China share a very strong desire to halt India's progress in this direction. In fact India has been the main factor that has influenced China and Pakistan policies toward each other. The two sides have a close understanding on the need to enhance strategic coordination, advance pragmatic cooperation and work together to meet challenges in pursuit of common development. Pakistan in particular viewed India as a potential challenger leading to use China to counter Indian power in the region.

China's position on Kashmir can't be delinked from its ever expanding relations with Pakistan. Although, the China's positions on Kashmir have not always been characterised by pro-Pakistan, but with expanding involvement in PoK, it can be expected that China would support its close ally ahead of India with which both Pakistan and China doesn't enjoy close relations.[76] By considering Kashmir as disputed territory between the two South Asian neighbours, China seems to reject Indian claim that Kashmir is its integral part.

References

1. Kerry B. Dumbaugh, "Exploring the China-Pakistan Relationship", Roundtable Report Prepared by CNA China Studies, June 2010, p. 5.

2. Aditi Malhotra, "The Red Shadow in Pakistan Occupied Kashmir", Scholar Warrior, Autumn 2011, p. 74.

3. Syed Waqas Haider Bukhari and Tahira Parveen, "China's Approach Towards Kashmir Conflict: A Viable Solution", Journal of Professional Research in Social Sciences, Vol. 1, No. 1, July 2014, p. 14.

4. Anil Kamboj, "Creation of Pakistan Occupied Kashmir and Present Scenario", World Focus, Vol. XXXVIII, No. 7, July 2017, p. 10 and Kewal Krishan, "India, Pakistan and China Border Dispute With Special Reference to Jammu and

Kashmir", Journal of Global Research and Analysis, Vol. 3, No. 2, December 2014, p. 4.

5. Ibid., p. 15.

6. Jabin T. Jacob, "China and Kashmir", p. 19, available at *<https://www.ideals.illinois.edu/bitstream/handle/2142/15471/China_and_Kashmir.pdf?sequence=2>.<https://www. ideals. illinois. edu/bitstream/handle/2142/15471/China_and_Kashmir. pdf?sequence=2>.*

7. Syed Waqas Haider Bukhari and Tahira Parveen, n. 1, pp. 15-16.

8. Prashant Kumar Singh, "Revisiting China's Kashmir Policy", IDSA Comment, available at *<https://idsa.in/idsacomments/Revisiting Chinas Kashmir Policy_pksingh_011110>.*

9. Mohan Malik, "The China Factor in the India-Pakistan Conflict", Parameters, Spring 2003, pp. 35-6.

10. Refer to, "India and Future Global Order", Paper produced at the Section for Policy Planning in the Department for Security Policy, Norwegian Ministry of Defense, November 2009, pp. 17-18, available at *<http://www.regjeringen.no/upload/FD/Dokumenter/India-studie_ssek_301109.pdf>.*

11. Lisa Curtis, "China's Military and Security Relationship with Pakistan", Testimony before the U.S.-China Economic and Security Review Commission, 20 May 2009, available at *<http://www.heritage.org/research/testimony/chinas-military-and-security-relationship-with-pakistan>.*

12. Harsh V. Pant, "The Pakistan Thorn in China-India-U.S. Relations", Washington Quarterly, Vol. 35, No. 1, Winter 2012, pp. 85-6.

13. T.V Paul, "Chinese-Pakistani Nuclear/Missile Ties and Balance of Power Politics", The Nonproliferation Review, Vol. 10, No. 2, Summer 2003, p. 24.

14. A S Chonker, "An Eye For an Eye - The Answer to the Chinese Predicament in Jammu And Kashmir", Claws Article, No. 1835, 8 December 2017, available at *<http://*

www.claws.in/1835/an-eye-for-an-eye-the-answer-to-the-chinese-predicament-in-jammu-and-kashmir-as-chonker.html>.

15. Quoted from "Chinese Troops Around Kashmir Posing Threat", Canadian Asian News, Vol. 15, No. 197, 15-30 April 2011, pp. 1 and 3.
16. Syed Waqas Haider Bukhari and Tahira Parveen, n. 1, p. 16.
17. Bahauddin Foizee, 'Kashmir's Geopolitical Significance is Growing Day by Day', Geopolitical Monitor, 24 May 2018, available at <*https://www.geopoliticalmonitor.com/kashmirs-geopolitical-significance-is-growing-by-the-day/*>.
18. B. Raman was quoted in Banyan, "China and Kashmir – The Chinese Connection", The Economist, 29 August 2010, available at <*https://www.economist.com/banyan/2010/08/29/the-chinese-connection*>.
19. J. Korbel, Danger in Kashmir (New Jersey: Princeton University Press, 1966), p. 331.
20. Monika Chansoria, op cit., pp. 75-6.
21. Syed Waqas Haider Bukhari and Tahira Parveen, op cit., pp. 19-20.
22. Monika Chansoria, "China's Current Kashmir Policy: Steady Crystallisation", Claws Journal, Winter 2016, pp. 68-9.
23. Ahmad Bhatty Maqbool, "China's Emerging Role in the World", Peace Initiatives Vol. V, No. III-VI, May -December 1999, p. 163.
24. The Hindu, 14th January 2002.
25. Kissing Contemporary Archives, (London, 1949), p. 104.
26. Aziz Qutubuddin, "Relations between Pakistan and People's Republic of China", in Ahmed Sherwani Latif, (ed.), Foreign Policy of Pakistan (Karachi, 1964), p. 82.
27. Pervaiz Ali Mahesar, Ali Khan Ghumro, Ghulam Mushtafa Khuskh and Abdul Hamid Mahesar, " International Journal of Scientific Research and Innovative Technology, Vol. 3, No. 3, March 2016, p. 23.

28. Farzana Shakoor, "The Kargil Crisis: An Analysis", Pakistan Horizon, Vol. 52, No. 3, July 1999, p. 61.

29. Syed Waqas Haider Bukhari and Tahira Parveen, op cit., p. 21.

30. John Garver views on China's Policy towards Kashmir was quoted in Savita Pande, "Sino-Pakistan Strategic Relationship : Implications for India", Scholar Warrior, Autumn 2015, p. 19

31. Jingdong Yuan, "China's Kashmir Policy", China Brief, Vol. 5, No. 19, September 2005.

32. Syed Waqas Haider Bukhari and Tahira Parveen, op cit., pp. 15-16.

33. See, 'Pakistan Occupied Kashmir: Changing the Discourse', IDSA PoK Project Report, New Delhi, May 2011, p. 9.

34. Ibid., p. 11.

35. Anil Kamboj, "Creation of Pakistan Occupied Kashmir and Present Scenario", World Focus, Vol. XXXVIII, No. 7, July 2017, p. 11.

36. Aditi Malhotra, "The Red Shadow in Pakistan Occupied Kashmir", Scholar Warrior, Autumn 2011, p. 74.

37. Jaiveer Singh Negi, "Gilgit-Baltistan-China-Pakistan-Economic Corridor: Implications for India", in Sanjay Kumar et al. (eds.), India-Pakistan Relations: Past, Present and Future, New Delhi: G B Books Publishers and Distributors, 2018.

38. Bahauddin Foizee, n. 17.

39. M. Ganapathi, "Contours of India's Foreign Policy: An Overview", Indian Foreign Affairs Journal, Vol. 12, No. 1, Jan-March 2017, p. 49.

40. Avinash Godbole, "India-China Relation: Enhancing Engagement Promises Better Future", which featured in a debate titled, 'Future Trajectory of Sino-Indian Relations', Indian Foreign Affairs Journal, Vol. 11, No. 1, Jan-Mar 2016, p. 16.

41. Monika Chansoria, "China's Current Kashmir Policy: Steady Crystallisation", Claws Journal, Winter 2016, p. 70.

42. Ibid., pp. 71-72.

43. Anil Kamboj, op cit., p. 12.

44. Netajee Abhinandan, "Turbulence in PoK: The China Factor", World Focus, Vol. XXXVIII, No. 7, July 2017, p. 53.

45. O. P. Gulia, "History of India-Pakistan Relations Through Chinese Prism", in Sanjay Kumar et al. (eds.), India-Pakistan Relations: Past, Present and Future New Delhi: G B Books Publishers and Distributors, 2018.

46. Aparna Pande, Explaining Pakistan's Foreign Policy: Escaping India, New York: Routledge, 2011.

47. O. P. Gulia, op cit.

48. Ahmad Faruqui, "The Complex Dynamics of Pakistan's Relationship with China," Islamabad Policy Research Institute, Summer 2001, *<http://www.ipripak.org/journal/summer2001/thecomplex.shtml>*.

49. Jiang Zemin Speech titled, "Carrying Forward Generations of Friendly and Good Neighbourly Relations and Endeavoring Towards a Better Tomorrow for all", Islamabad, 2 December 1996.

50. Muhammad Ishaque Fani, "Pakistan-China Security Relations and Mutual Ventures", JRSP, vol. 46, No. 2, 2009, p. 81-6.

51. Urvashi Aneja, "Pakistan-China Relations: Recent Developments (Jan-May 2006)", IPCS Special Report 26, June 2006, p. 2, *<http://www.ipcs.org/pdf_file/issue/1365648021PCS Special-Report-26.pdf>*; also refer John W. Garver, "The Future of the Sino-Pakistan Entente Cordiale", n. 6, pp. 389-90.

52. Tariq Mahmud Ashraf, "Future Sino-Pak Relations and the War on Terrorism", *<http://www.grandestrategy.com/2008/04/future-sino-pak-relations-and-war-on.html>*.

53. Talat Masood, "Guns vs. butter: Finding the balance," The News (Islamabad), February 18, 1996.

54. Shen Chun-Chuan, "Peking's Relations with India and Pakistan", Issues & Studies, Vol. 25 No. 9, September 1989, p. 32.
55. Rakesh Datta, "The Kargil War-China Factor", in Rajendra Nath (ed.), Musharraf's War, New Delhi: Lancer's Books, 2003, p. 236.
56. Lisa Curtis, "China's Military and Security Relationship with Pakistan", Testimony before the U.S.-China Economic and Security Review Commission, 20 May 2009, *<http://www.heritage.org/research/testimony/chinas-military-and-security-relationship-with-pakistan>*.
57. Robert G. Wirsing, "The Enemy of my Enemy: Pakistan's China Debate", Asia-Pacific Center for Security Studies Special Assessment, December 2003, p. 4, *<http://www.apcss.org/Publications/SAS/ChinaDebate/China Debate_ Wirsing.pdf>*.
58. Kerry B. Dumbaugh, "Exploring the China-Pakistan Relationship", Roundtable Report Prepared by CNA China Studies, June 2010, p. 2.
59. Swaran Singh, "Introduction", in Swaran Singh (ed.), China-Pakistan Strategic Cooperation: Indian Perspectives (New Delhi: Manohar, 2007), p. 22.
60. See "India in UNSC? No Way, Say Pakistan, China", *<http://www.rediff.com/news/slide-show/slide-show-1-pak-china-unite-against-indias-unsc-bid/20101113.htm>*.
61. Kerry B. Dumbaugh, n. 43, p. 4.
62. "U.S.-China Relations: Seeking Strategic Convergence in Pakistan", n. 7, p. 1.
63. See "Text of Pak China Joint Statement", October 17, 2008, n. 5.
64. Urvashi Aneja, n. 14, pp. 3-5.
65. Sanjeev Kumar, "PM Gilani Visit to China: Symbolic or Substantive", Indian Council of World Affair, New Delhi, 26 May 2011, *<http://www.icwa.in/pdfs/VPGilaniVisit.pdf>*.
66. Bhatty, "China's Peaceful Rise and South Asia", n. 4, p. 33.
67. Jamal Afridi, "China-Pakistan Relations", *<http://www.*

pakistantalk.com/forums/strategic-issues/3953-china-pakistan-relations.html>.

68. R.N. Das, "China's 'All-Weather Friendship' with Pakistan: Implications for India", IDSA Comment, New Delhi, 4 January 2011, <*http://www.idsa.in/idsacomments/Chinas allweatherfriendship withPakistanImplicationsforIndia_rndas_ 040111*>.

69. Isaac B. Kordon, "China and Pakistan: Emerging Strains in the Entente Cordiale", Project 2049 Institute, Arlington, Virginia, 25 March 2011, p. 11.

70. Devki Nandan, "Sino-Pak Nuclear Nexus and India's Concerns", Centre for Air Power Studies Issue Brief, 16 July 2010, pp. 1-3.

71. Upendra Choudhury, "The Indo-USA Nuclear Deal and its Impact on India's Ballistic Missile Programme", South Asian Strategic Studies Institute Research Report 17, June 2008, pp. 16-17, <*kms1.isn.ethz.ch/serviceengine/Files/ISN/99928/.../RR+No+17.pdf*>.

72. Harsh V. Pant, "The Pakistan Thorn in China-India-U.S. Relations", Washington Quarterly, Vol. 35, No. 1, Winter 2012, pp. 85-6.

73. Sherry W. Wangwhite, "China's Reactions to the India Deal: Implications for the United States", Thesis Submitted to the Naval Postgraduate School, Monterey, California, December 2007, pp. 63-4.

74. Issam Ahmed, "China-Pakistan Deal Raises Fears of Nuclear Proliferation", <*http://www.csmonitor.com/World/Asia-South-Central/2010/0701/China-Pakistan-deal-raises-fears-of-nuclear-proliferation*>.

75. Refer to "Pakistan Supporting Syrian Nuclear Programme: Ex-Israeli Army Gen", Indian Express, 13 November 2011, available at <*http://www.indianexpress.com/news/pak-supporting-syrian-nuclear-programme-exisraeli-army-gen/875154/*>.

76. Jabin T. Jacob, n. 6.

4

China's Water Strategy

Water, one of the most essential components for life is needed to ensure food security, feed livestock,progress industrial production and to conserve the biodiversity and environment. Growing human population, severe neglect coupled with over-exploitation of the resource and gross mismanagement, is making it a scarce commodity - forcing the world to gradually move towards potable water crisis. 'The 2030 Water Resources Group'in 2009 revealed that globally, the current withdrawals of water of about 4500 km^3 exceed the availability of about 4200 km^3 [1]. By 2030 a global deficit of 40% is forecast[2]. Asian sub-continent being the driest continent considering its population density and availability of fresh water reserve would continue to witness intra- state and inter- state stresses to meet its water demands, leading to internal and external tensions, especially in case of trans border rivers.

China is the biggest trans-border water provider in the world. Waters from China flow down to India, Pak, Kyrgyzstan, Kazakhstan, Russia, Bangladesh (BD) and the SE Asian nation'sup to Vietnam. The demand of water for economic and industrial growth is increasing every year;coupled with it is the rising pollution of existing water sources, resulting in reduction of per capita availability of fresh water. China being water abundant nation has minimal external water dependency unlike India which has 33.4% external dependency[3] being a lower riparian State. It is pertinent to mention that North and NE China is water scarce with 2/3rd of crop lands, in contrast to Southern China which is water abundant with 1/3rd of crop lands. It is in this context that China hasembarked upon the biggest hydraulic initiative of diverting the waters from South to address the existing and foreseeable water crisis in its Northern regions.

S No	Country	External flow Mn/ m^3	Total Mn/ m^3	External Dependency (% age)
1.	China	17,169	28,40,000	0.90 %
2.	India	6,47,220	19,07,760	33.40 %
3.	Pak	1,70,300	2,25,300	75.59 %
4.	Bangladesh	11,05,644	12,10,644	91.30 %
5.	Vietnam	5,24,710	8,91,210	58.90 %

All the lower riparian States and the related biodiversity would have an adverse impact if the waters of Indo- China trans-border rivers were to be diverted to Northern China.It is, therefore, axiomatic that the major water diversion projects by China on itstrans-border river, Tsangpo/ Brahmaputra, are analysed thoroughly to infer its impact on India and measures to be instituted to overcome the same, which this Paper attempts to.

Part I : Tibet & Trans Border Rivers

Tibet's high altitude, huge land mass and vast glaciers endow it with the greatest river system in the world. Tibetan plateau with 46,000 glaciers at an average altitude of 13000 ft is the earth's 3rd largest ice mass[4]. The net hydrological flows in Tibet are 627km^3/ yr out of which 577 km^3 flow into other countries (92%). Given the low precipitation in Tibet, higher proportion of river flows originates from the glaciers. The Tibetan Plateau is the greatest water system globally and is the primary fresh water resource to Northern India and China (Yellow R and Yangtse R) which are the most populous and fast growing economies in the region. China and India with eight other SE Asian nations and 47% of the world's population are heavily dependent on the Tibetan waters[5].

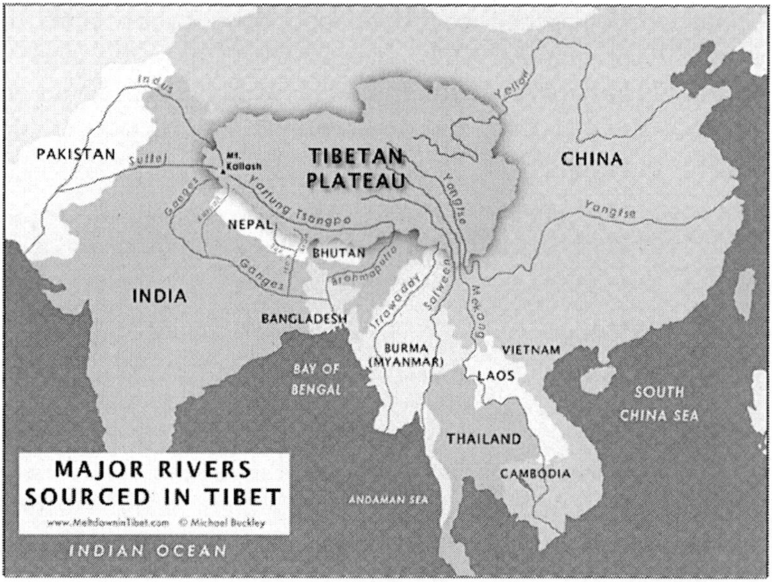

Six major Asian river basins begin in the Tibetan Plateau: the Indus (India, Pakistan); the Ganges (Nepal, India, Bangladesh); the Brahmaputra (India, Bangladesh); the Salween (China, Burma, Thailand); the Mekong (China, Laos, Thailand, Cambodia, Vietnam); and the Yangtze (China)[6]— Tibet is without question "the most incredible water tank one can imagine[7]." Indus, Sutlej and Tsangpo/ Brahmaputra are the

	ORIGIN	TIBET	INDIA	PAK/ B'DESH
INDUS (3180 KM)	Mt Kailash	358 KM	1114 KM	1708 KM (PAK)
SUTLEJ (1450 KM)	Raka Lake	240 KM	680 KM	526 KM (PAK)
MATSANG TSANGPO/ BRAHMAPUTRA (2880 KM)	Angsi Glacier/ Mansarovar Lake	1625 KM	918 KM	337 KM (B'DESH)

three major Indo-China trans-bdr rivers originating from the Chinese controlled Tibetan plateau. Additionally Karnali and Arun are the other two major rivers originating from Tibet which join the Ganges after draining through Nepal.Water discharge of Indus, Sutlej and the Brahmaputra, the three significant rivers,which originate in TAR, is a matter of concern for India. While the waters of Indus and Sutlej drain into Arabian Sea through Pak, Brahmaputra transits its course through the North Eastern States and Bangladesh before draining into the Bay of Bengal.

More than 60% of water in all the three rivers is added due to rainfall and other tributaries after they enter India. Most significantly 66.7% of the waters in Tsangpo are added post it enters India as Siang, while traversing 918 km with catchment area of 34%. This is primarily due to pattern in annual rainfall which in Tibet is 400mm and India is 3000mm,significantly increasing the water inflow into Brahmaputra. The data generated by Chinese writings depict annual flow of 168.9 BCM (Billion Cubic mtrs) of Tsangpo into India, whereas as per the Indian estimates it is 200 BCM.The Chinese plan of diverting 118 BCM of these waters towards Chinese main land would result in significant depletion in the waters of Brahmaputra, directly impacting the downstream navigation, ecology, irrigation patterns and fertility of land. The number of projects on Tsangpohasalso increased significantly from 28 in 2008 to 39 in 2012. China claims that these projects are 'run of the river' with no major lakes being formed; still the effect on downstream India is significant to raise concerns.

Part II: China-Necessity of Water Diversion

Asia's Water Problem

The availability of freshwater in Asia is not even half of the global annual average of 6,380 m^3 per inhabitant making it the driest continent in the world[8]. When the estimated reserve of rivers, lakes, and aquifers are added up,

Asia has less than one-tenth of the waters of South America, Australia and New Zealand, not even one-fourth of North America, almost one-third of Europe, and moderately less than Africa per inhabitant. Yet the world's fastest growing demand for water, for food, industrial production and for municipal support is in Asia, which now serves as the locomotive of the world economy[9].

The world's global water demand is set to increase by 55% in next 30 years. Asia continues to draw on tomorrow's water to meet today's needs. Worse still, Asia has one of the lowest levels of water efficiency and productivity in the world. Against this background, it is no exaggeration to say that 'water scarcity is set to become the defining crisis of Asia by the mid century, creating obstacles in the path of its continued rapid development, economic growth and its environmental sustainability'[10].

Chinese Water Crisis

Water Facts: China is one of the 13 countries that faces acute water crisis in the world. The per capita water share in China is 2300 m^3, which is *1/4th* of the worlds average or 121st in the world. 70% of the rainfall in China precipitates in four months, and over 2/3rd of that water is wasted in floods and free flow. There has been five times increase in water usage in China since 1949[11], further worsening the water situation. It also has a demographic problem - it hosts 20% of the world's population and holds 6% of the world's water resources. China is, thus, hard-pressed to implement the Brahmaputra project as an answer to its growing water woes arising from uneven distribution of water resources, demographic explosion, industrial upsurge, rapid expansion of cities, and greater demand for irrigated agriculture farming[12].

Uneven Distribution of Water Resources: The per capita water availability in Northern China is only 757 m^3/yr, less than 1/4th of Southern China. A study by UN pegs[13]

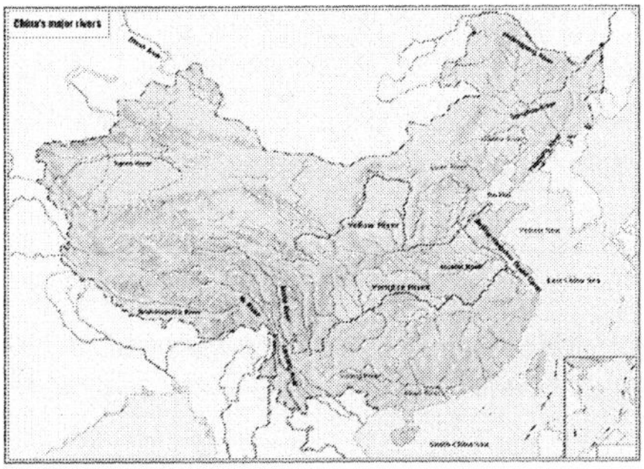

countries and regions with water availability per capita below 1,000 m^3/ yearas 'water scarce' regions. The average rainfall in South is 2000 mm/year in contrast to the average rainfall in North ie,200- 400 mm/yr. Resultantly, Yellow R (Northern China)supports 550 mnpeople and 2/3rd of the crop lands, but has supply of only 1/5th of the water; whereas the Yangtse R (Southern China) supports 700 mn people, 1/3rd of the crop land and has supply of upto 4/5th of China's total water. On an average, 70% of the total water extractions in the world are to support agriculture, which explains the water scarcity in the Northern regions of China.

Primitive Irrigation Practices: The resource imbalance coupled with primitive irrigation practices of ponded water culture - main source of evaporation (wastage of fresh water) results in poor productivity. China uses 66% more water than any developed country for producing same amount of wheat. Over 1/5th of the China's crop land suffer from salineness (accumulation of highly soluble sodium, magnesium and potassium salts), which are left behind due to evaporation. Today only 5% of Chinese have adapted to modern irrigation practice of drip and sprinkler irrigation system, which ensure optimum utilization of water for grain productivity and nullifies salineness due to excessive evaporation.

Pollution: Currently, 45000 Mn tons of untreated wastewater enter China's rivers every year. Approx 700mn, more than half of China's population, consume drinking water contaminated with animal, industrial and human waste. 80% of domestic and industrial waste water is released untreated in the rivers in China which has badly polluted

88% rivers of PRC; many of them are biologically dead, unfit even for industrial and agricultural use. At an average 25Km^3 of water in China becomes unfit for consumption every year[14] due to pollution there by aggravating its water scarcity.

Desertification: Desertification has taken place at an alarming rate and has gobbled up almost 18% of China's landmass. Xinjiang province (16,60,000 sq km) is primarily dry land because of its distance from the ocean. It has 570 rivers that flow inland andsurface water reserve available is 5800 crore m^3. Annual desertification rate has been registered at 350 sq km and if this desertification continues to spread eastwards; the most densely populated area in the world may turn into desert before arrival of the next century.

Living Standards: According to US Agricultural Department, Chinese consumption of meat has quadrupled in last 30 yrs. The production of same amount of meat protein is 10 times more water intensive than the plant protein, eg, a kg of chicken requires 3,900 litres of water, a kg of pork 4,900 litres and a kg of beef 15,000 litres[15]. Urbanization drive undertaken to propel the economy is set to increase the middle class having a multiplication effect on domestic water wastage due to washing machines and dish washers. It will also increase the number of high water consuming industries.

Effect : Water Shortage: The water resource usage is expected to peak in 2030 when the population peaks. This coupled with increase in pollution, poor discipline in management of potable water and effects of global warming would put undue strain on existing water resources which hasforced the Chinese think tanks to consider the water diversion projects from South to North in an attempt to solve the problem.It is noteworthy that 92% water of the Tibetan rivers flow into South and South East Asia, hence firstly; it is logical to think of diverting the water resources of Tibet to quench the thirst of main land China, secondly; any water diversion project amounting to reduction in the water flow of Tsangpo/ Brahmaputra, Mekong or Salween would affect the complete South Asian region and has a possibility of creating tensions between neighbours who share the waters of Tibetan trans-border rivers.

Part III : Water Diversion Projects in China – An Analysis

Historical Perspective

The Chinese psyche has historically laid great value in dreaming and commissioning grand schemes under their emperor of the time. Claude Arpimentions that this mentality lead to creation of the Great Wall, the grand cnl, Three Gorges dam,Gromo-Lhasa Railway Line and now the South-North Water Diversion Projand the Great Western Diversion[16]. China has been known to make canals and divert water historically. The Grand Canal, also known as the Beijing-Hangzhou Grand Canal, is the longest canal (1,776 km) or artificial river in the world. Starting at Beijing, it passes through Tianjin and the provinces of Hebei, Shandong, Jiangsu and Zhejiang to the city of Hangzhou linking the Yellow R and Yangtze R. The oldest parts of the canal date back to the 5th century BC, although the various sections were finally combined during the Sui Dynasty (581-618 AD).

South-North Water Project

The Project: The South-North Water Projecthas three routes- Western, Central and Eastern and is the biggest hydraulic initiative undertaken by China. It forms part of the 10 biggest construction projects costing above 27 Bn in the world. *The project is to link Yangtse R, Yellow R, Huaihe Rand Haihe R sys with the overall aim to provide water to*

Beijing, Tianjin, Hebei, Henan and Shangdong with the cost of $ 62 Bn[17]. It envisages diversion of 44.8 Bn m3 of water annually (Eastern- 14.8 BCM, Central - 13 BCM and Western - 17 BCM).

- **Eastern Route**: Construction on the Eastern route officially began on December 27, 2002, and water was to reach Tianjin by 2012.It basically consists of an upgrade of the Grand Canal. Water from the Yangtze R is proposed to be drawn into the canal in Jiangdu, which has a giant 400 m^3/s pumping station and then pumped up by stations along the Grand Canal and through twohorizontal tunnels, 9.3 m diameter 70 m long[18], under the Yellow R, from where it can flow downhill to reservoirs near Tianjin. The route is expected to initially provide water for the provinces of Shandong, Jaingsu and Anhui. The completed line will be slightly over 1,152 km long, equipped with 23 pumping stations with a power capacity of 454 MW taking 14.8 BCM of water to Tianjin.
- **Central Route**: The route is from Danjiangkou Reservoir on Han R (tributary of Yangtse R), to Beijing. This route is built on the North China plains and, once the Yellow R has been crossed, water would flow to Beijing by gravity. The construction on this route began in 2003/04 and by 2008, the 307 km long northern stretch of the Central Route was completed at a cost of US $ 2 bn. The whole project was expected to be completed around 2010; this has recently been set back to 2014 to allow for more environmental protections to be built. The completed line will be approx 1,267 km long, providing 9.5 BCM of water annually and subsequently 12 to 13 BCM annually.
- **Western Route**: The route is also called the Big Western Line which involves diversion of internal rivers of China. It aims to divert 17 BCM of water

from the headwaters of the Yangtze R (the Tontian, Yalong and DaduRs) into the headwaters of the Yellow R. To move the water through the drainage divide between these rivers, huge dams and long tunnels are needed to cross the Qinghai-Tibetan Plateau and Western Yunnan Plateaus. The Tongtian diversion line would be 289 km long, the Yalong 131 km, and the Dadu 30 km.

Project Controversy: Since the introduction of the South – North Project, it has created widespread controversy. Opponents object to it on the grounds that it is a waste of resources and would create large number of migrant people.It could waste massive quantity of water through evaporation and pollution and the project's huge cost would make the water prohibitively expensive for consumers[19]. The dry season could cause the Yangtze R to suffer from water shortages and would be detrimental to Yangtze R's inland transportation.

The Great Western Diversion

General: It is assessed by experts that Yangtse waters alone would not be adequate to flush out/ rejuvenate the sluggish Yellow R and solve North China's water problem. This impelled the Chinese leadership to launch the gigantic inter connected scheme of *damming YarlungTsangpo (Brahmaputra), Salween, Mekong and tributaries of Yangtse (as per Western Route) and transfer their waters to North China along the Great Western Route*[20]. The project was the brain child of Gao Kai, a veteran hydrographer, who researched on the project for 17 years[21]. It was in 1988, the PLA got interested in the project and Zhang Jinong (Minister for Water Resources) established the Preparatory Committee. The first official survey was conducted in May - Jun 1999 in form of an expedition; its report was prepared and presented on 07 Oct 2000 which received supportof the State Council, PRC's highest state institution and accorded its approval. The survey approved the feasibility and concluded the water source to be stable and secure[22].

The Project: The project is named as Shoutian[23] - 'Shou'- from SHOUMATAN (gorge near Tsethang in Central Tibet where the first dam to intercept YarlungTsangpo will be built) and 'Tian' – from TIANJIN, (terminal point where the Yellow R merges in the Yellow Sea). 'The Great Western Diversion Project'envisages diversion of the Tsangpo, Mekong and Salween trans-border rivers to Yellow R and the arid NW and Northern regions of China at an estimated cost of $ 125.4 Bn. Out of this, 118.80 BCM is proposed to be drawn from Tsangpo, 48 BCM from Salween and 30 BCM from Mekong. The length of the route is likely to be 1339 km, with eight tunnels (longest- 60 Km). If implemented, it would supply water to 65% of the Chinese territory.

Yellow R- Its Significance: This project will enable diversion of water to the Yellow R, which according to Mao Tse Tung is the most important waterway in China. The river has only 2% of the water flow of the rivers in China, but it irrigates 15% of the entire China's agricultural fields.Despite this, the Chinese have treated the river shabbily; approx 13 Crore Cubic m of waste is dumped into Yellow R annually. Sedimentation through sand deposition has seen lowering of its depth from 6 to 13 m in last 50 yrs.

The Plan: There are many versions of the plan to divert waters of Tsangpo/ Brahmaputra, the most logical is as under :-

- **First** - to create a reservoir on Tsangpo by damming it to divert enough volume of water northwards and canalising water towards end of the Great Bend towards Medog, for generation of 40,000 MW of hydro power.

- **Sec** - create a system of tunnels and canals and pump water from the reservoir with the help of the power generated to Yellow R through the Salween, Mekong, Jinsang and DaduRs.
- **Third**- create reservoir at Lajia Gorge (Yellow R) ; pump up water to Qinghai Lake making Lajia and Qinghai as major reservoirs.
- **Fourth** - canalise waters from Qinghai lake to East Turkestan towards Tarim Basin, Urmqi and Karamay; to Inner Mongolia towards Badian desert; and along the Yellow R to Tianjin.

Hydropower at the Great Bend- Concern for India: The project involves a tunnelto be created to divert the water before the Great Bendto the end of the bend which would be 15- 20 km[24] (min distance as per google earth is 37 km) with a drop in altitude of 2500 m[25] reducing the distance of flow from 200 km (across the complete bend) to 37 km. The

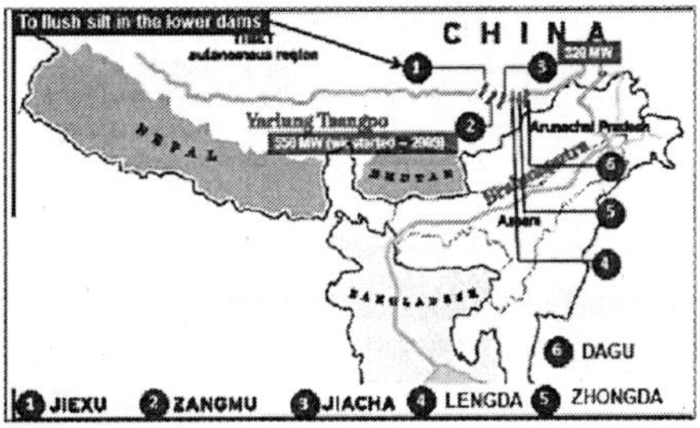

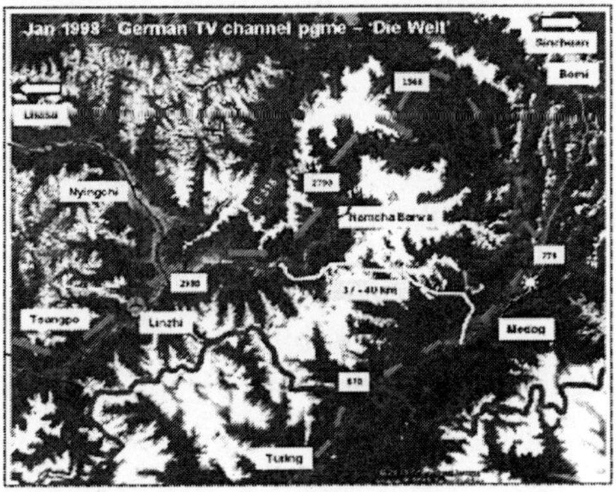

energy created by the water in such short distance would allow generation of 40,000 MW[26]. This power is proposed to pump water through the mountains up North into the Western Route of the diversion plan. Lake created as a result of the project would be more than 100 km upstream and would extend upto the Kongpo region. China has already connected Medog through a roadto Eastern Highway and has clear intentions on embarking on this project as depicted in the National Power Grid Plan - China 2020[27].

The Nuclear Angle: In 1995, the Chinese Academy for Engineers and Physics after study of the project concluded that tunnelling for diversion of Tsangpo waters for 'The Great Western Route' was possible only through nuclear explosions. It is may be recalled that the US and erstwhile USSR carried at least 155 Peaceful Nuclear explosions (PNEs) from 1961- 1988[28], and concluded that PNEs were the best for large scale excavations as the energy released by the lowest nuclear explosion was more beneficial than the largest conventional explosion. Though no PNE has been carried out across the world for the last 15 yrs, the precedent does give justification to China for use of nuclear explosion in their national interest.

Chinese Behaviour on Trans-Border Rivers

Damming of Tsangpo/ Brahmaputra : China has already dammed various tributaries of Tsangpo; there are four projects above 1000 KW already functioning. China has planned six projects on the main stream with Jiexu being the upper most; waters of which will be used for flushing silt from the lower dams. The details are shown in the figure alongside.

Salween River: Salween is a free flowing trans-borderriver into Myanmar from China which has not been dammed till now. China has been carrying out feasibility study for multiple power projects on the river. Myanmar also carried out the study and started rehabilitation of people from the project site; resentment and protests by the people and environmentalists forced the Chinese companies to halt the project. China finally has announced 13 projects on the river, five of which have been earmarked as priority in the 2001-15 five year plan.

Mekong River: The Mekong River originates in Tibet, flows through Myanmar (Burma), Laos, Thailand, Cambodia and Vietnam, before finally discharging into the South China Sea. China is engaged in an extensive programme of dam-building on the river and has already constructed five dams with varying capacities on the river. All countries on the Mekong River watershed, with the notable exceptions of China and Myanmar (Burma), belong to the Mekong River Commission (MRC). In developing the upper Mekong for navigation and hydropower projects, China has acted unilaterally and without consultation with downstream nations[29].

Critical Analysis: Great Water Diversion Project

There are divergent views in the Chinese govt about the feasibility of the project; critics feel itmay be impractical due to the u/m issues:-

(a) Since Yellow R cannot receive such influx of water, a reservoir would have to be made on the river and a number of existing lakes would have to be connected (Qinghailake and Erhai lake). Wang Hao (Engineer in Chief of China Institute of Water Resources and Hydropower Research) opined that - the 300 m high Dam would have to be constructed on the Qinghai - Tibet plateau (elevation over 4000 m) which is technically impossible.

(b) Chinese Academy of Engineering (CAE)[30] in its study on Sustainable Development of China's Water Resources in 21stCentury underscored two potential areas of error in the proposed project :-

(i) The project only plans to channel the water into Yellow R disregarding all the inland rivers of North and the NW China.

(ii) The project violates the laws of nature and disturbs the adaptive ecological environments; as it envisages natural arid zones of the NW China to be converted into wet lands.

(c) **Qian Zhengying,** former Minister of Water Resources (1979 -82) informed the State Council that in near future there would be no feasibility - technical or economical for The Great Western Route.

(d) The bio-diversity along the Tsangpo R is an ecological marvel attained after millions of years; it won't be prudent to disturb it.

(e) **Wang Shuchang,** former Minister for Water Resources (1989 -2007) felt that solution to China's water problem lay in building a water sustaining society instead of creating water diversion projects.

(f) It is estimated that cost involved in diverting Brahmaputra's water would be higher than alternative of desalination of sea water.

Part IV – Impact on India & Our Approach

Exploitation of Brahmaputra in India

Whilst, it is true that the major water diversion projects by China would affectan approx reduction of 20% of Brahmaputra waters; however, it is pertinent to mention that out of total catchment area of 5.8 lac sq km of Brahmaputra, 50% is in Tibet, 34% in India and 16% in BD. India needs to exploit these catchment areas/ drainage/ tributaries -Siang, Lohit, Dibang, Subansiri, Kamala, Rong, Kameng and others, for generation of hydel power and other uses. *These make the mighty Brahmaputra the size that is; not Chinese waters*[31]. India's anxiety over Chinese overtures also stems from the fact that out of Arunachal Pradesh's estimated potential of 50,064MW of hydel power, less than 1% or 405MW, has been harnessed so far[32]. Moreover, about

65% of the water is added to Brahmaputra in India, due to high precipitation as compared to the Tibetan Plateau; therefore the water loss to India may not be significant, notwithstanding the other bearing effects of the water diversion projects by China.

UN Provisions- Water Sharing

UN Convention on Shared Waters -1997: The law of the Non Navigation Uses of International Water Courses[33] was adopted in 1997 by the UN General Assembly. It concludes that cooperation rather than conflict has been the rule in international water relations and violence over water is rare. The u/m facts have been elucidated in the said convention:-

(a) 145 countries are riparian to one or more of the world's 263 international basins.

(b) 1/3rd of the 263 basins(formal management institutions established in 117 basins)involve sharing by two countries and19 involve five or more sovereign states.

(c) 40 % of the world's population lives along these basins which contribute to estimated 60% of the global fresh water.

(d) Population growth has resulted in a near 80% decline in per capita water availability over past century.

Cooperation Management Network: The convention lays stress on cooperation management between the riparian states[34] and emphasizes an agreement to be reached by the States with certain safeguards. It must have an adaptable management structure - a flexible structure with scope for public participation and provision for extending benefit to non signatories. The clear and flexible criteria for water allocations and water quality management need to be ensured for equitable distribution of benefits. Concrete mechanism to enforce treaty provisions and detailed conflict resolution mechanism also need to be suitably factored in this cooperation management network. Apropos, last 50 years has seen 37 acute water disputes and 150 water treaties[35].

Behaviour of Upper Riparian States across the World

Effectiveness of Legal Provisions: Existing legal provisions for water sharing, at the international level, are characterised more by their weakness than their substance. In short, most agreements remain bilateral, monitored by joint commissions and the game is 'free for all', dominated by the upper riparian states. Chinese thinking on the issue is reflected in the native Chinese adage, 'upstream does not suffer' and supports the Chinese tendency to take unilateral action in matters of water exploitation[36].

Getting this pre-eminent riparian power to accept water-sharing arrangements or other cooperative institutional mechanisms has proven unsuccessful in any basin. In fact, as epitomised by its planned or actual construction of a separate cascade of upstream dams on several major international rivers, including the Mekong, Salween and Brahmaputra, China is increasingly headed in the opposite direction — toward unilateralist actions impervious to the concerns of downstream nations[37].

U.S: The US affected the diversion of Colorado R, a trans-border river with Mexico, by 1963 by diverting 9.3 BCM of water[38]. The interests of the lower riparian Mexico were not considered while planning and execution of the project. The Upper Basin - provides water to Wyoming, Colorado, Utah and New Mexicostates. 90% of the sup water is spread into land irrigated for crops, 10% is for urban and other users. The Lower Basin provides water to California, Arizona, and Nevada and 85% is utilised for agricultural purposes.

Turkey: The country enjoys upper riparian advantage and is the nation with most dams after China. It has planned construction of 22 dams and 19 hydropower projects on Euphrates and Tigris and is working to get addl 1.8 mn hectares of land under irrigation. Syria and Iraq, the lower riparian are in no position to challenge.

Israel: It is the most water scarce country in the world. During the Six Day War in 1967, it captured the water rich Golan Heights and aquifer controlling waters of West Bank. It was also in control of Jordan R head works. Israel still controls the Golan Heights which provides water security and power of water diplomacy with its neighbours in the region.

Indo – China Water Sharing Arrangements

Existing Water Sharing Mechanisms: India and China have no water treaty, as signed by India and Pak (Indus Water Treaty) to formalise the sharing of the trans-border river waters. However, a MoU was signed between the two countries to share hydrographic data of Sutlej in 2002, post the Pare Chu flooding disaster and Brahmaputra in 2005[39], to facilitate preventive action to be undertaken downstream during monsoons in case of flash floods which in the past have resulted in massive loss to life and property. In May 13, a MoU was signed during the recent visit of Mr Li Keqiang, the Premier of China, on 'provision of information by China on water level, discharge and rainfall from its three hydroelectric projectss upstream of Brahmaputra', which in the present scenario is not enough.

Complexities on Border Issues and Upper Riparian Status: China does not consider Arunachal Pradesh to be a part of India and considers it as Southern Tibet. India has been administering the State since the colonial era and it recognizes the Mac Mohan line as the boundary. China is the upper riparian State and according to basic principlesof customary international law (not written but practiced) it has the first right to exploit the basin resources; Ripa in Latin means 'Bank of stream'. The Law of Riparian Nations states that 'Propriety of water rights go to the owner of land contiguous to the river with reasonable logic of sharing the waters with the lower riparian's'[40]. It allows China reasonable water share without defining reasonableness, hence the ambiguity on the water sharing issue.

Impact of Diversion on Lower Riparian Nation- India

The Indian concerns over plans to divert the Brahmaputra were not unwarranted. The two components of the diversion scheme would include the construction of the world's largest hydroelectric plant on the Great Bend of the river on the Tibetan plateau; the second is the diversion of the waters northwards across hundreds of km to China's northwestern provinces. Diverting Tsangpo would result inan overall reduction of minimum 20 % in the water flow of Brahmaputra R. River morphology is the single most majorcasualty of damming and diversion of the river. The impact on the lower watercourse will broadly be in terms of reduced water channel and its related effects, biodiversity along the areas of lake formation and downstream, rehabilitation of local populace, disturbance of ecological fragility triggering landslides and earthquakes. The implications and impact of such project are being discussed in u/m paras.

Logistics Sustenance: Damming upstream has created capabilities with China to flood the downstream at will. Natural disasters and poor quality of workman ship may puncture the dams having catastrophic effects (major loss to life and property worth mns) on downstream India. This would trigger loss of revenue directed towards rehabilitation and reconstruction. All the roads follow valleys and water drained by the river will impact these roads due to flooding, having a direct impact on logistics sustenance and habitat in the region.

Reduced Water Channel: Reduced water flow would have an adverse impact on fresh water availability on the lower riparian States – India and Bangladesh. Threat to navigation in National Waterways of lower riparian Statesie, National Waterway-2 on Brahmaputra R from Sadiya to Bangladesh border for 891 km would be affected. Irrigationchannels, community pools downstream may dry up reducing the fish catch and crop yield in the region, directly impacting the food security. There is likely to be an increase in pollution as reduced flow would not be able to wash away the waste discharge fed into the river from habitation along it. Moreover, lowering of water table would reduce the fresh water availability.

Biodiversity/ Ecology: Effect on bio- diversity would be further aggravated by loss of forests, plants, wildlife, birds - their migration patterns, fishes, insects and host of other rare living organisms. Rare species found in a part or section of the river owing to altitude, temperature and silt/ mineral pattern in the river would get destroyed and lost forever.

Seismic Zone: The Himalayas (including the Tibetan Plateau) were formed by the collision of Indian plate with the Eurasian plate and fall in the highly active seismic zone prone to intermittent earthquakes. Major changes to the river courses would have an adverse impact on the frequency of earthquakes and is likely to be a cause of mass scale destruction of life and material. The seismic hazard mapping shows the area to be falling in Seismic zone 5[41] (max chances of a calamity), hence the risks of massive flooding and loss to life and property if the dam is built on Tsangpo.

Effect on Water State in India: The per capita availability table wrt India depicts a serious problem. One perspective of how water is likely to haunt us is report in *The Economist (2009)*– citing official estimates – that India will run short of water by 2050

Year	Population (Mn)	Per capita water availability (M^3/yr)
1951	361	5177
1955	395	4732
1991	846	2209
2001	1027	1820
2025	1394	1341
2050	1640	1140

(when the population is expected to peak at 1.7 billion), unless massive improvements are made[42]. The land under irrigation is also going to expand and the water usage accordingly. We need to address the matter of water security seriously and devise policies to conserve water with efficient methods, as also to critically examine the Chinese plan to embark upon the project of diverting Tsangpo waters, and institute measures and undertake actions to ensure that our interests are not harmed and optimal utilisation is made of the Brahmaputra waters.

Recommendations

China being the biggest dam builder in the world[43] has built power projects on almost all the trans-border rivers except Salween R (which is being planned to be dammed by 2015). It has diverted waters to balance out water availability in its water parched Northern regions and has plans to build more water diversion projects. Water is essentially required by China to sustain its growth momentum and hence the likelihood of implementation of the project for diverting waters of the three trans-border rivers of Tsangpo, Salween and Mekong. Most severe impact of the reduced water availability would be to the lowest riparian States – India, Bangladesh, Myanmar, Thailand, Cambodia and Vietnam. This could strain relations, impact economic interdependencies, bilateral and multilateral trade and host of other issues. Hence a via media has to be found to resolve the water crises of China while the security interests of the lower riparian Statesie, India, amongst others, are preserved. Inter alia, politico- diplomatic effortsand efforts at the national level need to be initiated to arrive at an action plan to be periodically reviewed.

Rohini Nilekani in her well-reasoned article, 'Is Water the Next Oil?' speaks of people's involvement, quoting a Chinese proverb ('Tell me, I forget. Show me, I remember. Involve me, I understand)[44], as the way forward to resolve the crisis. People must see themselves as not only part of the problem but also part of the solution. It is, therefore, incumbent on both the Chinese and Indian governments to make radical, science-based policy changes as soon as possible. Unless they do so, devastating water shortages will result within decades for billions of their citizens. Recommendations wrt engagement with China on the water diversion projects and actions to be undertaken are discussed in the succeeding paras.

Political and Diplomatic Efforts

(a) **Institution Building**: Institutions and forums by the water sharing nations need to be created in Asia. Regional cooperation water related mechanisms like -inclusive basin organisations; mechanism to expand rain fed agriculture; building Asian norms and rules; integrated planning to promote sustainable practice and careful balance between rights and responsibilities need to be initiated.

(b) **Lower Riparian Partnership**: India must take the lead in building lower riparian partnership in Asia. We need to conduct and publicise joint studies on adverse impact of water diversionand to quantify waterrequirement by each of the riparian State and its effect.

(c) **Joint Studies**: Joint studies may be initiated to quantify the impact of extensive damming on Brahmaputra waterways. Since generation of hydro power is also a necessity, quantification on the number and type (dam height, reservoir capacity and surface area of the lake) of dams which can be built with suggested locations,without major impact on the river morphology, should be spelt out.

(d) **Data Base**: The world water data base is not authenticated and acceptable to all. We should jointly initiate hydrographic data base for trans-border water systems which holds as an authority for all future interactions. The data base must include - sourcing, discharge, degradation, siltation to the impact that water related infrastructure would have on the environment.

(e) **Diplomatic Intervention**: Seek UN intervention for violation of the UN Convention on Shared Water Basins of 1997 by China and sensitise the region and world community to stop funding the Great Western Diversion for the adverse impact it has on India.

(f) **Joint Monitoring Mechanism:** India must push to establish joint monitoring mechanism on river basins on all trans-border rivers (Indus, Sutlej and Brahmaputra), for its equitable and justifiable use amongst riparian states.

(g) **PNEs**: Ensure that China is not allowed to carry out PNEs to construct tunnels for the water diversion projects.

National Level

(a) **Water Conservation**: We need to carve out effective policies for optimal use of available fresh water and to mitigate the wastage. National policy on water conservation should be enforced.

(b) **Recycling of Water**: Recycling of waste water should be the norm in every modern house hold and water harvesting especially rain harvesting should be encouraged.

(c) **Precedent**: We have an excellent precedent in negotiating treaties and implementing international norms on trans-border waterways; these need to be underscored to garner international support and to influence change in attitude of the Chinese. Poor water sharing resolution record within Indian States needs to be addressed and justified water sharing arrangements be put into place at the earliest. Examples of fair treatment by India (upper riparian) to lower riparian states in the region, which need to be appropriately leveraged, are as under[45] :-

(i) **Indus Water Treaty** with Pak.

(ii) Treaties with Bangladesh on sharing of Ganges waters.

(iii) The project of 'Interlinking of Rivers'has been shelved by India on concerns raised by BD and environmental issues.

(iv) India's acceptance of award by UN based arbitrator on Baglihar project in J&K.

Conclusion

The Himalayan waters have been a major source of life and prosperity in China and the Indian sub-continent. The envisaged increase in population, industrialisation, global warming - resultant receding glaciers and depleting ground water levels would increase the stress on fresh water availability in the trans-border rivers. Any reduction in flow caused by the water diversion projects will be a cause of dispute between the higher and lower riparian countries in 21st century. Focussed efforts also need to be undertaken to exploit the large catchment areas of Brahmaputra in India for hydel power generation, as the loss/ reduction of Brahmaputra waters entering India is about 20% as result of water diversion projects by China.

Whilst, a 'water war' in the near term seems quite unlikely[46], the core issue of the declining availability of water and the increasing demand for it is, nevertheless, a very serious, as well as complex and interlinked issue. Quite to the contrary, there is a realisation at both ends that territorial and other differences in perception need to be set aside, to enhance mutual trust and cooperation between China and India to tackle the various challenges they face. Any solution that is found will, therefore, have to be networked and international, rather than stand-alone. The dependence on water from the high Himalayas is such that China, and the South and Southeast Asian countries (the so-called lower riparian states), especially India have to collaborate instead of getting involving in conflict.

The current concern of dam construction activity over Tsangpo and its likely diversion by China have already involved India in worrisome tussle on control of waters. India as a nation will have to protect its rights over waters of trans-borderrivers for a sustained economic growth. Sustained diplomatic efforts by India need to be initiated to influence the Chinese thought and conduct on the trans-border river issue. As the study is on the current dynamic subject, it needs to progressively collate data on balance of the trans-borderrivers and study the Chinese behaviour on all these rivers continuously to formalise our action plan.

References

1. Yogendra Narain Roy, Diversion of Brahmaputra Waters to North China, Dialogue April – June 2010, Vol II No 4
2. *Ibid*
3. Dr Brahma Chellaney, Water: Asia's New Battleground; Georgetown University Press, Sep 13
4. Lester Brown , 'Tibet and China: Climate Crisis at the Earth's Third Pole'
5. Kimberley Layton, 'Tibetan Waters: Coming Conflict?', Institute of Peace and Conflict Studies, July 2009
6. Ibid
7. Claude Arpi, '*Born In Sin: The Panchsheel Agreement. The Sacrifice of Tibet,*'Mittal Publications, August 2004
8. Dr Brahma Chellaney, Asia's Water Crisis and the New Security Risks, Journal of USI, Vol CXLI, No 587, Jan – Mar 12
9. Ibid

10. Dr Brahma Chellaney, Water: Asia's New Battleground, Introduction
11. Study Reportby Organisation for Economic Cooperation & Development (OECD), 2006
12. P Stobdan,: '*China Should Not Use Water as a Threat Multiplier*', IDSA Comment October 23, 2009
13. *http://www.un.org.ezp2.lib.umn.edu/waterforlifedecade/scarcity.shtml, May, 2012,*
14. Food and Agriculture Organisation of the UN, Information System on water and agriculture, China 2010
15. Nathanial Matthews, China's Water Crisis needs better farming, not the South-North Water Transfer, Jun 13; *www.thethirdpole.net*
16. Claude Arpi, Water War in South Asia? Brahmaputra: Dam & Diversion, October 2003
17. Raj Mehta, Re-plumbing China: Leading to the World'sFirst Water War?, CLAWS Journal Summer 2010
18. South to North Water Diversion Project, Article in *www.water-technology.net/projects/south-north/*, Sep 2008
19. The Inquirer, Philadelphia: China to resettle 330,000 people, 19 October 2010
20. Yogendra Narain Roy, Diversion of Brahmaputra Waters to North China, Dialogue April – June 2010, Vol II No 4
21. Controversial Plan to Tap Tibetan Waters, Southern Weekend, translated by Shao Da for China.org.cn, 8 Aug 2006
22. *Ibid*
23. Claude Arpi, '*Himalayan Rivers: Geopolitics and Strategic Perspectives*,' Issue: Vol 23.2, June 23, 2008
24. German TV channel ZDF programme - 'Die Welt' - 'The World', in Jan 1998- blog of Claude Arpi, 31 Aug 2013
25. Yogendra Narain Roy, Diversion of Brahmaputra Waters to North China, Dialogue April – June 2010, Vol II No 4

26. BL Seth, 'Passive Neighbour', comment on *www.down toearth.org.in*, Nov 2011

27. National Power Grid Plan – China 2020; Practical Steps for Developing Renewable Energy in China's 12th Five-Year Plan' Haibing Ma , 02 Jul 2011

28. M. D. Nordyke, The Soviet Program for Peaceful Uses of Nuclear Explosions, UCRL-ID-124410 Rev 2,Sep 2000

29. Raj Mehta, Re-plumbing China: Leading to the World'sFirst Water War?, CLAWS Journal Summer 2010

30. Study -Chinese Academy of Engineering (CAE) on Sustainable Development of China's Water Resources in 21st Century, 2000

31. P Stobdan,: '*China Should Not Use Water as a Threat Multiplier*', IDSA Comment October 23, 2009

32. Utpal Bhaskar, '*India firms up its strategy on Brahmaputra water diversion*'; www.livemint.com/politics, 20 Nov 2013

33. ***Convention on the Law of the*** Non-Navigational Uses of International Watercourses, New York, 21 May 1997; *http://legal.un.org/avl/ha/clnuiw/clnuiw.html*

34. Ibid

35. Trans boundary waters, *http://www.un.org/waterforlifedecade/transboundary_waters.shtml*

36. Vikas Joshi, '*China*'s Water Crisis, its Management and Implications for India', published in an Indian Army Service magazine, 2009

37. Dr Brahma Chellaney, Asia's Water Crisis and New Security Risks, Journal of USI, Vol CXLI, No 587, Jan – Mar 12

38. Paul Stanton Kibel, Jonathan R. Schutz, 'Rio Grande Designs: Texans' NAFTA Water Claim against Mexico', Berkeley Journal of International Law Volume 25 I Issue 2 Article 5, 2007

39. n. 37.

40. Gabriel Eckstein, '*Application of International Water Law to Trans*

boundary Groundwater Resources, and the Slovak-Hungarian Dispute Over Gabcikovo-Nagymaros', Suffolk Transnational Law Review, Volume 19, at page 67, Winter 1995

41. Yogendra Narain Roy, Diversion of Brahmaputra Waters to North China, Dialogue April – June 2010, Vol II No 4

42. B Shantanu, 'Nightmare at Noon – What if I Had No Water to Drink?' December 1 2009, *http://satyameva-jayate.org*

43. Dr Brahma Chellaney, Asia's Water Crisis and New Security Risks, Journal of USI, Vol CXLI, No 587, Jan – Mar 12

44. Rohini Nilekani, 'Is Water the Next Oil?', Yale Global Online Magazine, May 31, 2007

45. Dr Brahma Chellaney, Asia's Water Crisis and New Security Risks, Journal of USI, Vol CXLI, No 587, Jan – Mar 12

46. Raj Mehta, Re-plumbing China: Leading to the World's First Water War?, CLAWS Journal Summer 2010

5

China Global and Regional Environment

China like any other country cannot escape its geography. All countries have to adapt themselves as per their regional realities. The neighbours are permanent and cannot be wished away. The regional environment of China is defined by cooperation as well as conflict. The biggest trade partners of China were its closest neighbours. Similarly its most fierce opponents were also its neighbours.

In olden times the geography of China largely insulated it from its rivals with the exception of Mongolia. The Mongols were China's biggest tormentors through most part of history. However, over a period of time the tormentors have been incorporated in the Chinese mainstream. Inner Mongolia has become a province of China. What we today know as Mongolia is no more a threat.

Japan was the elephant in the room from the turn of the previous century leading to brutal occupation and oppression of China. The Nanjing massacre is probably the worst symbol of Japanese occupation of China. The Japanese learnt from Western war fighting techniques before China and therefore were militarily superior. During the Second WW, the Western powers were rather grateful that China absorbed most of the offensive capability of Japan and as such they had to largely content with Germany alone.

This history of China-Japan relations is important to understand as the Chinese people at large remain distrustful of the Japanese in spite of Japan becoming a defensive nation post WW2. The deep rooted animosity and trust is unlikely to go away any time soon. The rise of China, continued conflict over islands and maritime boundaries and the previous history has propelled Japan into remilitarising itself along with seeking alliances with countries like USA and Australia. In case it is perceived by Japan that USA is unable to protect its interests, it may even chose the nuclear option.

Russia is the other elephant in the room. While both countries are communist and thus supposed to be ideological allies, this has not prevented them from being competitors. The reason is simple-both aspire for domination of the region. Russia of course has been a superpower earlier while China aspires to become one. The Chinese demographic invasion of Russian Far East is also a reality and remains a potential flash point. Because of the Western sanctions and the rising economic clout of China, Russia has been temporarily forced to seek tactical alliance with the latter. However, this is purely a marriage of convenience and is likely to go away sooner than later.

India and China were largely insulated from each other for most part of history as they were divided by the Tibetan plateau. There was little trade and as such no cause for military or political interaction. However, for most part of history these were the largest economies in the world. Both were also ancient civilisations.

Now with Tibetan plateau becoming part of China and connectivity even otherwise opening up both nations have become neighours for the first time in history. They are also jostling for regional dominance. China does perceive rise of India to be inimical to its interests. There are good reasons for that. Both countries share the same regional space and are seeking dominance. India with its vast markets, cheap labour and technological prowess can become an economic competitor to China. In its quest for becoming a global power, China perceives India to be a allying itself closely with USA and thereby assisting the latter in balancing China.China has tried its best to contain India to South Asia by propping up Pakistan.

Image of a Hegemon

China has no doubt emerged as a regional power and is slowly challenging the international order to emerge as a Global power. However, in the process of establishing its sphere of influence in its immediate neighbourhood, it has alienated most of its neighbouring countries. It is perceived as a bully. While all countries, including India, do want the Chinese investment, they also want China to respect their sovereignty. China's behaviour in South China Sea has sent a message that China will forcibly take whatever it fancies. Similarly its CPEC initiative ignoring India's sensibility provide an indicator of China's behaviour. This has made the neighbouring countries to be vary of China and has forced them to keep their strategic option for alliance with other counties open. May be if China had used diplomacy instead of coercion, it would have won itself many more allies of a more permanent nature.

Global Aspirations

The global aspirations of China are of course being viewed seriously by the sole superpower of the day USA. Paradoxically China's rise was largely fuelled and supported by US multinational companies. However, over a period of time China has emerged from the shadows to claim its place in the comity of nations.

As China becomes, again, the world's largest economy,

it wants the respect it enjoyed in centuries past. But it does not know how to achieve or deserve it.

For all this ambition, China is not bent on global domination. It has little interest in polities beyond Asia, except in as much as they provide it with raw material and markets. Talk of China's "neo-colonialism" in Africa, for instance, is much exaggerated. The country's stock of direct investment there still lags far behind Britain's and France's and amounts to only a third of America's. Though China's influence is undoubtedly growing, its engagement is not imperial but transactional.

Chinese foremen have abused African workers; Chinese companies have run illegal mines and annoyingly undercut local traders with cheap Chinese goods. But these are the problems of bad business, not of grand strategy. Unlike Europe's colonial powers of yesteryear, China has no strategic vision of keeping all others out of its bit of the continent, nor any hypocritical "civilising mission". When it perceives it could have a problem with its image, it responds pragmatically: building hospitals, paying for malaria-prevention programmes, laying down railways. In Africa and Latin America it is focusing more on taking stakes in local companies, not just buying up land and resources. It is also making forays into the use of soft power through a number of Confucius Institutes all over the world that try—in frequently ham-fisted ways—to show that China and its culture are benign.

Clan-focused Confucianism and the fear bred by communism have persuaded the Chinese to mind their own business: sweep the snow from in front of your own house, goes the old saying, don't worry about the frost on your neighbour's roof. If it adopts similar attitudes to the world at large, that may be because China faces problems on a global scale within its own borders: it has more poor people than any other country save India. When 160m of your own citizens are living on less than $1.25 a day, and many people are beginning to complain more openly about your nation's domestic problems, the development needs of Africans can seem less pressing.

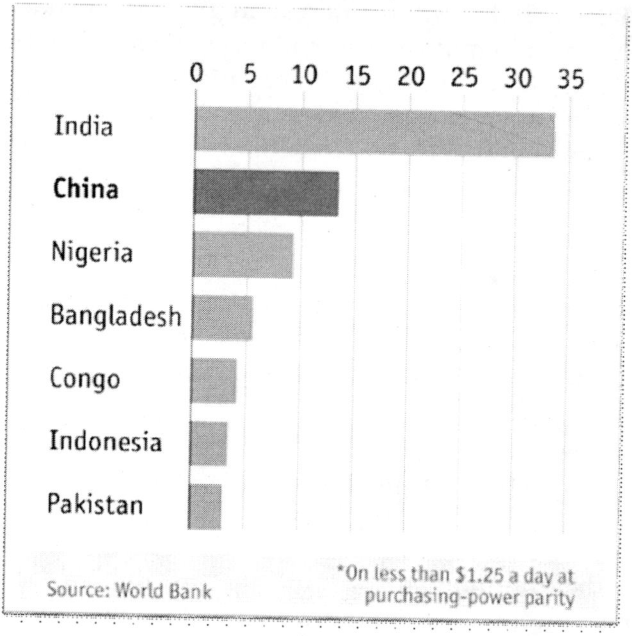

Accordingly, there is a tension in Chinese foreign policy. The country wants to have as little involvement abroad as it can get away with, except for engagements that enhance its image as a great power. It will act abroad when its own interests are at stake, but not for the greater or general good. Its navy has started to take part in anti-piracy operations off the Horn of Africa and in UN peacekeeping in Africa. In 2011 it sent a ship to co-ordinate the evacuation of 36,000 Chinese workers from Libya. More such actions may follow as its companies get more deeply involved in the world, but only if they are seen as either low-cost or absolutely necessary. Acute awareness of its domestic weaknesses acts as a restraint, as does the damage China sees done by the militarisation of America's foreign policy in recent years.

In a wide range of fields, what China is against is a lot clearer than what it is for. It vetoed the interventions Western powers sought in Syria and Darfur and has taken no position on the Russian annexation of Crimea (despite having a dim view of any sort of centrifugalism at home). At the 2009 climate summit in Copenhagen China made sure no deal emerged that would even suggest it might have to slow its industrial growth. There and elsewhere it showed itself ready to block but not ready to build. As a former senior official in the Bush administration says of Chinese engagement at the G20, "They love to show up, but we're still waiting for their first idea."

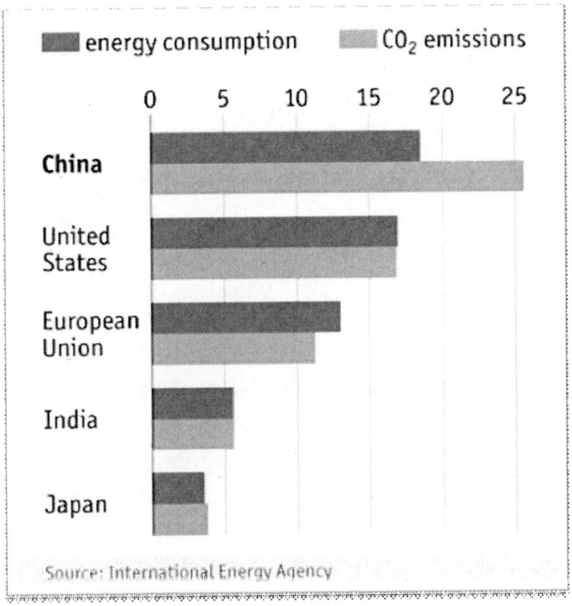

Genesis of Pak-China Linkages and Collusivity

"The real challenge in crafting lies in detecting the subtle discontinuities that may undermine a business in the future. And for that there is no technique, no programme, just a start mind in touch of with the situation". - Henry Mintzberg

China and Pakistan have long been strategic allies. Their collaboration and cooperation in all spheres has been comprehensive and has stood the test of time. India has somewhat inimical relations with both China and Pakistan including unsettled border issues. Therefore their collaboration as also collusivity can only have adverse strategic implications for India. For decades, Beijing's secretive ties with Islamabad have run closer than most formal alliances. Founded on a shared enmity with India, China's backing to Pakistan has gone so deep that it was willing to offer the ultimate gift from one state to another: the materials that Pakistan's nuclear scientists needed to build the bomb. Pakistan acted as China's backdoor during its years of diplomatic isolation, the bridge between Nixon and Mao, and the front-line in Beijing's struggles with the Soviet Union during the late stages of the Cold War. Now, Pakistan is a central part of China's transition from a regional power to a global one. The country lies at the heart of Beijing's plans for a network of ports, pipelines, roads and railways connecting the oil and gas fields of the Middle East to the mega-cities of East Asia. Its coastline is becoming a crucial staging post for China's take-off as a naval power, extending its reach from the Indian Ocean to the Persian Gulf and the Mediterranean Sea. Penetration by Pakistan's intelligence services into the darkest corners of global jihadi networks are a vital asset to China as it navigates its growing interests in the Islamic world, and seeks to choke off support for the militant activities that pose one of the gravest threats to China's internal stability.[1]

Symbiotic Relationship

There is a need to understand as to how this relationship is mutually beneficial. After all if it was one sided or more favourable to one of the nations, it would have withered. However, the fact that it has stood the test of time is indicative that both counties have gained from this semi alliance. Pakistan is perceived by China to be its gateway to the Islamic bloc of countries. It helps to trap India within South Asia rather than permit it to emerge as a challenger to China. Pakistan also fulfils the Chinese aspirations to gain a land route to the Indian Ocean obviating its Malacca dilemma. Through Pakistan, China also attempts to gain influence in the Af-Pak region and monitor the extra regional presence in Afghanistan. At the same time China wants influence to limit Pak role in any possible support to ETIM. Pakistan also helped China gain access to USA as a backdoor intermediary during the early turbulent years of its existence. Pakistan also provided China access to some Western weaponry and equipment which could then be copied by its manufacturers. On the other hand Pakistan has found an all weather ally in China which supports it in all forums. China creates the two front dilemma for India reducing Indian threat to Pakistan. China has been generous in transfer of technology as also direct military aid. However, its most significant help is in the field of nuclear and missile technology, which Pakistan may not have been able to master on its own. China has also repeatedly come to rescue of Pakistan in terms of economic aid. However, the extent of Chinese economic support to Pakistan is debatable and in terms of trade, it may well be China which benefitted more. China also vetoes any resolution in Security Council which goes against Pakistan. Hafiz Saeed being a case in point. The recent precondition of accepting Pakistan also, in case of Indian entry to the NSG underscores the level of Chinese support to Pakistan.

Initial Relations

Sino-Pak relations were in a dormant state in 1947. India in fact perceived itself to be the closest ally of PRC / China. India was amongst the first countries to grant recognition to PRCin 1949. Nehru repeatedly extended a hand of friendship to China. China on the other hand viewed this relationship differently. China perceived India to be the most powerful country in South Asia, which may challenge China's rise subsequently. The Chinese therefore followed a policy of containment right from the beginning. Chinese priority was a complete control over its frontier territories of Tibet and Xinxiang. In fact much of China's strategic thinking was shaped by Mao-who believed that a rising nation must continue to push against its frontiers. This thinking was partly shaped by his experiences of the Century of Humiliation as also the Chinese civil war. Tibet as also the Southern boundary of Tibet constituted one such frontier. Therefore China was not content only with the annexation of Tibet-it also wanted to push further southwards. However, China was yet weak militarily and did not want to be openly hostile towards India. They thus needed the benign Sino-Indian agreement of 1954. Nehru's visit to China in 1954 also brought to fore irreconcilable differences between India and Pakistan. Pakistan thus entered long term strategic calculus of China as the only country which can balance India. India at that time remained oblivious of this Chinese design. In fact, consequent to Chinese occupation of Tibet, India accepted that Tibet is a part of China. This state was possibly driven by beliefs of the then Prime Minister Nehru as also the Indian ambassador to China, Mr Panniker. They both believed China to be a long term Indian ally. Surprisingly, in the initial years the Pakistani leadership was not as well disposed towards China as they clearly were worried about Chinese territorial ambitions. The Pak tilt in this period was decidedly towards USA. Post the Chinese annexation of Tibet, the CIA covert operations to train the Tibetan guerrilla force for an uprising in Tibet against the PLA were directed from Peshawar. India on the other had provided the sustenance for PLA in Tibet in terms of food grains. During the visit of Ayub Khan to India on 24 Apr 1959, he proposed for a joint strategy for defense against China which was refused by Nehru. Pakistan also tried to develop cordial relations with USSR at this stage but without much success. The Bandung conference in 1955 did normalize Sino-Pak relations to some extent but not to the extent of turning it into an alliance. Strangely the Karakoram highway was started by the Chinese in 1959, the exact year that the Ayub Khan's proposal was rebuffed by Nehru as also the year when Dalai Lama fled to India. Thus the highway is indicative of the long term strategic calculus of China. The road was opened to public in 1979- as USSR invaded Afghanistan.

Post 1962 Sino-Indian Conflict

1962 proved Pakistan correct with respect to the Chinese threat from the North. This proved to be the turning point in Sino-Pak relations. The shift was accentuated by three factors. First, by this stage Sino-Soviet friendship was falling apart and China needed new friends. Second, by befriending Pakistan the Chinese hoped to counter-veil India as also grow closer to USA. Pakistan, also realized that it cannot wish away China being their neighbour. Third, and the last reason, was that the Indian defeat in 1962, brought to fore the urgency of settling the border issue with China. Post 1962, Pakistan went on to normalize its relations with China and after ceding of the Shaksgam valley resolved its border problems with China in 1963. China similarly understood and condoned Pakistan's reasons for joining SEATO/ CENTO. Pakistan thus shifted its position from being skeptical about China to becoming its ally. In fact, by settling and demarcating the border with China, Pakistan also somewhat legitimized its illegal occupation of PoK and the Northern Areas. Thus seeds of Chinese intervention in the J&K dispute were sown at this stage. Chinese were cautious about making any statement on J&K till 1962 as they were concerned that India may similarly comment about Tibet. However, in 1964, they made statements about ill treatment of Muslims in J&K, signalling their support for Pak position. In 1964, Chou en Lai visited Pakistan and used Pakistan to message to USA about its intentions regarding the on-going conflict in Vietnam. He stated that, China does not want a conflict in South East Asia, however will retaliate only if bombed & will then use full might at point of choosing. In this manner China tacitly condoned US involvement in Vietnam. Thus use of Pakistan as an intermediary between China and USA was established in late sixties and early seventies. This process was taken further during the Nixon era when Pakistan facilitated a number of high level secret negotiations between China and USA, finally resulting in UN recognition of China as a permanent member of the Security Council in 1972. The worsening of Sino-Indian relations were also partially co-terminus with deteriorating China – Soviet relations. This is a little vexing as by this stage India was not very close to Soviet Union[2].

Nuanced Support From China

Inspite of the all-weather friendship which was developing between China and Pakistan, the Chinese support to Pakistan was not unconditional. Pakistan realized that USA would not be underwriting all their security concerns against India. Infact USA had militarily helped India in the 1962 war. Post 1962 Pakistan perceived that China could now militarily support them against a common foe in India. This hope was belied in 1965 war wherein, China provided only verbal support to Pakistan. Mao then asked Pakistan to be prepared to wage a long drawn guerrilla war against India. Similarly, even in 1971 inspite of all the help that Pakistan was providing to China, the latter refused to bail out Pakistan militarily. The reasons for such Chinese behavior may well have been their internal political compulsions as also the fact that the Chinese armed forces were not very strong. China was also actively seeking the permanent seat in UN Security Council in 1971, which it would not have risked by unprovoked military action against India. Even during the Kargil war, Pakistan was heavily banking on the Chinese support which did not really materialize except for a few isolated statements.

Strategic Engagement: 1971-1990 and Beyond

This period was defined by the Soviet expansion in Afghanistan and the peak of cold war. Presence of Soviet troops in Afghanistan made Pakistan a frontline state for both USA and China. China funneled arms to the Afghan mujahedeen through Pakistan. China truly became strategic ally of Pakistan extending it military hardware, monetary support as also the ultimate gift of nuclear and missile technology. China on the other hand used Pakistan to get closer to USA against USSR. In fact USA clandestinely propped up China as a counter weight to USSR. The Tiananmen incident in 1989 did weaken the USA-China relationship to some extent. Post 1991, after the breakdown of the Soviet Union, USA continued its economic relationship with China in the process making it an economic superpower. China and Pakistan friendship also continued. Chinese support to Pakistan after its nuclear explosion was indicative of the degree of friendship and alliance between the two countries. However, like before Chinese support to Pakistan remained nuanced during the Kargil war.

There are no values systems in the Sino-Pakistan collaboration. It is purely based on the same strategic, security concerns & necessity. It is an all-weather strategic partnership with a common destiny. The FTA of 2003 and the treaty of Friendship, Cooperation and Good Neighbourly Relations in 2005, further cemented the relations between the two countries. In this treaty China reaffirmed the status of Pakistan as a strategic ally, whereas Pakistan restated its One China stance. Present Chinese security concerns are mainly in the East in the South China Sea, East China Sea& USA. The principle objective of China is to win local wars, presently, for which they have recently reorganized the PLA. China has realized that expeditionary capability was the key to the success and economic rise of Western nations in the previous century. China is therefore keen to emulate the same model for which it needs allies. China has been seeking a land access to the Indian Ocean to boost its presence there. Countries which can make this possible are Pakistan and Myanmar. China has therefore tried to develop friendly relations with them, Pakistan being the most successful story. The coastline of Pakistan today offers the opportunity to China to give a strategic reach to the PLAN. China also has problems in the province of Xinjiang. It is 1/6th of China's land mass; however, it is important due to being home to its Nuclear Industry, being the largest gas producer and 2nd largest oil producer in China. Its network of communications enables China to access wealth of Central Asia. China believes that Pakistan plays an important role in Xinjiang. China projects Pakistan as a friendly Islamic country. Pakistan gives access to China to the larger Muslim/ Islamic community & does not criticize China's iron hand policy on Muslims in Xinjiang.

The China Dream[3]

(*Zhôngguómèng*) is a term popularized after 2013 within Chinese strategic thought that describes a set of personal and national ideals in the People's Republic of China and the Communist Party of China. It is used by journalists, government officials, and activists to describe the role of the individual in Chinese society as well as the goals of the "Chinese nation". The Belt and Road Initiative (OBOR)[4] was accordingly launched with great fanfare as part of this China dream. OBOR has over a period of time become the signature initiative of Xi Jinping. He has attached certain personal credibility to its success. CPEC is a part of this OBOR initiative. CPEC is somewhat different from other alignments of OBOR, in that the alignment is over extremely difficult terrain and through disputed territory. Both nations have chosen to push for it in spite of obvious legal as well as physical hurdles. Clearly CPEC fulfils geo-economics as well as geostrategic needs of both nations. Their close relations naturally made Pakistan a prime contender for the CPEC. Gwadar is the culmination point of CPEC where the

OBOR and the Maritime Silk Routes converge. Gwadar is located at a strategic place and control over Gwadar provides enhanced expeditionary capabilities to the Chinese Navy. Gwadar in times to come is likely to become a strategic naval base for PLAN. The relationship based on the shared common animosity towards India further gains from CPEC as it enhances the physical connectivity between the two nations. Moreover, Pakistan's economy desperately needs the infusion of this FDI for its infrastructure primarily its power sector. China also made a new regional monetary system by announcing the formation of AIIB. This posed a direct challenge to IMF as also ADB which had Western / Japanese domination. Many projects under CPEC are to be funded by AIIB funds thereby earning revenue for the Chinese. Some of the investments had interest rates as high as 6% which have however, been since reduced to 1% to 2% in most cases. Even investments by private Chinese companies were secured by China by seeking sovereign guarantees from Pakistan for repayments.

China in the garb of security will also be able to deploy PLA troops on Pak soil[5]. This gives it a strategic edge in Afghanistan, Pakistan as also against India. Troops also provide China traction against any endeavors by Pak Army to provide support to ETIM. The Chinese footprint in the Indian Ocean is indirectly supported by CPEC.

In summation Sino-Pak relations have weathered the vagaries of time and have emerged even stronger. Pakistan has become China's Israel in a manner of speaking. The relationship is symbiotic with both countries benefitting from it.

China -Pakistan Economic -Challenge for India

While India must always be wary of Chinese and Pakistani cooperation, the latest developments should not be perceived by Delhi as a direct threat to its interests or security. Despite a deep-rooted regional rivalry and innate suspicion between India and China, both nations share myriad common strategic and economic interests. It can be argued that common interests far outnumber issues which put the two powers at odds.

- It is these very interests which make the likelihood of either China or India initiating any sort of offensive highly improbable. In fact, India stands to benefit from greater Chinese involvement in Pakistan.
- China's expanded economic footprint in Pakistan will not come at India's expense. Beijing and Delhi enjoy stable and widening economic ties worth roughly $70 billion dollars annually, almost six times greater than current Sino-Pakistani trade volumes.
- Even at the apex of the CPEC, trade between Islamabad and Beijing is not expected to exceed $20 billion. Fears that Pakistan will usurp India as China's most prominent regional economic partner are wholly unfounded. The superpower will remain China's most important economic partner in the region for the foreseeable future.
- Pakistan's economic growth and stability is vital to Indian and Chinese regional interests alike. A prosperous and surefooted Pakistan is more likely to liberalize trade barriers with India and promote regional economic integration.
- More importantly, a financially viable Pakistan, capable of delivering power and basic services to its citizens, will be better positioned to combat the plethora of violent Islamist operating in its territory. This is, perhaps, the greatest advantage for India should the CPEC be realized.

Should India be threatened by China's footprint in Central Asia?

- With the drawback of US troops from Afghanistan, the United States has welcomed the prospect of greater Chinese involvement in the region. Though the United States has not given Beijing a carte-blanche to do as it pleases, Washington does recognize that China is one of the few states with the capital and regional credibility required to promote true economic integration and security cooperation in restive Central Asia.

- If the United States is not overtly threatened by a Chinese presence in Afghanistan, there is little reason why India should be overly fearful of a Chinese presence in Pakistan. China is the only nation with the political clout and financial capacity to restore a semblance of internal stability in Pakistan.
- A deeply invested China may also help foster a more peaceable coexistence between Islamabad and Delhi. With its economic interests vested in regional stability, China may come to represent a convenient and powerful interlocutor for both India and Pakistan, mitigating the possibility of future conflict.

Deepening Sino-Pakistan Ties - A strategic threat to India?

- Both China and Pakistan represent India's most formidable regional rivals. Ongoing and unsettled border disputes continue to dampen Indo-Sino relations. Furthermore, China's naval expansion into the Indian Ocean and Arabian Sea, coupled with fears of encirclement by the People's Liberation Army Navy (PLAN), have stimulated unprecedented growth in India's naval capabilities.
- With China now solidifying its sphere of influence over Pakistan and Central Asia, India could legitimately perceive an erosion in its status as a regional superpower.
- This perception is partially unfounded. While the successful development of the Gwadar Port will

elevate Pakistan and China's status in Central Asia, India still maintains considerable clout and even leverage over China.

- India's loss in Central Asia will be balanced by its network of strategic allies in Vietnam, Singapore, Myanmar, South Korea, and most notably, the United States. As such, India would in no way find itself in a position of weakness when negotiating with China.

Implications of Increasing Chinese Footprint in India's Neighbourhood

China and India share the extended neighbourhood. Many small countries who are India's immediate neighbours also think of China as their neighbour. Over a period of time China's influence in these small countries has been constantly increasing. China has emerged as their largest trading partner in most cases. China is also willing to make substantial investments as also provide economic aid.

In addition to this cheque book diplomacy, China has also been generous with military aid in terms of providing military hardware. Some of the hardware is being gifted while some other is being sold at lower rates than similar weaponry from Western sources.

The crowning effort by China has been in the form of OBOR wherein, physical connectivity between these countries and China has been enhanced along with an even greater economic dependence.

Naturally this caused certain apprehensions and concerns in Indian strategic community. Many nations such as Nepal which had deep historical linkages with India were now perceived by some as tilting towards China. Similarly nations such as Sri-Lanka and Maldives were perceived to be indirectly aiding the Chinese in strategic encirclement of India.

Most nations in Indian neighbourhood are developing

nations and as such seek economic aid/ investment. Therefore it was natural for them to seek such economic cooperation from both China and India. The former obviously has much deeper pockets. The fact also remains that being sovereign nations India's neighbours can align with China if they so perceive it to be in their national interests.

The question is whether India should be greatly alarmed and take counter measures. While there is no doubt that India should continue to engage our neighbours in constructive economic and strategic partnerships, the worry of Chinese engagement seems to be overstated.

To start with, most countries in the neighbourhood have come to realise that Chinese investments are often expensive and the repayments difficult. Classic example is that of Hambantota port in Sri Lanka where the repayments were not possible by Sri-Lanka and the country was forced to sell some equity stakes of the port to China. Thus countries like Myanmar are rethinking the extent of investment they were previously seeking from China. Chinese investments are often also routed through Chinese firms, thereby not really helping in creation of local jobs. The prospect of the permanent presence of Chinese nationals to oversee these projects also has to be considered.

Nationals of countries like Nepal and Bangladesh could seek jobs in India. Similar concessions are unlikely to be provided by China. Chinese investments are really a one way affair.

Even in terms of military hardware, quite often the countries may not really be getting the value for money. Even for gifted hardware, the countries may have to fork out money for spares etc and in the long term such aid may turn out to be expensive.

India has always been benign towards its smaller neighbours and always willing to walk the extra mile. We should stay the course rather than get into competition with China. Let the neighbours decide the relative merits of engaging with the two big neighbours. The verdict is more likely to be in favour of India.

China in Indian Ocean

The Indian Ocean is the world's third largest body of water and has become a growing area of competition between China and India. Escalated activities such as port development and military exercises and rhetoric could endanger stability in a critical region for global trade flows.

India has treated the Indian Ocean as an ocean of peace and stability. Now that China has decided that it is going to become one of the major player in the region, India has reasons to worry because China will come to India's immediate neighbourhood.

Importance of the Indian Ocean

- The Indian Ocean littoral has the potential to become the leading source of new global growth over the next 20 years.
- One-third of the world population lives in the region, including one-quarter of the UN members.
- It provides critical sea trade routes that connect the Middle East, Africa, and South Asia with the broader Asian continent to the east and Europe to the west.
- A number of the world's most important strategic choke points are found in the Indian Ocean.
- Indian Ocean channels carry 2/3rd of the world's oil shipments, 1/3rd of the bulk cargo and half of all container traffic.
- Nearly 40 per cent of the world's offshore petroleum is produced in the Indian Ocean.
- The Indian Ocean hosts heavy mineral deposits, and fisheries are increasingly important for both exports and domestic consumption.

- China and India are dependent on energy resources transported via the secure sea lanes in the Indian Ocean to fuel their economies.
- India imports nearly 80 percent of its energy, mostly oil from the Middle East.
- For New Delhi's press to maintain economic growth, its dependency on the safe transport of resources will likely intensify.
- The region is home to some of the most intense conflict-prone areas and hosts various nuclear powers of the world.

India and China in Indian Ocean

- China's growing global influence and India's rapid economic rise have heightened the ocean's strategic value.
- Both countries have developed initiatives to bolster infrastructure and other connections in the region.
- Each country is seeking to strengthen ties with smaller regional states to secure their respective security and economic interests.
- Since launching counter-piracy operations in 2009, Beijing has become increasingly active in the region.
- Beijing's regional vision outlines its One Belt, One Road plan.
- China's ties with regional states have deepened, including the influx of Chinese capital into construction projects in Bangladesh, Myanmar, Pakistan, and Sri Lanka.
- Beijing's forays into the Indian Ocean are driven by China's excess capacity challenges, incentivizing Chinese firms to compete in and open new markets abroad.
- India sees itself as the natural preeminent regional

power.

- India has doubled-down on maintaining stronger diplomatic, economic, and security ties with IOR maritime states.
- It is meant to strengthen India's economy, establish its role a driver of regional growth, and simultaneously diminish China's growing appeal.
- It is India's neighbourhood that holds the key to its emergence as a regional and global power.
- China's movements in the region have been described by the "string of pearls" metaphor, which holds that China is taking on economic and investment projects with Indian Ocean states to secure ports or places for its military stations.

Impact of Chinese Influence on India

- The Indian Ocean is the only ocean which has been named after one of the countries. So, this indicates the important presence of India in this zone.
- About 7000 km of India's coastal land borders around the Indian Ocean. Most of its trade through sea-route occurs through this Ocean and some of the islands belonging to the Indian Territory lie in this Ocean, whose safety is also a primary responsibility of India.
- China's increased presence can mean a great harm to this position.
- Chinese are increasing their trading posts all around the Indian Ocean and also exploring mineral and oil resources in these areas.
- India has a competitive and cooperative relationship in many countries of Africa and Southeast Asia which might get affected due to Chinese presence.
- China has become the first or second major trading

country with all these countries in the Indian Ocean region and Australia as well.

- There could possibly be China-led alliances, Chinese client states and the establishment of Chinese spheres of influence, affecting India's clout in the region.
- With China, stepping up its political and economic footprint in the region, revisionist claims in the land and oceanic space could be brought up again like the issue of Doklam and Arunachal Pradesh.
- With the presence of Chinese strategic bases, there will be constriction of the Indian strategic manoeuvre space within its own geographical area.
- India has legitimate strategic concerns because any conflict in the Indian Ocean will have ramification in the whole region.
- It may hamper regional security situation and in such case, India's relationship with IOR countries may get disrupted.
- There is global maritime security interest involved in the region and many nations want India to balance the assertive and rising China and like it to get involved in the dispute to maintain peace and security in the region.

India's current strategy in the Indian Ocean

- India is moving to shore up its position against a more assertive Chinese presence by developing its own 'string of pearls'.
- New Delhi recently signed a strategic pact with France, with each opening their naval bases to the other's warships across the Indian Ocean.
- That gives the Indian navy access to strategically important French ports including one in Djibouti that offers easy access to key oil supply and trade routes.

- Prime Minister Modi finalised an agreement for a new base in Seychelles and negotiated military access to facilities at Oman's port and airfields.
- India signed an agreement with Singapore and Indonesia for naval cooperation.
- India has expanded its bases on Andaman and Nicobar Islands.
- India has realised that it needs to match China's assertiveness, and that includes expanding its reach into the Pacific.
- India is creating a security grid with the littoral countries so that militarization of the Indian Ocean can be prevented.
- For Delhi, having a counter power-projection capability in the South China Sea is now seen as critical to its strategic deterrence against Beijing.
- India has also stepped up aid to littorals through its **Project SAGAR** (Security and Growth for All in the Region), which is designed to revive India's ancient trade routes and cultural linkages around the Indian Ocean. It is a counter-move to China's maritime silk road.
- India is seemingly increasing its alliance with the US to deal with Beijing; most recently the Quad.

What More India Should Do

- The idea of selling the illusion of China as a villain in Asia may not work beyond a point.
- Instead, view China as part of the solution to the region's challenges.
- A mutual 'complex interdependence' in economic, security and other domains should be strengthened by initiating structured consultations. E.g. the current India-China joint anti-piracy missions in

the Gulf of Aden.

- India should certainly focus on the Indo-Pacific and consider cooperating with China, even while being part of the Quad.
- India also needs to strategize a plan to nudge China towards playing a role so as to ensure a stable regional security order.
- This is particularly in the context of its role in Pakistan, where China has to balance trade and terrorism.
- Despite this strategy of mutual trust, the role of military strength in guaranteeing national security cannot be underestimated.
- Thus, India would be better served by adopting a more nuanced strategy of 'smart-balancing' China.
- It is suggested that India should use its $70 billion-strong trading relationship with China as a bargaining chip to check Chinese behaviour.
- India needs to plan its own sea and road linkages with its neighbouring countries.
- Indian Ocean RIM Association should be a force multiplier for India's interests and for this, bilateral relations with all countries in this region has to be revived.
- Maintaining peace and stability of the Indian ocean is very important.
- The militarization of Indian ocean must be prevented.
- A proper framework must be developed by the littoral countries to deal with any type of crisis be it natural or any other.

CPEC A Self Goal By China and Pakistan?

There has been considerable excitement in the strategic circles of India as also China and Pakistan ever since China announced CPEC as a part of its 'Belt and Road (OBOR)' Initiative. China of course is looking for better opportunities for investment as US treasury bonds became fraught with risk after 2008. For China, OBOR was thus the perfect vehicle to invest their surplus capital, deploy additional infrastructural capacities, get employment for Chinese workers as also get geostrategic leverage; all this while integrating more and more number of countries embedded in the Chinese economic system.

CPEC also fulfils all the above stated economic objectives for China. In addition for Pakistan, it brings the much needed investment in its infrastructure. Furthermore, for both the countries it also meets critical geostrategic and security requirements. Pakistan stands to gain as Chinese military presence in the garb of protecting Chinese commercial interests deters the Indian military superiority. For China Gwadar port meets its requirement of a naval base in the Indian Ocean. This gives boost to the Chinese power projection as also expeditionary capabilities. What is even better from the Chinese perspective is that this port has an overland connectivity with Chinese mainland.

The above mentioned facts will tend to indicate that CPEC is a win-win formulation for both China and Pakistan. However, it is not so. As the alignment of CPEC passes through PoK, it has immediately raised some legal and moral dilemmas for both China and Pakistan. It is noteworthy that Pakistan does not claim PoK to be its integral part. For China also PoK at best remains a disputed territory and at worst is a part of India. The fact that this project is being touted as a corridor means that its passage through PoK has come in sharp focus and raises questions about the legitimacy of OBOR.

There is a need to examine certain facts. CPEC is not about connectivity and a very miniscule portion will be spent for upgrading road and rail infrastructure. Most investments will be in the power sector as also Gwadar port. The connectivity through PoK in fact came in 1979 through Karakoram Highway (KKH). It further got upgraded in 2009-2014 to all weather status, in spite of all Indian protests (For record, the Chinese development of KKH was as legally and morally incorrect then as it is now).

In case the Chinese had called their future investments in Pakistan as 'Foreign Direct Investment (FDI)' instead of 'CPEC' they could have easily invested the same amount in Pakistan without raising heckles anywhere. After all each country in the world is seeking FDI from China and no one could have objected to Chinese FDI in Pakistan. However, CPEC raises the spectre of a geostrategic intervention by China in the region –which China in any case was quietly doing. CPEC has however given a rallying handle to all whose interests are negatively affected by China. It has in fact brought into sharp focus, the creeping action of China to gain a foothold in the region, brushing aside legal Indian claims. It has also mobilised negative public opinion in Pakistan as also it has become a talking point in countries like Iran and Russia. Thus in the larger analysis CPEC has been a self-goal by both China and Pakistan, they could have easily achieved all that they seek to achieve by remaining low key about it.

China – Taiwan Summit: A Possible Explanation

The handshake was long, 82 seconds, almost awkwardly so, and the smiles were stretched too, for the cameras. On Nov 7 2015, on the neutral and friendly ground of Singapore, Xi Jinping, President of China and general secretary of the Chinese Communist Party (CCP), and Ma Ying-jeou, President of Taiwan and representative of the Chinese Nationalist Party or Kuomintang (KMT), held a brief but historic summit. Big authoritarian superpower engaged small young democracy.[6] Of course since then the government in Taiwan has changed, but it will be interesting to analyse this event still.

The event and its possible reasons have been exhaustively debated the world over. Many possible explanations have been offered. It was at the time widely expected that the KMT will lose to DPP in the Jan 16 elections in Taiwan (which happened). The DPP is known for its hard-line stance against mainland China, unlike the KMT. Thus perhaps this summit was possible only in the limited window available before the Taiwanese elections and the opportunity was seized by both sides, more so by PRC. Once DPP came to power, as was expected, the window for the summit may have closed for some time.

What is it that the summit brought to the table for Xi Jinping or for PRC? The Chinese President was able to emphasize the fact again that the two political systems are supported by a single set of people and that deep cultural and family ties exist. In a manner he appealed to the concept of *Greater Chinese Nationalism*. He also conveyed that mainland China is not an enemy of Taiwan. While this may not have allayed the fears of the Taiwanese political class with respect to the Chinese military intentions, the message would have resonated well with the people of both countries. With increasing trade ties there is much greater people to people movement between the mainland and Taiwan and thus better integration. While the Taiwanese would very much like to maintain their independent political identity, they would also on a people to people basis seek greater contact with the mainland and vice versa.

The Taiwanese president would have possibly agreed to the meeting with an eye on the forthcoming elections. By meeting his Chinese counterpart as an equal, he may have conveyed a strong image of himself and his party to the voters. He could assert his independence without being confrontationist with the Chinese. This was a very nuanced stance – and not the totalitarian position which the DPP has adopted. In a manner the Taiwanese also again projected themselves on the world stage, something of which the

USA will have to take note of. The position of USA on independence of Taiwan has been rather muted in the past even though they remain committed to underwriting its security concerns. The summit may also have been driven by private desire of President Ma – to shine once before fading into sunset.

Thus both sides gained in their own manner. Cross straits relations are complex at best of the times. Tumultuous events such as this summit can therefore be always interpreted in multiple manners. The above is only one possible explanation.

China's Support To Pakistan Over Terrorism

China's Permanent Representative Liu Jieyi has reiterated Beijing's claim that Pakistan based JeM Chief Masood Azhar does not qualify as a terrorist who would have to face UN sanctions. Speaking to reporters on Friday after assuming the rotating presidency of the Security Council, Liu asserted that Azhar did not meet "the Council's requirements" to be considered a terrorist. Asked about China exercising a virtual veto at the UN sanctions committee by putting a hold on Azhar being declared a terrorist subject to a range of punitive actions, Liu said: "Individuals and orgnisations on the sanctions list of the United Nations would have to meet the requirements. It is the responsibility of all the members of the Council to make sure that each requirement is followed." Pressed further about in what way Azhar fell short of being a terrorist, Liu said: "The Council's requirements." Implying he did not meet them, Liu would not go into details.[7]

This is not the first time China has thwarted Indian attempts to bring to fore Pak complicity in spread of international terrorism. China in a bid to further strengthen its strategic linkages with Pakistan, has been shielding it in international forums. This time however, India seems to have taken a serious note of this Chinese stance. There were recent press reports about Indian government contemplating tightening of restrictions on Chinese companies in India as a response to the Chinese actions in United Nations.

Chinese press has been suggesting that a move of this nature would ultimately hurt Indian interests and would slow down Chinese FDI in India. The Chinese would therefore hope to continue to exploit the lucrative Indian markets while at the same time hurting Indian interests elsewhere. To an extent our own wavering policies are to be blamed for this situation. The Chinese are encouraged towards this behaviour because they have been getting away with it in the past. While it's no one's case that we should be jingoistic and belligerent, yet we can also not be taken for a ride. A firm response is needed. Many in the Indian establishment may disagree but by not giving a rejoinder to the Chinese actions we would only be encouraging it.

India today can be confident of its economic prowess and the growth potential of the Indian economy is not hostage to Chinese FDI. On the other hand it is China who is in greater need of expanding its economic footprint in India. We should therefore not let them beat us in the mind game and convince us otherwise. The world is watching India closely in anticipation of its rise as a global player. Taking occasional hard-line positions and defending them even at a cost is the price we have to be prepared to pay in case we have to be a power to reckon with. The world respects only the currency of power and strength.

India-China relations are mired by psyche of 1962 conflict, lingering border dispute, Tibetan issue and Pakistan - China nexus. China perceives that India is part of a Grand Encirclement design being woven by the US to contain China. Besides unprecedented military modernization, it is carrying out massive military oriented border infrastructure in Tibet, making forays into POK and Indian Ocean and increasingly leveraging Pakistan card to countervail India. There is also the build-up of China-Pakistan Economic

Corridor (CPEC) which passes through disputed territories and the Chinese development of Gwadar port in Pakistan are strategic concerns for India. Their forays in building up ports in Sri Lanka, Myanmar and Nepal reflect their creeping assertiveness on the border regions of India. These developments do not augur well for India's security. It is, therefore, imperative for India to carry out an in – depth study of war waging potential of China and seek measures to safeguard its vital national interests and strategic objectives.

The Chinese strategic encirclement of India also results from the fact that in addition to being a strategic competitor, India is also an economic competitor. The Chinese grand design is therefore to contain India strategically only to South Asian region by propping up proxies such as Pakistan as also by developing influence and leverage with all other smaller neighbours of India. Concurrently China seeks to limit India's economic growth as well while at the same time using the advantage of vast Indian markets.

The border dispute has been kept alive as a pressure point as also to keep India tied down on its Northern frontiers, while China goes on developing a global expeditionary capability. China has also indirectly aided and abetted terrorism and internal instability in India by providing weapons and funding to various terrorist groups in India's North East as also by providing Chinese weapons to Pakistan for funnelling them to the terrorists in J&K.

How Other Countries Can Survive the US-China Competition

The world is now faced not only with the implications of China's rise to superpower status and its growing economic clout and the challenges this raises, but also with a United States that is pursuing an inconsistent foreign policy and a growing sense of ongoing and increasingly strategic rivalry between the U.S. and China. This new reality is placing many smaller countries in a new and unfamiliar position, having to navigate and promote their own interests while balancing the demands of the two competing superpowers.

The realignment of global and regional actors is extremely dynamic, creating unprecedented threats, risks, and opportunities. As the United States is perceived to be decreasing its involvement in Asia and in the Middle East, regional regimes are increasingly eyeing China as a potential regional game-changer in the spheres of trade, economy, energy, as well as defense and foreign policy.

Viewed from Israel, these developments present opportunities and challenges. Asia's economic growth and demand for technology and innovation offer access to the world's most dynamic economic region. On the other hand, Israel has traditionally been oriented toward the United States and Europe, from both an economic and cultural perspective, and therefore needs to develop an understanding of how to effectively engage with Asia. In addition, Israel must balance its growing ties with China with its obligations to the U.S. alliance.

In recent years, China has become substantially more active in the Middle East, including through the Belt and Road Initiative, and this trend is likely to continue. China's economic engagement with Israel has grown substantially too, including Chinese investments in strategic infrastructure and technology. China has also become more active in promoting Chinese culture and soft power in Israel. These developments have raised sensitivities with the United States and highlighted the need for Israel to develop an independent, long-term strategic policy regarding its relationship with China.

With the global geostrategic landscape changing rapidly, many countries are feeling pressured. In Europe, for example, countries such as Britain, Germany, and Spain are feeling the crunch as the United States actively works to persuade allies to block the involvement of Huawei and other Chinese tech companies in 5G networks.

This phenomenon is relevant not only for technology issues. Many small to medium-sized countries, including Australia, Singapore, Israel, and other countries in Europe, Asia, and the Middle East (particularly in the Gulf), that have a strong connection with the United States are also seeking a closer economic relationship with China. These "stuck in the middle" countries should seek to learn and actively engage with one another. For such smaller powers the evolving challenges of an ongoing state of aggressive competition between the world's two leading powers are substantial and require astute handling.

But this state of global and regional geopolitical uncertainty creates new opportunities as well. Smaller countries should identify and grasp the new opportunities that this changing landscape presents. Taking a proactive approach, smaller countries should aim to move away from the old divides, and to create new coalitions within and between regions, in particular the Asia-Pacific and the Middle East.

Such new coalitions can take a number of different forms, for example, the establishment of a new ASEAN-Middle East Innovation Forum. This would be a multilateral coalition focused on strengthening relations and cooperation between countries in Southeast Asia and the Middle East by bringing together unique capabilities and technological innovations to deal with the real needs in both regions, including water desalination, food safety, green energy and clean technology, healthcare, education, science and technology.

Such broader cross-regional cooperation could also provide an effective platform for joint promotion of regional and global solutions to transnational problems such as climate change, crises management, people smuggling and immigration, and terrorism. It could also act as a platform to bring together countries that do not normally sit at the same table.

Another way to step out of the familiar boundaries of state-to-state diplomacy could be to engage in city diplomacy – transcending the limitations and constraints of states, and creating agile joint frameworks directly with cities, metropolitans, and provinces. This approach could help in finding quick and effective solutions for pressing needs and interests.

As the competition between the two superpowers seems likely to continue into the foreseeable future, smaller countries need to join forces to develop a greater understanding of the challenges involved and create innovative new forms of cooperation.

References

1. Andrew Small, The China-Pakistan Axis: Asia's New Geopolitics (London: C Hurst & Co Publishers Ltd, 2015).
2. '<i>The China-Pakistan Axis'.
4. One Belt, One Road'.
5. Diplomat, 'Pakistan's Army Seeks Greater Authority Over China-Pakistan Economic Corridor Administration'.
6. ZohelAbdoolcarim, TIME 09 Nov 15
7. 'Masood Azhar Doesn't Meet Criteria To Be Banned As Terrorist: China', NDTV.com, accessed 8 April 2016, *http://www.ndtv.com/india-news/pathankot-attack-mastermind-not-a-terrorist-china-reiterates-at-un-1306529.*

6

Conclusion

Both China and India have a long and great history that goes back thousands of years, both are not mere societies; they are oldest civilisations. Both countries had extensive cultural contact since the first century, especially with the transmission of Buddhism from India to China; many scholars from both sides visited the other side for cultural and religious exchanges. Trade relations via Silk Road acted as economic contact between the two regions. Both the Asian giants had some contacts even before this period. References to people called the *Chinas,* now believed to be Chinese, are found in ancient Indian literature. The Indian epic *Mahabharata* contains references to "China", probably referring to Qin Dynasty.

The records of the grand historian, Zhang Qian and Sima Qian make references to "Shendu", which may have been referring to the Indus Valley, originally known as "Sindhu" in Sanskrit. In sixth century B.C., the birth of Confucius and Sakyamuni opened a new period of exchanges between the two civilizations. During the 7th century, Tang Dynasty gained control over large portions of Silk Road and Central Asia, when a diplomatic mission to northern India was sent by Wang Xuance.

Both civilizations also shared scientific knowledge. In eighth century, Indian astronomer Aryabhata's astronomical signs were translated into Chinese in the book "Kaiyuan Zhanjing" compiled by Gautama Siddha, an astronomer in Chang'an of Indian descent. It is also believed that he translated the Navagraha calendar into Chinese. There were scores of inventions and discoveries made in both China and India much before it caught the thoughts of Europeans.

It is generally said that history has two eyes – one is chronology and the other is geography. In other words time and space are significant factors in determining the historical process; particularly, a country's geography largely determines its historical events.The above statement is tailored made and fits a typical example of the Sino-Indian relations into its folds.

During the Ming Dynasty, navigator General Zheng's arrival at Calicut in early 15th century is also a testimony of China's ancient maritime linkage with India. He was a Chinese diplomat and expressed his respects to the local deities and customs; in Ceylon he erected a monument honouring Buddha, Allah and Vishnu.

Before the age of European colonization, China accounted for about 33 percent of the world's manufactured goods and India for about 25 percent. China under the Song and Qing dynasties was the world's superpower. Under the Guptas and Mughals, India's economic, military, and cultural prowess also was an object of envy.

For five centuries-thirteenth to seventeenth-however, most parts of India were under Muslim rule, though with varying degrees of effectiveness in different regions of the country. But at no single point of time was the whole country ruled exclusively by the Muslims. On the other hand the five hundred yearlong Muslim rule did not fail to influence Indian political and cultural life in all its facets. Naturally, the interaction of Muslim culture with the Hindu way of life, backed by the superimposition of Muslim rule in India, gave rise to a sort of a common Indian culture.

On the face of it the influence of Islam on Indian culture is to be seen in all spheres oflife, in architecture, painting, music, and literature; in social institutions like marriage ceremonies, in eating habits, in gourmet and cuisine, sartorial fashions and so on. In actual fact, Hindus and Muslims lead their own lives, mostly in isolation from one another, except for personal friendships. Even living together for a thousand years has not welded Hindus and Muslims into one people. A thousand years of Muslim contact failed to Islamize India. India, therefore, provides a good study to evaluate the achievements and failures, atrocities and beneficences, fundamentalism and secularism of Muslim rule and Muslim people. In the appraisement of Muslim rule, Muslim religion also cannot escape scrutiny, for the former was guided by the latter, the one being inseparable from the other. This makes the assessment of the legacy of Muslim rule in India an extremely controversial subject. Its contribution comprises of both bitterness and distrust on the one hand and on the other a composite common culture.

The idea of Pakistan was as old as the Muslim rule in India. Mohd. Ali Jinnah is reported to have said that the seeds of Pakistan were planted when the first Hindu converted to Islam in India. Zulfiqar Ali Bhutto reiterated the same conclusion in still clearer terms. The study of Mughal and British periods will show that the seeds of Pakistan took root in the sub-continent from the time Muslims consolidated their position in India. The creation of two sovereign states of India and Pakistan merely formalised this existing division.

However, whatever the point of time or the genesis of Partition, never before was India geographically divided on religious basis in the course of its long history. Aurangzeb died in 1707, and the Mughal state began a long, slow process of crumbling from within and without. Increasing peasant revolts and sectarian violence threatened the stability of the throne, and various nobles and warlords sought to control the line of weak emperors. All around the borders, powerful new kingdoms sprang up and began to chip away at Mughal land holdings.

Around the 18th Century a number of significant events took place in the world. One such event was the Industrial Revolution which took place in England. It gradually spread to other countries of Europe also. It was followed by the discovery of new sea and trade routes. One such sea route was to India, discovered by a Portuguese called Vasco da Gama in 1498. As a result, the English, French, Portuguese and the Dutch came to India for trade.

The 18th century was a period of internal power struggle in India and with the declining power of the Mughal Empire, the British officials were provided with the perfect opportunity to establish their hold over Indian Territory. They did these through numerous wars, forced treaties, annexations and alliances with the various regional powers all overthe country. Their new administrative and economic policies helped them consolidate their control over the country. Their land revenue policies helped them keep the poor farmers in check and get huge sums as revenues in return. They forced the commercialisation of agriculture with the growing of various cash crops and the raw materials for the industries in the Britain. With the strong political control, the British were able to monopolise the trade with India. They defeated their foreign rivals in trade so that there could be no competition. They monopolised the sale of all kinds of raw materials and bought these at low prices whereas the Indian weavers had to buy them at exorbitant prices. Heavy duties were imposed on Indian goods entering Britain so as to protect their own industry. Various investments were made to improve the transport and communication system in the country to facilitate the easy transfer of raw materials from the farms to the port, and of finished goods from the ports to the markets.

Railways were one such big investment which was

considered as an investment surplus of England. English education was introduced to create a class of educated Indians who would assist the British in ruling the country and strengthen their political authority. All these measures helped the British to establish, consolidate and continue their rule over India. The Industrial revolution helped the English merchants accumulate a lot of capital which they now wanted to invest in setting up industries and trade with India.

The mass production of goods through machines that we witness today was pioneered through the Industrial Revolution which occurred first in England during the late 18th and the early 19th century. This led to a massive increase in the output of finished products. The East India Company helped in financing and expanding their industrial base. During this time there was a class of manufacturers in England who benefited more from manufacturing than trading. They were interested in having more raw materials from India as well as sending their finished goods back. Between 1793 and 1813, these British manufacturerslaunched a campaign against the company, its trade monopoly and the privileges it enjoyed. Ultimately, they succeeded in abolishing the East India Company's monopoly of Indian trade. With this India became an economic colony of Industrial England.

China on the other end also faced somewhat similar problems. In the beginning of 13th century Genghis Khan conquered part of China to the north from Huan He. Sung dynasty was rooted in 1279 when Hubilai conquered the whole of China and became Emperor. He founded the Mongol Yuang dynasty and moved the capital to Khanbalik, modern Peking. In 14th century the Mongols were driven from China and replaced by Ming dynasty. Ming Emperors ruled till 17th century which was marked by development of architecture and marine expeditions to Yava, Sri-Lanka and even Persian Gulf and Africa. In 1644 China was conquered by Manchus and the following 150 years were the period of stability and peace, but in the beginning of 19th century

Opium War was initiated by Britain and the British troops occupied Shanghai and Nankin and later Hong Kong. The end to the boxer's revolution against the 8 flag army laid a huge tax burden on the Chinese government (more than they made in taxes) and was one of the final nails in the coffin for the Qing Dynasty, even though it would take a few years for it to disappear.

In 1894 the war with Japan started and China lost Korea, Taiwan and Pescador islands. Qing dynasty of Manchus was uprooted in 1911 by revolutionary movement of Sun Yat-sen and in 1912 China was declared as Constitutional Republic.Further chaos and failure in administration led to a period of warlords gaining control of parts of China. The Treaty of Versailles in 1919 also treated China in a heavy-handed manner making western thinking and ideas an anathema in China.In 1916 Japan invaded China and power passed to Japanese. In 1917 China took part in World War I in exuberance of false promises made to it for getting back its lost territory.

In 1925 Sun Yat-sen died and national government was headed by YuanKaishi who ruled the country for ten years. Japan conquered Manchuria in 1933 and guerrilla war commenced. In 1935 Mao Zedong became the leader of communist party. In 1945 after Japanese capitulation the civil war broke out which ended in 1949 by creation of People's Republic of China which was headed by Mao Zedong. The humiliation suffered by the Chinese in the hands of the westerners and raiders from the northwest had changed the psychology of the Chinese who by now had become assertive in nature.

The British East India Company in India was founded in 1600, while Akbar was still on the throne. Initially it was only interested in trade, and had to content itself with working around the fringes of the Mughal Empire. As the Mughals weakened, however, the East India Company grew increasingly powerful.

The gradual westward expansion over the centuries under Mongol and Qing dynasties extended China's influence over Tibet and parts of Central Asia (now Xinjiang province). In contrast, India's boundaries shrank following the1947 partition that broke up the subcontinent's strategic unity that went back two thousand years to the first Mauryan Empire.

Both India and China began their journey of independent governance almost at the same time, India in 1947 and the People's Republic of China in 1949.

The means adopted to secure freedom by China and India provides indication of the approaches adopted by them to cope with the international order. The basis of relationships established by the two states bilaterally with other states was also founded in that historical context. China had won its freedom through an armed struggle. Its military was committed to an ideology and the military leaders. Marxist-Leninist revolutionary thought provided the underpinnings to much of China's post-independence policy of military power as an instrument of internal and external policy and was not an entirely new element in Chinese political management. The Marxist theology provided a perfect patina for a widespread and traditional military content in China's national life.

India on the other hand chose the route of non-violence and of political struggle through constitutional means to wrest its freedom from colonial rule. Its leaders fought for its independence by means of negotiations and debate instead of armed struggle, as for the Indian military, its leaders were expressly advised by the political leadership to keep well out of the freedom struggle that was being waged.

The ancient cultural contacts between the two nations were through a transfer of religious thoughts, intrepid travelers of ancient times carried images of India to China. There is little to indicate that a reverse flow of images, religious beliefs and learned treatises occurred. It is useful to remember that much of the India-China interaction took place through geographic areas in the western reaches of ancient India and which no longer form part of India. Trade between India and China formed a very small part of the totality of their relationship. In military terms, the two nations shared no commonalities in doctrine and organizational concepts. Perhaps the only shared military experience between India and China was the Mongol invasions of their territories.

Traditional thoughts run deep in civilisational responses. Consequently, they indicate through the approaches and emphasis of state policies, a deeper and psychological national preference. The Indian text leans heavily on the defensive while the Chinese emphasises on the offensive. Arthashastra and Bingfa provide the clues from the past to the two nation's policy preferences of the present. As Kautilya saw it, the army was only one amongst seven major elements of the state's power. He recommended alliances and coalitions as the means to stabilise the state's security. Sunzi saw war as 'a matter of vital importance to the state ..." He warned the ruler against allowing the state into fighting a protracted war. One might even say that China has been the true "Realist" state and India the "Idealist" in the use of power to further national interests.

The initiative on Non-Alignment, the choice of the UN as a forum to settle the Jammu and Kashmir issue even when it was winning the war, the restraint in the nuclear weapons field, the initiatives on MARC, are indicative of the underlying Indian belief in negotiation and tolerance as the essential element of state policy. The Chinese approach stands out in contrast. It is of victory by use of force in pursuit of its objectives, an unwillingness to tolerate dissent in internal policies, of using protracted *wars* in other countries through encouragement to dissident groups and the preference for demonstrated military strength in its neighbourhood.

India's partition in 1947 and the Chinese occupation of

Tibet in 1950 have allowed China to extend its reach and influence into a region where it had, in terms of history and civilisation, previously exercised no influence at all. There had been talks, agreements, treaties and conventions amongst Britain, Soviets, Chinese and the Tibetans on the border delimitation during the period, better called as the period of the "great game." However it was not considered as serious until the Chinese occupation of Tibet in 1950.As a result of this, the two nations came into close physical contact for the first time and clashed. China-India relations have been tense ever since.

Since the days of Jawaharlal Nehru (1889–1964), independent India had entertained hopes of a joint Sino-Indian leadership of Asia as a counter to Western influence, but the Chinese showed no enthusiasm for sharing leadership of Asia with anyone, least of all India,after all, the main objective of China's Asia policy is to prevent the rise of a peer competitor to challenge its status as the Asia-Pacific's sole "Middle Kingdom." As an old Chinese saying goes, "one mountain cannot accommodate two tigers." Checkmated in East Asia by three great powers—Russia, Japan, and the United States—Beijing has long seen South and Southeast Asia as its spheres of influence and India as the main obstacle to achieving its strategic objective of regional supremacy in mainland Asia.

Tibet has always been the core issue in Sino-Indian relations. The revolt in Tibet leading to the flight of the Dalai Lama to India in 1959 came as a rude shock to the Indian leadership; however China has always been very suspicious of India in this regard. Even during the 1962 conflict, Chinese leaders, including Mao, acknowledged that the conflict was not about the boundary or territory but about Tibet.

Although the 1962 Sino-Indian war per-se has not been discussed in the course of this research, it is imperative that some important lessons drawn out after the war be penned down just to correlate with the border issue and the historic and cultural aspect of Chinese and Indian character.

Firstly; it was a failure of *"Grand Strategy"* vision of the government who lost sight of military as an instrument for attaining national goals and objectives. International idealism, pacifism and Nehruism espoused by national leadership then naturally disfavoured a strong military role; yet, the environment in the region was of power-centric realism rather than liberalism. Thus, the exercise of raw power by a resurgent PRC led by Mao Dzedong, with the motif of 'power flows through the barrel of the gun', internally as well as externally, was not fully appreciated in New Delhi. This led to the neglect of military capability as well as isolation of army leadership from national security decision making.

Secondly; it was a failure of*"brinkmanship"*which has a role in military strategy, it is a psychological ploy and has to be based on rational logic of inter se capability of enemy and own forces. Where the differential is limited, brinkmanship can be adopted to effect by a marginally weaker force; however, in the case of very wide variation in force potential, brinkmanship can be disastrous.

Thirdly; absence of good *"civil-military relations"*, are a bane of democracies, particularly when a nation plans or goes to war. This is also true in countries where supremacy of political over the military is well acknowledged, as in India.

Fourthly; lack of systematic management of *"higher defence"*, as a function of governance includes the military represented by the Ministry of Defence, foreign affairs and intelligence. These three primary arms are supported by finance. A viable structure for defence management post-independence was not in place.

Fifthly; absence of integrated battle in terms of *"Air Force"* was missing. Close air support which is the main component of an integrated battle especially when numerically inferior should have been activated.

Sixthly; Gross deficiencies were noticed in the process of promotions and selection of officers for *"higher military command"* appointments in 1962.This ignored principles of merit and experience. The recommendations of the service chiefs were set aside even in respect of principal staff officers, such as the Quarter Master General (QMG). Thus, no institutionalized system was in place, and hurriedly, square pegs were fitted into round holes.

The argument that culture influences national security policy was adequately showcased in the existence and character of Chinese strategic culture and causal linkages to the use of military force against external threats in the war with India. The use of *"grand strategy"* was displayed by China when, besides internal preparation for war it also used its political clout to wither away any interference from the power blocks, and ended the war precisely when there was a chance of any interference, i.e., after the Cuban missilecrisesended. On the other hand India was not even adequately prepared because it was surprised and deceived by China, when Nehru failed to assess the Chinese threat and shunned military inputs of an impending attack.

The Indian political class took a lesson from this and saw a complete reversal of similar mistakes in the 1971 war with Pakistan, when Indira Gandhi ceded to the advice of Gen Sam Manekshaw and the General gave her Bangladesh on a platter.

In the modern times, as the personal revolutionary ideas of great personalities fade and situations change the thinking towards more legal and global viewpoints, the Chinese have also changed their perceived logic behind the Great Cultural Revolution. While acknowledging the wrongs it had done; the positive side of it has emerged only after lapse of time. Probably Mao is said to have identified is the relationship of the modern state, especially the Communist state to the people it governs. Chinese may come to regard him as they do the early emperor Qin Shihuang, who's excesses were acknowledged by some as a necessary evil. Largely agricultural societies like China and India, and even some incipient industrial societies, the public must be able to understand the core issues of governances and always kept in touch with the political class either directly or through a interface. In formal and aristocratic societies, the relevant public may be limited, but some form of tacit consensus by those who are to carry out the directives is needed. Any governance by means of imposition may not sustain the test of longevity. In the present global context, the complexity of the legal framework has become increasingly impenetrable. This should automatically reduce the approachability factor between the leader and the led; it is seen that directives issued by political class is left to fissures opening up between the political and the bureaucratic classes and between both of those and the general public.

Mao's Cultural Revolution attempting to solve this in superfast mode, immediately wrecked the Chinese society, but in the long run provided a sense of common spiritual experience missing in the contemporary era. A Chinese scholar and government advisor Hu Angang feels that the reforms that Deng made in 1970s and 1980s was actually a relapsed outcome of immediate failure of Mao's Cultural Revolution. The Chinese approach to the world order was vastly different from the system that took hold in the west and a shadow of it, imbibed by India by virtue of the long colonial rule.

China had for over a thousand years a fully formed imperial bureaucracy recruited by competitive examination, permeating and regulating all aspects of economy and society. The modern concept of international relations emerged in the sixteenth and seventeenth century, when the medieval structure of Europe dissolved into homogeneous states of almost equal strength. No state was strong enough to impose its will; no religion retained so much authority to sustain universality because of the rise of sovereignty and legal equality of states became the basis of international law and diplomacy.

However, China, it seems was on a different path because it was never engaged in a sustained contact with another country on the basis of equality. Its world revolved around its geographical sphere, which was taken virtually as a law of nature or the Mandate of Heaven; the concept of the 'Middle Kingdom'. It always strove for tributary states to recognise China's special status. It believed that the neighbouring peoples benefited from contact with China so long as they acknowledged the suzerainty of the Chinese government whose organization reflected a hierarchical approach to world order. In its imperial role, China displayed impartiality, but never equality with its neighbors.. China has extracted some land out of all the border negotiations that it has held with other nations including Russia. However the Sino-tajik boundary negotiations in the Pamir region is particularly important for India as the area lies in the region is particularly important being in close proximity to India's sensitive borders of the north J&K, across Afghanistan.

Controversial issue of China-Pakistan nuclear nexus of providing unrelenting support to the nuclear weapon and missile programs of the Pakistan Armyresulted in Indian nuclear explosions of1998 and thereafter by default, a changed attitude of China and the world's strategic position on India emerged. The efforts to stabilise bilateral relations put the engagement between Delhi and Beijing on a more positive footing. The periodimmediately succeeding the blasts saw rapid expansion of the bilateral economic cooperation trade jump from barely $2 billion to $70 billion but with a trade imbalance. Both sides also announced a strategic partnership agreement and a set of principles to resolve the boundary dispute. Cooperation on common multilateral issues such as global warming and developing an agenda for emerging powers through the BRICS was the highlight of the decade.

Mutual suspicions on Tibet and Kashmir intensified, coupled with territorial transgressions by China in the garb of unclear perception of contested boundary. Last decade also revealed China's reluctance to support the U.S. initiative to integrate India into the nuclear global order and a determination to support Pakistan's quest for nuclear parity with India. India now eminently suited for permanent membership of the UNSC affirmed its willingness and capacity to shoulder the responsibilities of permanent membership of the UNSC. Having mustered adequate support including that of permanent members, China felt this not so impressive to be able to provide comprehensive support to India as compared to India's open and full support to China during its own membership in mid-1950's.

With India's ascent in the global hierarchy and U.S. attempts to carve out astrong partnership with India, China's need for Pakistan is only likely to grow. In the aftermath of the cold-war, Russia's influence in the region may have dithered any of the four nations to expect Russia playing a strategic role in the region, but it still is an historical all - weather friend and major exporter of defense material to India, possessing second largest nuclear arsenal; it cannot be ignored.

The Sino-Indian relationship has experienced strategic indulgence of the other three countries in a way that has affected either of the five very significantly, yet not always with a positive result. Such indulgence has only grown in the past and is likely to further aggravate relations in future rather than solving them.

Strategic vision of expansion for energy caused friction between the two into the maritime domain of the Indian and Pacific Oceans.

This quick synopsis of the complex dynamic in India's relations with China underlines the repeated attempts at constructing a cooperative partnership and how they are threatened by an intractable contest over territoriality of the two republics. Adding to this complexity is an persistent tension in the domestic Indian policy discourse on China. On the one hand are optimists who view China either through the prism of anti-colonial philosophy; on the other are those who simply demonize China and are unwilling to engage it even in national self-interest. This tension produces constant swaying in Delhi between hopes of forming a solid partnership with Beijing and deep rooted skepticism about an unavoidable conflict with China.

As China rises to become a great power, the challenge for India is to find a convincing policy that recognises the possibilities for greater collaboration, as well as absolute potential for conflict. A quarter century ago, India's notion of parity with China did not seem an unrealistic one; however this challenge is now more acute due to the widening gap between India's power abilities and those of China.

Due to absence of any major and authentic information on the 30 years of talks on the boundary issue with China and finally unresolved borders with China. At present only following can be comprehended.

- First, a long, barren but continuing process goes with the Chinese interest to keep India under strategic pressure. In diligently seeking to drag out the negotiations open-endedly, Beijing is following the principle, "negotiate to engage the other side, not to reach accord." This principle dovetails with China's broader two-pronged strategy to present a friendly face while building up its power-projection force capability through military, economic and diplomatic means.
- Second, China persuaded India in 2003 to shift from the practical task of clarifying the frontline to the abstract mission of developing "principles," "concepts" and "framework" for a border settlement. This shift was designed to release Beijing from its commitment in 2001 to exchange maps with India of first the western sector and then of the eastern sector — a pledge it had already breached by missing the mutually agreed deadlines.

- Third, India has sadly retreated to a more and more defensive position, bringing itself under greater Chinese pressure. Nobody is suggesting India adopt an aggressive posture. But if New Delhi is to engage Beijing on equal terms, the latter cannot have a monopoly on outrageous territorial claims that it forces into the negotiations agenda to put the ball in India's court and stall progress.

It is strongly felt that border-talks process has yielded what it could — an agreement to maintain peace, tranquillity and stability along the Indo-Tibetan frontier, and the initiation of modest military-to-military cooperation. The process offers little more. Staying put in a sterile, everlasting process cannot become an end in itself for India. Indeed it only emboldens China to be publicly obstinate and intimidatingly revanchist.

The conflicts of the past between China and India were not of nations but between states following different policies to secure themselves. Now that the two states are in a better environment of "Realist-Idealist" mix, specific measures can be looked at. The border dispute should now be formally and finally settled. This will need accommodation from both sides and that should not be an insurmountable problem given the new circumstances. Resolve of boundary dispute and the military perspective which so dominated the India-China relations in the last 50 years would be balanced by the larger contexts of economy, trade, and international cooperation. It would be a condition which both Kautilya and Sunzi would have approved.

The rich historical experience and the broad vision, which are common qualities of big countries, serve as the basis for China and India to take a long-term view and live in amity with each other. With joint efforts in the past few years, the two sides have gradually found a way to maintain peace and tranquility on the disputed border areas, and have learned to deal with the situation in a reasonable and mature manner. Both agree that the common interests between China and India far outweigh their differences and that the two countries should enhance mutual trust rather than increasing mutual suspicion. Both China and India are big countries in size and in population. Together, the populations of our two countries exceed 2.5 billion and account for nearly 40% of the world's total.

Today, China's GDP is four times as large as that of India, and Beijing spends three times more than India on defense. While India's economic growth rates in recent years have been impressive, China has grown much faster over a much longer period. The inevitable expansion of the gap, for the foreseeable future, presents India with a number of strategic imperatives.

Any Indianstrategy towards China must be steeped in realism and must be based on coherent, logical and legal foundations: building comprehensive national power, expanding cooperation with China wherever possible, preventing the territorial conflict from damaging the bilateral relationship, widening consultations with Beijing on regional security, and protecting against non-peaceful rise by establishing stronger economic, political, and security partnerships with other powers.

Swami Vivekananda had said, "We are responsible for what we are, and whatever we wish ourselves to be, we have the power to make ourselves. If what we are now has been the result of our own past actions, it certainly follows that whatever we wish to be in future can be produced by our present actions; so we have to know how to act."

In recent years, India-China relations have maintained a good momentum in their development, with co-operation the key factor. The two sides have sought to continue raising the level of mutual political trust and promote the in-depth development of bilateral co-operation. The current situation suggests that co-operation between the two countries has mainly focussed on economic areas of interest, although pragmatic co-operation has also been gradually promoted in the areas of politics, boundary negotiation and non-traditional security.

Present day Sino-Indian relations stand at a crossroads. On one hand, there is growing military and economic competition, while on the other there is increasing co-operation (on certain issues, at least). There is wide latitude for further co-operation and this paper strives to broadly identify the most promising threads of convergence for mutual strategic benefit. The only way for that to happen, however, is for the two countries to realise the responsibility that comes with their status as rising powers. By working together, they can best tap existing and future opportunities to build mutual trust and respect. In view of its position as the other rising Asian power, the world is now looking towards India to maintain peace, stability and development in the South Asian region and to keep a check on China's growing assertiveness. If both India and China can embrace the responsibility that comes with that, and facilitate greater regional integration, a lot can be done. But first, we need to understand the current state of affairs between the two countries and the complexities involved. The following is a model used to represent areas identified as areas of divergence. (Please note that the issues identified are not listed in order of importance). The challenge for both countries is to find ways to convert the divergences into convergences. They are not entirely doomed to impossibility, despite a history of "mutual suspicion".

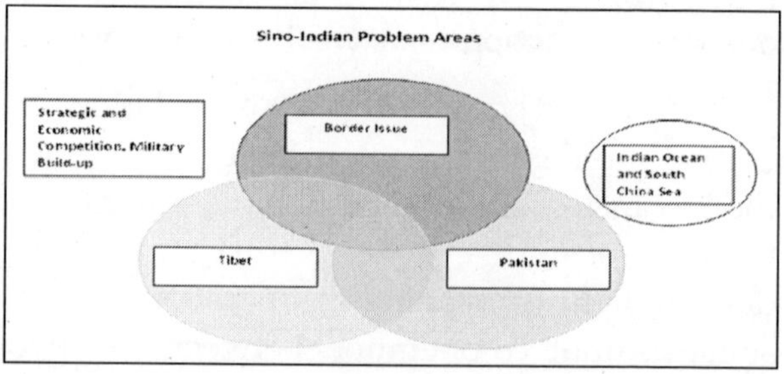

Determining the Nature of the Present Relationship and How it Might Evolve

Prime Minister Jawaharlal Nehru's "Hindi-Chini Bhai-Bhai" (Indians and Chinese are brothers) slogan of the 1950s lost its meaning after the 1962 border war, the first and, so far, only military confrontation between the two countries. But, despite years of estrangement, the overall nature of the relationship is not one of enmity. Indeed, the 50 subsequent years of wariness hardly figures in the long history of relations between the two countries and peoples. It is also true, however, that, since 1962, the two have shared a tenuous relationship with mutual mistrust being the most common sentiment.

The nature of the Sino-Indian relationship at present could be well explained by the notion of "Balance of Threat" propounded by Stephen M. Walt in 1985, where he modified the already established "Balance of Power" theory to better explain alliance systems. Walt suggested that alliances made by states are determined by their perception of a common threat from other states (or other alliances). Nation-states thus seek balance by forming alliances against a perceived threat to preserve their security. 'The proposition that states will join alliances ... to avoid domination by stronger powers lies at the heart of traditional balance of power theory.' He also notes that states ally with other states that are either at parity with or weaker than them, since 'allying with a dominant power would mean placing one's trust in its continued benevolence. The safer strategy is to join with those who cannot readily dominate their allies... to avoid being dominated by those who can.'

Using the above, we can better understand what is happening in the Indian Ocean Region, as well as the South China Sea. Even so, the motives behind China's so-called "encirclement" of India in the Indian Ocean Region and India's growing presence (or even "intrusion") into the South China Sea towards the wider Asia-Pacific, are not always clear; whether they are seeking economic gains or to create a sphere of influence respectively, or, perhaps, simply as a counter-balancing move. However, exclusive alliances between either China or India with dominant powers do not feature prominently; there are more incentives for the two in a strategic partnership.

The unresolved "border issue" has always been a thorn in Sino-Indian relations. The increasing militarisation on both sides of the border has not been a positive step towards resolving the dispute; neither are China's activities in the Pakistan-Occupied Kashmir (POK) area. According to a 2010 report, China has deployed approximately three hundred thousand troops within the region. Undeterred by the Chinese show of force, Indian Defence Minister A.K. Anthony declared, 'if they can increase their military strength there, then we can increase our military strength in our own land.'

'Tibet has always been the core issue in Sino-Indian relations. Even during the 1962 conflict, Chinese leaders, including Mao, acknowledged that the conflict was not about the boundary or territory but about Tibet.' The collapse of the scheduled high-level talks on the border issue because they would coincide with the Dalai Lama's visit to New Delhi for the World Buddhist Conference in November 2011, confirmed once again that Tibet remains an irritant in the relationship. China's close alliance with Pakistan can also be assessed against the same theoretical backdrop. China has traditionally valued Pakistan as a strategic hedge against India. To some China scholars, Pakistan is a low-cost secondary deterrent to India; for Pakistan, China is a high-value guarantor of security against India.

China's military modernisation programme parallels, and is funded by, its impressive economic growth. India's acquisition of aircraft carriers and Inter-Continental Ballistic Missiles (ICBMs) testifies to the fact that it is willing to meet any challenge posed by China. India's testing of its *Agni*-V ICBM and the repeated references to its ability to reach

Beijing, were emphatically matched by Chinese state-run newspapers, saying that 'India would stand no chance in an overall arms race with China'. Such exchanges exemplify what appears to be a building arms race.

Areas of Common Interest and How They Might Further Develop

India and China have a unique "arms-length" relationship, although both have been able to identify and co-operate on wider global issues, such as climate change, and increasingly they have been successful in consolidating economic ties. 'China and India have been instrumental in solidifying resistance from emerging market and developing economies for pursuing alternative agendas in trade and climate talks. In the process, they have been perceived as obstructionists, particularly by the G-7. From their own vantage points, both have been driven to their current postures by domestic concerns.' Both "Asian Giants", have managed to co-operate while tiptoeing around contentious issues and have taken care not to amplify any misunderstandings.

For both, their economic resurgence is directly linked to overseas trade and energy demands, most of which are seaborne, along with which come maritime threat perceptions. 'The importance of the maritime global concern about security and the economic growth of both China and India automatically translate to a convergence of interests that underlines the need for [them] us to strengthen co-operation in the maritime domain.'

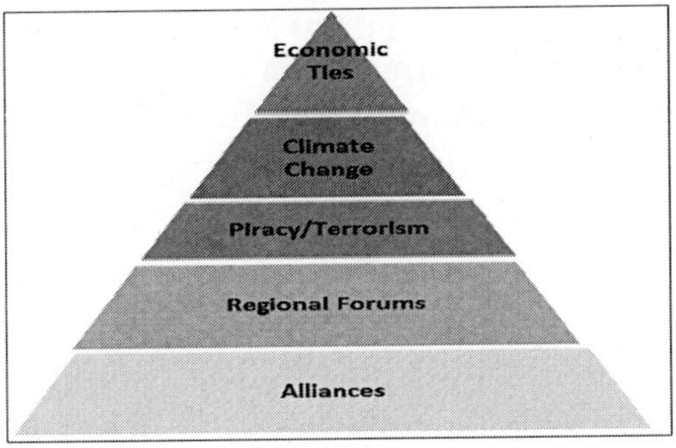

Conceptualisation: Areas of Co-operation (Apparent and/or Likely)

Instability in the Indian Ocean Region could hamper global economic prosperity and, therefore, issues such as piracy, drug trafficking, climate change and the Security of Sea Lines of Communication (SLOCs) could be some common concerns inviting co-operation. The Indian Ocean Rim Association for Regional Co-operation (IOR-ARC) could serve as a good platform; India is currently the Chair and China is a dialogue partner. Enhanced relations through ASEAN are beneficial for both India and China and can be helpful in strengthening economic linkages between them. In the years to come, according to the Asian Development Bank, 'the combined national wealth of India, China and ASEAN could exceed that of the US and European countries put together.' But, India's current trade deficit with China also gives rise to fears that it might widen further under the proposed Regional Comprehensive Economic Partnership to be negotiated between the ASEAN countries and China, India, Japan, South Korea, New Zealand and Australia.

The BRICS grouping has also benefited Sino-Indian relations. At talks on the sidelines of the 2012 BRICS summit, Hu Jintao conveyed to Prime Minister Manmohan Singh that, 'it is China's unswerving policy to develop Sino-Indian friendship, deepen strategic co-operation and seek common development.' Despite that, China has not expressed overt support for India's bid for a permanent seat on the United Nations Security Council, perhaps not least because India had associated its bid with Japan – a direct sticking point in the relationship (China has not supported the Japanese bid for a permanent seat on the Security Council due to "historical baggage").

If China gives support to India's bid, both countries will then be able to reinforce each other's efforts to further the interests of the developing world, where both are already icons of development. Their impressive records of raising hundreds of millions out of abject poverty, in the midst of international crises, must be commended. Collectively, their two giant economies have become pillars of the global economy, supplying vital resistance to the financial tsunami that has swept the system since 2008.

From an Indian perspective, New Delhi is committed to efforts towards bridging the gaps in its relations with China. Former Foreign Minister S.M. Krishna proclaimed that, 'the government of India will work with China in areas such as trade, investment, cultural exchanges, science and technology co-operation, where both countries stand to gain from each other. We will continue to engage China in a constructive and forward-looking manner so that both countries can achieve a win-win situation.'

Benefits for Both Countries

A stable regional architecture is a pre-requisite for security and prosperity. In the Indo-Pacific, broadly defined, achieving and maintaining that is fundamental to the interests of both India and China. China can be the leader in East Asia, with India the net security provider in South Asia. Individually and collectively, both countries need to find ways to ensure that all the prospects of a resurgent Asia are realised. Given their similar developmental challenges and huge populations, the quest for a stable economic environment is not surprisingly a core concern for both countries.

The growth and prosperity emanating from a "resurgent Asia" will invite "interest" from countries in other regions and, similarly, may also invite interference. What is critical for both India and China is to fashion a solid strategic alliance, since, as Asian behemoths, what could trouble one could easily trouble – or maybe even topple a government – in the other. Continuing at arm's length may equally invite intervention and unwanted infringements.

In the Indo-Pacific, there are several broad, possible approaches to the rise of China. They range from balancing, to containment and "soft balancing". There is even the suggestion of countries band-wagoning against China. There is no clear evidence of deliberate containment or balancing behaviour at present. After all, if it were simply a matter of a rising power, countries in the region should also balance against a rising India.

Therefore, none of these notions are as clear cut as the concepts themselves would suggest, but there is another option: engagement. Countries would continue to underwrite their security interests with established powers like the United States, while continuing to invest and/or trade with China. It is an approach that Australia is very familiar with. After the financial turmoil that began in 2008, with major markets in Europe and the Americas in recession, the Australian economy was saved by China's thirst for resources. At the same time, Australia seeks to strengthen its military and strategic relationship with the US, reassuring Washington of its loyalty. Australia is also attempting to forge a deeper and more co-operative relationship with India.

Australia is critically positioned to not only benefit from a prosperous and secure Asia; it is also in the foreground of power projections. Linked by ANZUS, Australia is the springboard for Western and US influence into the Asian littoral from the East (USPACOM is the military gate). Physically, Australia is the other side of the Asian bottleneck squeezing the Indonesian archipelago and its various chokepoints. Australia's participation is critical to the health of any regional framework. It is in Australia's interests that Asia is stable, India is secure and China is prosperous. Australia, therefore, has a critical interest in promoting the positive changes in the region brought about by increasing prosperity and, to the extent that they contribute to stability rather than arms races, military modernisationprogrammes.

Ultimately, far from being a buffer state whose interests are wedged between great powers, the rise of the Indo-Pacific, and China and India in particular, offers an opportunity to help frame opinions and contribute to the emerging regional architecture. From the South Pacific to its Indian Ocean territories, Australia should encourage Sino-Indian engagement to be conducted in a balanced manner and on a level playing field.

Since the border clash of 1962, the only thing fired across the Sino-Indian borders has been rhetoric. A subtle arms race is perceived as being managed and both are wary of any third party intervention. Despite tensions, the apparent absence of direct conflict between China and its neighbours, including India, is helping the "new" Asia mature into a centre of global power and prosperity. Remaining overly focussed on border disputes will mean missed opportunities when the relationship between India and China needs to be widened and reinforced to serve as the pillar for regional security and prosperity.

This gives wide latitude to both countries for the maximum fulfilment of their national interests. Symbiosis is the key term. A prosperous and growing China is good for India. India will grow, too; projections have hinted that India could become the biggest economy in the world by 2050. South-South co-operation is a key aspect; both countries' pursuit of modernisation and development provides a natural focus for greater Sino-Indian economic co-operation.

What India needs to do is to engage with China economically and signal clearly that it will open up its markets if China is willing to return the favour. The two countries could not find a better strategic friend than each other. Deeper Chinese investments in India could also blunt Pakistani militarism and terrorism in India. In doing so, it would provide a more united front against terrorism, as China is acutely anxious about the Uighur insurgency in its western provinces. This is a strategic threat that, if left unattended, could easily destabilise China or India and stymie economic growth.

While the People's Liberation Army may have a disdain for India, that is but one view. Increasing contact and prosperity can help to balance that view and promote enhanced co-operation. Asia's rise is led by its economic growth, and leading that is China. China and India are both becoming major maritime powers. As they build large navies to secure their growing interests, both countries are roiling the waters of the Indo-Pacific: that vast expanse stretching from Africa to Australasia.

The United States, the dominant global power, is seemingly supportive of a stronger Indian strategic presence in the context of any unfolding Sino-Indian competition. Despite the huge asymmetries in the current naval capabilities of China, India and the United States, C. Raja Mohan argues that the three countries are locked in a triangular struggle destined to mould the future of the Indo-Pacific. What eventuates depends on India and China. Ultimately, it is they that will determine if the "Asian Century" is one of opportunity or debilitating competition. India's military engagement with the US and Japan is disheartening to China and should be considered carefully, even as New Delhi continues to make the most of its relationships with those two democracies and Australia.

China does not have the same threat perceptions about India that India has about China. Chinese Foreign Ministry military spokesperson Hong Lei gave a view from Beijing that the world has enough space to accommodate both China and India. Noting India's commemoration of the fiftieth anniversary of the 1962 war, Hong made the pronouncement that 'China and India are partners, rather than rivals. We have far more common ground than disagreements, more mutual interests than conflicts.' Chinese Defence Minister Liang Guanglie, after meeting with Prime Minister Manmohan Singh and Defence Minister A.K. Antony declared, 'During the talks, we have positively evaluated China-India relations and the ties between the armed forces of the two countries. And we have affirmed the co-operation between the armed forces.' Recently, however, on several occasions, Chinese activities in the Ladakh region across the Line of Actual Control have increased, causing turbulence in Sino-Indian relations. While Chian's exact intent is unclear, the danger is that such posturing could result in an armed conflict if it were to continue. To help mitigate such a possibility, a series of visits by high-ranking officials and delegates is scheduled on both sides to discuss the options for joint naval and air force exercises. Also, a possible agreement on Border Defence Co-operation that includes protocols such as prohibiting the exchange of gunfire could be concluded.

Nonetheless, to achieve a fully co-operative relationship, both countries must demonstrate the political will to re-assess and re-configure the narrative that defines it. In the meantime, they must also refrain from interfering in each other's internal affairs, such as the protests by China against the evolving India-Japan-US relationship. A strong India is the best thing that could happen to a rising China and vice versa.

We recommend following measures to improve India-China relations:

- Upgrading the current Sino-Indian Strategic and Economic Dialogue meetings to a higher level – for example, by having future dialogues led by the Chinese State Councillor and Indian National Security Advisor, with the full participation of diplomatic, economic and military policymakers;
- Strengthening co-ordination and communication in regional and global institutions;
- Nurturing a more positive image of each other, both in government and society;
- Working on non-traditional security issues, such as the maritime security co-operation, and making it a basis for better mutual understanding;
- Careful handling of sensitive issues – particularly such issues as the Tibetan independence movement, the South China Sea and the so-called "String of

Pearls"; and,

- Promoting open regionalism and rejecting the idea that East Asia and South Asia should be viewed as separate blocs and defined regions.
- Despite years of estrangement, the overall nature of the relationship is not one of enmity.
- If both India and China can embrace the responsibility and facilitate greater regional integration, a lot can be done.
- India and China have a unique "arms-length" relationship, although both have been able to identify and co-operate on wider global issues.
- Asia's rise is led by its economic growth, and leading that is China. China and India are both becoming major maritime powers. As they build large navies to secure their growing interests, both countries are roiling the waters of the Indo-Pacific.
- To achieve a fully co-operative relationship, both countries must demonstrate the political will to re-assess and re-configure the narrative that defines it.
- China and India have achieved tremendous progress in multi-sector co-operation.
- Notwithstanding that progress, challenges still exist in the bilateral relationship, however. This includes economic constraints, border disputes and perception problems.
- Difficulties aside, the two countries' common interests provide the bases for a brighter future for India-China relations.

Bibliography

Books

A.G. Noorani, *"Brezhnev plan for Asian Security"*, Bombay, 1975

A.M. Halpern, *"Policies Toward China: Views from Six Continents"*, London, 1965

A.O. Cukwurah,*"The Settlement of Boundary Disputes in International Law"*, Manchester,University of Manchester, 1967

Alaister Lamb, *"The Sino-Indian Border in Ladakh"*, Canberra, Australia, National University Press, 1973

Alastair Iain Johnston, *"Cultural Realism: Strategic Culture and Grand Strategy in Chinese History,"* Princeton, New Jersey: Princeton University Press, 1995

Albright David, *"Peddling Peril: How the Secret Nuclear Trade Arms America's Enemies"* ,Free Press, 2010

Alexander P de Seversky, *"Victory through Air Power"*, New York: Simon and Schuster, 1942

Anand Kumar, *"Tibet: A Sourcebook"*, New Delhi, Radiant Publishers, 1995

Arthur Cotterell,"China: A Concise Cultural History", London Johan Murray, 1988

Arthur M. Schlesinger, Jr., *"A Thousands Days: John F. Kennedy in the White House"*, Boston, 1965

B.L. Sharma, *"The Pakistan-China Axis"* New Delhi :Asia Publishing House, 1968

Berinder Verma, *"China-Pakistan Relations,"* Delhi, 1986

Bingyan li, ed., Shen Weiguang," *Applying Military Strategy in the age of the New revolution on Military affairs,"* The Chinese Revolution in Military Affairs, China, New China Press, 2004,

Bower Hamilton, *"A Journey Across Tibet"*, London, 1894,

BrahmaChallaney, *"Water: Asia's new battleground"*, Washington D.C. Georgetown University Press, 2011

Brahma Chellaney, Asia Jugergrnaut, Harper Collins, 2010

Carrington Goodrich,"*A Short History of the Chinese People*", Sturgis press 2007

Chellaney Brahma, *"Water: Asia's New Battleground"*, Harper Collins, Uttar Pradesh, 2011

Chu Chai and Winberg Chai,"*The Changing Society* of China", Chicago New American Library, Menter book, 1962

Clarke Michael E., *"Xinjiang and Chinese Rise in Central Asia—A History"*, Routledge, London, 2011

Clausewitz Carl von, ed., and intro.AnatolRapoport Baltimore, MD: *"On War"*, Penguin Books, 1971

Clausewitz Carl von, Machael Howard and Peter Paret, eds,"*On War*", and trans. Princeton University Press, 1989

D. Jagjit Singh, *"Relations between Pakistan and the People's Republic of China"* (Bombay, 1980

Dalvi J.P., Brig (Retd), " *Himalayan Blunder*", Orient Paperback.

David C. Wright,"*The History of China*"Westport Greenwood Press, 2001

David C. Wright, *"The History of China"*, Westport Green wood Press, 2000

David Shambaugh and Richard H. Yang ed. China's Military in Transition, Oxford, Clarendon Press, 1999

Dreyer Edward L,"*Early Ming China-A Political History*", 1355-1435, Stanford University Press, California, 1982

G. W. Chaudhary, *"Pakistan's Relations with India, 1947-1966,"* London, 1968,

G.S. Bhargava,"*Star Crossed India: Let Down by Leadership*", New Delhi, Kalpaz Publications, 2005

Gary K. Bertsch, (eds.), "*Engaging India: Strategic Relations with the World's Largest Democracies*", New York, 1999.

Gen Shankar Roy Chowdhury (Retd), "*To combat Red Terror, Tackle its Root Causes*", *The Asian Age,21*April , 2009

George Perkovich, *"India's Nuclear Bomb: The Impact on Global Proliferation"*, Berkeley: University of California Press, 1999.

Gondker Narayan Rao, "*The India-China Boundary: A Reappraisal*", London, Asia Publishing House, 1968,

Gupta M.L., "*A short History of China*", New Delhi, Reliance Pub. 1994

H. Qureshi, "*A Short history of Pakistan*", University of Karachi, 1992

Hari R. Gupta, "China and the Peace of Asia",New Delhi 1985

Harold A. Gould, and SumitGanguli, ed., "*The Hope and the Reality: U.S. India Relations – FromRoosevelt to Reagan*", New Delhi, 1992

Harold Isaacs, "*Scratches On Our Minds: American Images of China and India*",NewYork, 1958

Harpreet Mahajan, "*Arms Transfer to India, Pakistan and the Third World*", (New Delhi, 1982),

Harsh V. Pant, "*The U.S. India Nuclear Pact: policy, Process, and Great Power Politics*" Oxford, Oxford University Press, 2011

I.H.Qureshi, "*The Foreign Policy of Pakistan, in U.E*",eack and K.W. Thompson, ed., Foreign Policies in a Changing World , New York, 1963

Itty Abraham, "*Interpreting the Meanings of India's Nuclear Tests,*" in Scott D. Sagan, ed., *Inside Nuclear South Asia,* Stanford: Stanford University Press, 2009

J.A. Naik,"*India, Russia, China and Bangladesh,*" S. Chand & Co. (Pvt) Ltd., New Delhi, 1972

Jagannath P. Panda, "*China's Path To Power; Party, Military and the Politics of State Transition*", New Delhi,Pentagon Press, 2010.

Janki Sinha, "*Pakistan and Indo-US Relations, 1947-1958,*" Patna, 1978

Jyotsna Bakshi,"*Russia-China Relations: Relevance for India*",New Delhi, Shipra Publications, 2004

K. Sarwar Hassan, "*Pakistan and the United Nations*", New York,1960

K. Warikoo,(ed), "*Himalayan Frontiers of India: Historical, geo-political and strategic perspectives*", Routledge,Oxon, 2009,

K.M. Panikkar, "*The Founding of the Kashmir State: A Biography of Maharaja Gulab Singh 1792-1858,*" London, 1953

K.R. Narayanan, "*India and America: Essays in Understanding*", New Delhi, 1984,

Kissinger Henry, "*On China*", Penguin Group, USA, 2011

Kurien Nimmi , "*Emerging China and India's Policy Options*", New Delhi, Lancer, 2001.

Kux Dennis, "*India and the United States: Estranged Democracies-1941-1991*", US, National Defense University Press, 1992

Lamb Alastair, "*The McMahon Line*", A Study in the Relations between India, China and Tibet, 1904 to 1914, Vol-1 & 2; Morley, Minto and Non- Interference in Tibet, Great Britain, Routledge & Kegan Paul Ltd, 1966

Lawrence Ziring, ed., "*The subcontinent in World Politics,*" New York, 1978.

Li Li, "*Security Perception and China-India Relations*", New Delhi, K W Publishers Pvt Ltd, 2009

Liu Xinru, "*Ancient India and Ancient China; Trade And Religious Exchanges AD 1-600*", (1988) second impression, 1997, New Delhi, Oxford University Press.

Lorene's Kavic, "*India's Quest for Security*", Defense Policies, 1947-65, California, 1967

M.L. Gupta, *"A Short History of China,"* preface

Major General Yang Huan, *"China's Strategic Nuclear Weapons, Defense Industry of China 1949-89,"* Beijing, National Defense Industry Press, 1989,

Malik Mohan, *"China and India: Great Power Rivals"*, Lynne Rienner Publishers, First Forum Press, Boulder, CO

Mao Tse-tung, *"Problems of War and Strategy"*, from the selected Works of Mao Tse-tung, Peking: Foreign Language Press, 1967

Maxwell's Neville, *"India's China War"* Jaico Publishing House, Bombay, 1970

Melvyn C Goldstein, *"Tibet, China and the US- reflections on the Tibet Question"*,

Michael Franz, *"China, through the Ages: History of Civilization"*, USA, and West view Press, 1986

Mohammad Ayub Khan, *"Friends not Masters: A Political Autobiography,"* (London, 1967),

Mohan Guruswamy and ZorawarDaulet Singh, *"India China Relations: The Border Issue and Beyond"*, New Delhi, Viva Books, 2009.

Mohd Ayub Khan, *"Friends, Not Masters: A Political Autobiography"* Lahore, 1967

Muni S.D. and Tan Tai Yong (eds), *"A Resurgent China: South Asian Perspective"*, Routledge, India, 2012

Nehru Jawaharlal, *"The Discovery of India"*, London, Meridian Books Ltd, 1960,

Noorani A.G.,*"India-China Boundary Problem 1846-1947, History and Diplomacy"*, New Delhi: Oxford University Press, 2011

P.K. Fabian, *"Diplomacy Indian Style"*, New Delhi, Har-Anand Publications Pvt. Ltd., 2012.

P.M. Kamath, ed, *"Indo-US Relations: Dynamics of Change"*, New Delhi, South Asian Publishers, 1987

Pande Ira, (ed.), "*India and China - Neighbours, Strangers,*" Harper Collins, India, 2010,

Parshotam Mehra, "*Negotiating with the Chinese 1946- 1987: Problems and Perspective*", New Delhi, Reliance Publishing House, 1980

Peter Lyon, "*New States and International Order*", in Alan James,ed, "*The Bases of International Order*" (London 1973),

Peter Sahlins, "*Boundaries: The Making of France and Spainin the Pyrenees*", California, University of California Press, 1989

Prasad Bimal,"*Indo-Soviet Relations 1947-1972; A Documentary Study*",New Delhi, Allied Publishers Private Ltd, 1973

Py Ho and S.P. Lisowski, 2nd edition, "*A Brief History of Chinese Medicine*", Singapore, World Scientific Publication Pvt. Ltd., 1997

Qutubuddin Aziz, "*Relations Between Pakistan and People's Republic of China*", in Latif Ahmed Sherwani, ed., "*Foreign Policy of Pakistan,*"Karachi, 1964

R.K.Chaterjee,"*India's Land Borders: Problems and Challenges*", New Delhi, Srerling Publishers (P) Ltd, 1978

Rajagopalan Rajeswari Pillai, "*The Dragon's Fire: Chinese Military Strategy and Its Implications for Asia*", New Delhi, Rupa and co, 2009

Ram Rahul, "*Modem Tibet*", New Delhi, MunshiramManoharlal Publishers Pvt. Ltd., I 992

Rasgotra M & Chopra V.D, "*India's Relations with Russia and China: A New Phase*", Gyan Publishing House, 1997

Rasul Bux Rais, "*China and Pakistan: A Political Analysis of Mutual Relations,*"Lahore, 1978

Robert Andre LaFleur,Palmer, Warren Bruce Rapp, John A Robson and, Santa Barbara, "*China A Global Studies Handbook*" ABC clio, Globalstudie: Asia 2003

Robert D. Bernard, "*Nuclear Weapons and Limited War*", Washington 1986

Ross Robert S, "*Chinese Security Policy: Structure, Power and Politics*", Oxon, Routledge, 2009,

Rothermund Dietmar, "*An Economic History of India, From Pre-Colonial Times to 1986*", New York, Croom Helm with Methuen, Inc. 32, 1988.

S.P. Bajpai, "*India- China Boundary: Central Sector*", in S.P. Sen(ed): "*The Sino- Indian Border Question—A Historical view*", Calcutta, 1971

S.P. Singh, "*Political Dimensions of India-USSR Relations*",New Delhi, Allied Publishers Pvt. Ltd., 1987

S.S. Bindra, "*Determinants of Pakistan's Foreign Policy*", New Delhi. Deep and Deep Publications, 1988

Sali M.L.,"*India China Border Dispute*", New Delhi, APH Publishing, 1998

Sangat Singh, "Pakistan's Foreign Policy" Bombay, 1970

Sen Amartya, "*The Argumentative Indian; Writings on Indian History, Culture and Identity*", England, Penguin Books Ltd, 2005

Singh Bhavna, "*China's Discursive Nationalism: Contending in Softer Realms*", Pentagon Press, New Delhi, 2012

Singh Jaswant, "*Defending India*", Macmillan, India Ltd, 1999.

Sinha N.K.and Ray N.R.,"*A History of India*", Orient Longman Ltd., Calcutta, 1973

Sisir Gupta, "*Kashmir: A study on India-Pakistan Relations,*" Bombay, 1966

Smith A.Vincen, C.I.E.,"*The Oxford History of India*", Oxford, Oxford University Press, 1958

Srikant Kondapalli and Mifune Emi, "*China and its Neighbours*", New Delhi, Pentagon Press, 2010

Stein Arthur, "*India and The Soviet Union; The Nehru Era*",USA, University of Chicago, 1969

Stein Burton,"*A History of India*", UK, Blackwell Publishers Ltd., 1998

Steven Warshaw,"*China Emerges: A Concise History of China from Its Origin to the Present*", 11thRved, Berkeley Diablo press, 1988

Sudhakar Bhatt, "*India and China*" New Delhi: Popular Books Service, 1967

Surjit Mansingh, "*India's Search for Power*", Delhi, 1984

Susan L. Shirk (ed.), "*Changing Media, Changing China*", Oxford University Press, New York, 2011

Swarnlata Sharma, "*Tibet: Self-determination in Politics among Nations*", New Delhi, Criterion Publications, 1988

Tara Chand, "*History of the Freedom Movement in India*" NewDelhi, 1972

Tariq Ali, "*Pakistan and Bangladesh: Results and Prospects*" in Robin Blackburn, ed., Explosion in subcontinent, (London) 1975

V.P. Malik, and Schultz Jorg, "*The Rise of China: Perspectives from Asia and Europe*", New Delhi, Pentagon Press, 2008,

V.V. Balabushevich and BimlaPrasad, ed., "*India and the Soviet Union: A Symposium*" New Delhi, 1969,

William J. Barnds, "*India, Pakistan and Great Powers*"New York,1972

Wolfram Eberhard, "*A History of China*", IIIrd rev ed, Berkeley university of Colifornia Press, 1969

Zulfiqar Khalid, "Pakistan in the Pamir Knot, Geostrategic lmperatives", Lahore, Vanguard, 1987

News Papers, News Online and Periodicals

1. bdnews 24.
2. Business Standard
3. China Daily
4. Diplomat
5. Economic Watch
6. Frontline
7. Hindustan Times

8. Indian Express
9. Kabul Times
10. Monitor
11. New York Times
12. Pakistan Times
13. Patriot
14. Peking Review,
15. Penguin Viking
16. Pravda,
17. Ribao Peoples Daily
18. Telegraph,
19. The Dawn
20. The Economic Times
21. The Hindu
22. The News Nation
23. The Seattle Times
24. The Statesman
25. The Tribune
26. Tibet Press Watch
27. Times of India
28. Xinhua

Journals

1. Asian Survey
2. BIISS Journal
3. Canadian Institute of International Affairs
4. Chinas Economy Yearbook
5. Executive Intelligence Review, Washington

6. Far Eastern Survey
7. Foreign Policy Journal,
8. ICJ, Tibet
9. Indian Defence
10. Indian Defence Review
11. Institute for National Strategic Studies
12. Institute of Defence Studies and Analysis, (IDSA), New Delhi)
13. Institution of South Asian Studies, Singapore
14. International Security
15. International Studies, (New Delhi),
16. IOSR Journal of Humanities & Social Sciences(JHSS),
17. IPCS
18. Journal of Contemporary Research in Management
19. National Bureau of Asian Research
20. National Defense Research Institute
21. National Institute of Advanced Studies, Bangalore
22. National Maritime Foundation
23. NDC
24. Pakistan Horizon
25. R.G.S.J
26. South Asia Analysis Group
27. South Asian Strategic Studies Institute
28. Soviet Review
29. Strategic Analysis, New Delhi
30. *The Asian Age*
31. The Wall Street Journal
32. USI Journal (New Delhi)
33. Washington Quarterly
34. World Focus

Index